SELF-ESTEEM

Chris Mruk's background in psychology consists of several decades of clinical and academic experience. The former includes working as a crisis intervention specialist for St. Lawrence Hospital of Lansing, Michigan, providing comprehensive psychological and testing services in several community mental health settings, directing a college counseling center at St. Francis College in Pennsylvania, and serving as a consulting psychologist to Firelands Regional Health System, Sandusky, Ohio. His academic background consists of undergraduate training in traditional psychological methods at Michigan State University and graduate work in phenomenological psychology at Duquesne University. Dr. Mruk has published several chapters and a number of articles on self-esteem, phenomenology, and the psychology of computerization. He teaches full time as a professor of psychology at Firelands College of Bowling Green State University in Ohio, where he has been since 1984. Dr. Mruk also offers seminars and continuing education programs for mental health professionals. His e-mail address at the time of this writing is cmruk@bgnet.bgsu.edu.

SELF-ESTEEM:

Research, Theory, And Practice

SECOND EDITION

Christopher J. Mruk

FREE ASSOCIATION BOOKS / LONDON

First published in the United Kingdom 1999 by
FREE ASSOCIATION BOOKS
57 Warren Street, London W1P 5PA

ISBN 1–85343–459–0 (pbk)

Typeset in the United States of America
Printed in the EC by J.W. Arrowsmith, Bristol

Contents

Preface

Given the vast amount of professional and popular literature on the topic, it would seem that the field of self-esteem should abound with second editions. As of this writing, however, the number of professionally oriented books advancing to this stage can still be counted on one hand. The invitation to write one after a few short years came as a surprise and brought with it a sense of responsibility. Like most authors, I wanted to say some things presented in the first edition more clearly, but my primary motivation for a second edition comes from wanting to update the book in a way that may keep it contemporary for some time. Thus, there are two kinds of revisions to be found in this new edition.

The first goal concerns an attempt to refine the book. I have had time to think about what I said as well as how I said it in the first edition, and I have made an attempt to clarify some things and modify others. For instance, I now call the form of the phenomenological method I use "integrated description" (Mruk, 1994), meaning that I attempt to uncover the underlying structure of a given human phenomenon, in this case self-esteem, then show how existing quantitative and qualitative research is accounted for within that framework. Similarly, I have trained several therapists in the use of the self-esteem enhancement program offered in the last chapter since the first writing and found that it may be possible to simplify the procedures, or at least make them more flexible in ways that clinicians may find useful. And, of course, I continue to struggle with some issues that are what I like to call "self-esteem puzzles," such as how to classify the various types of self-esteem people come to have, or how far to explore self-esteem from a developmental rather than a clinical perspective.

Second, there have been some important developments in the field during the past few years that require attention. One of them concerns what might be called an "anti-self-esteem movement" or a "self-esteem backlash." By this phrasing I am referring to the fact that today there is a body of material that criticizes enhancing self-esteem, especially in educational settings, and even the very concept of self-esteem as a desirable human characteristic. This trend seems to have emerged in response to the popularization of self-esteem that occurred in the last decade or so. As we shall see, I do think there is a way to deal with these developments, but this new body of literature is sure to become significant in the history of the field, as is other work linking self-esteem and aggression. Other material completely new to the second edition includes published research supporting the self-esteem enhancement program offered at the end of the book.

Those who are familiar with the first edition will find that the second has been revised rather extensively. Chapters 1 and 5 received the most attention. For example, chapter 1 begins with only three major reasons to study self-esteem instead of five, and one of them is completely new, reflecting recent developments in the field. In addition, the entire chapter has been rewritten to create a more harmonious introduction to the problem of defining self-esteem and finding one that works. Similarly, chapter 5, which concerns a phenomenological theory of self-esteem, has been developed further than before. It now includes more information on clinically significant self-esteem problems as well as on the development of self-esteem. The other four chapters have been updated to reflect new findings, new ideas, and even new controversies that have emerged during the past five years or so, for this period has been a very busy one in the history of the psychology of self-esteem. Of course, it is inevitable that by the time I completed this work, I wanted to start all over again. After all, with more than 7,648 publications in its body and more emerging each month, this field can never really be covered in complete detail. Consequently, I have not spent as much time with certain areas as I would like, such as self-esteem in the educational setting or the cross-cultural dimensions of self-esteem. Instead, like the last edition, this one is oriented toward clinical and academic audiences, although I believe that anyone who writes reasonably well can communicate with anyone who reads reasonably well.

In a certain sense, this entire book is a phenomenology of self-esteem: from research, through theory, to practice. The following pages, then, can be likened to a natural scientist's laboratory notebook in that they present one scientist-practitioner's search through the human land-scape called self-esteem. The chapters are carefully arranged in a logi-cally progressive fashion. That is, the phenomenon is first researched and defined in terms of its general structure (chapter 1). Then, the major issues and methodological issues associated with researching self-esteem are examined (chapter 2), which, in turn, enables us to identify more credible findings (chapter 3). Next, the leading theories of what self-esteem is and how it works are identified and considered (chapter 4). Following that, the research findings and theoretical points of view that result from the work we have done so far are integrated into a phenomenological theory of self-esteem (chapter 5). We finish by examining how a self-esteem enhancement program based on the theory stands up to pre- and posttesting with nonclinical and clinical populations (chapter 6). While this "scholarly" approach builds a better argument because it addresses the research and theoretical issues asso-ciated with self-esteem before turning to the practical possibilities, it can seem somewhat laborious for busy clinicians who may want to get right to the point as quickly as possible. Although I do not recommend doing so, it is possible to modify the reading order by moving from chapter 1 directly to chapters 5 and 6, providing the others are picked up when more time is available.

Perhaps the most pleasurable task in writing a book is the opportunity to acknowledge people who helped along the way. A second edition means that some new names will be added. Above all, the following pages still remain dedicated to my family—to the one that raised me and to the one that came along later. Thanks to my mother, Veronica, my father, Joe, and my brother, Steve, for teaching me to hope, work, and care for self-esteem, respectively. A similar sense of gratitude goes to my second family, Dee, Pam, and Tina Bradshaw. This context of care and support continues through my wonderful partner, Marsha, who is also dedicated to enhancing self-esteem in her professional career as a director of behavioral health care delivery systems.

I cannot escape the special debt that is still owed to my mentor and friend, Tony Barton, but my own development as a professional over time shows me that I am also indebted in this way to Connie Fischer, both of whom were among my teachers at Duquesne University. The strong feeling of gratitude toward those who constituted my "existential community" while working on the original manuscript still remains, especially toward Frank and Mary Ann Salotti and Bob and Pam Harmount. To these names I must now also add Virginia Oliver, Jeff Welsh, Julie Hakim-Larson, Will Currie and the staff at the library of Firelands College, Bowling Green State University, and the people involved with the Firelands Regional Health System, such as Patty Martin, where I still do my clinical and consulting work.

Not as many students shared in the project this time, but two of them still deserve special attention. They are Karen Page Osterling, who was employed as the copy editor while drafting the second edition, and Leona Hope Preston, who was one of my first graduates. A word of thanks goes to Dorothy Kouwenberg, the foreign subsidiary rights manager for Springer Publishing Company, who arranged the Spanish edition of the original book. Of course, every book requires a publisher, so I remain indebted to those who helped with the first edition. To that group, I need to add a few names and elaborate on another. I am grateful to those at Springer who worked directly on the book with me, including Bill Tucker, the talented senior editor, Jeanne Libby, the production editor who sped things along nicely, and Laura Daly, the copy editor whose thoughtful suggestions improved the manuscript. Also, it is my pleasure to thank Dr. Ursula Springer, the publisher, whose penetrating mind and impressive energies have touched the very direction of scholarship in psychology. Last, but never the least, I again must express my gratitude to those individuals who have allowed me to share their tragedy and triumph through our clinical work together: Your courage allows psychology to be more than a social science.

1

The Meaning and Structure of Self-Esteem

Why is there a need for another book on self-esteem? This very reasonable question was asked in a review of the first edition (Aanstoos, 1995) and is even more relevant now that it is several years later. After all, according to one PsycINFO database search I did in 1998, there were some 7,648 articles and books on the topic, so why, indeed, should there be a need for even one more? The fact is that there are at least three good reasons to take up the topic once again, and each one of them involves a different methodological challenge. Therefore, in addition to providing the rationale for more work on self-esteem, I will point out what is required of the method that is necessary to address each concern. This approach lays the foundation for the major point of this chapter, which is to define the meaning and structure of self-esteem so that we can better understand this important, complex human phenomenon.

A most compelling reason for studying self-esteem, and the one that interests me the most as a clinician, is a practical one. Self-esteem appears to be connected to two broad dimensions of human behavior. On the one hand, this vital human phenomenon is often understood in relation to positive mental health and general psychological well-being. We shall see that research in this area correlates high self-esteem with such things as positive ego functioning, good personal adjustment, an

1

internal sense of control, the likelihood of a favorable outcome for psychotherapy, healthy adjustment to aging, individual autonomy, and a tendency toward androgyny (Bednar, Wells, & Peterson, 1989; Coopersmith, 1967). On the other hand, the lack of self-esteem is often related to a number of important negative possibilities with which we need to be concerned, such as feelings of inadequacy, a sense of unworthiness, increased anxiety, depression, suicide, child abuse of all types, exploitative relationships among adults, and certain mental health disorders (Coopersmith, 1967; Skager & Kerst, 1989). The hope is that if we understand how self-esteem is related to behavior, enhancing self-esteem could make a significant difference in individual lives and, perhaps, to society in general. Of course, this practical justification for looking at self-esteem means that the method we use to study it must allow us to see how self-esteem is actually lived by real people in real situations.

Another major reason for continuing to study self-esteem is that it is a foundational topic for much psychological research, theory, and practice. Indeed, the roots of this field go back to at least 1890, which makes it one of the oldest themes in psychology, and over a century later it is still regarded as an indispensable concept in the social sciences (Wells & Marwell, 1976). As such, there is a very large body of literature on self-esteem, and it comes from almost every major theoretical perspective. For example, psychodynamically oriented authors uncover insights about self-esteem as a developmental process (Adler, 1927; White, 1959). Cognitive-behaviorists frame self-esteem in terms of problem-solving skills and various coping strategies (Bednar et al., 1989; Pope, McHale, & Craighead, 1988). Social psychologists focus on attitude formation, especially self-protective ones such as "self-handicapping" (Snyder, 1989; Tice, 1993). And humanistic psychologists emphasize the experiential dimensions of self-esteem, particularly in terms of self-acceptance (Branden, 1969; Jackson, 1984). Today, however, the field seems to be in need of taking a new step forward:

> The future development of self-esteem research will depend on two key factors—*consensus* and *accumulation*. The task is to combat the disparateness of the literature, where much of the research is carried on in analytical and empirical isolation from the remainder, and cross-comparisons are difficult. (Wells & Marwell, 1976, p. 251)

With so many publications already in this field, surely some degree of "accumulation" has occurred. That is not to say that the goal of reaching a consensus has been achieved, because there are several factors that make this a very difficult challenge. For example, there are several complex methodological issues involved in researching self-esteem scientifically. A case in point is that many of the findings with which we have to work in reaching toward a consensus are qualitative, while many others are primarily quantitative, which means that the task of integrating them requires careful thought. As we shall see in this chapter, the fact that researchers have defined self-esteem in several different ways creates another, particularly important, set of research and theoretical problems. Ultimately, only a method that is capable of describing the very structure or "essence" of self-esteem can hope to lead to a theory comprehensive enough to make sense of the research and theoretical diversity that characterize this field.

The third reason that researching self-esteem is still important today is because it has considerable social significance. As Wells and Marwell (1976) concluded in their massive review of the literature on self-esteem,

> First of all, self-esteem seems to us to be a vital and broadly relevant conceptual tool for both psychological and sociological perspectives. . . . [H]ow people think of and evaluate themselves, both as a consequence of basic social conditions and as a predisposition for subsequent behaviors, is an essential behavioral construct for interpreting human conduct. Its interpretive importance is revealed not only by its frequency of occurrence in academic literature, but by the strength and variety of its application in popular debates as well. Self-esteem seems to be emerging as one of the key "social indicators" in current analysis of social growth and progress. (p. 250)

In other words, self-esteem is a valuable concept for social scientists because it helps psychologists, sociologists, social workers, counselors, and others to integrate the complex interplay of personal and social factors involved in determining human behavior. The fact that we do not have an abundance of such intellectual tools makes this one all the more important.

Today, however, two converging forces have pushed the social significance of self-esteem well into a much larger social arena. One of them originated with a group of academicians and politicians in California who emphasized to the public the possibility of a link between individual self-esteem and major social problems, such as substance abuse, welfare, and teen pregnancy. Or as Mecca, Smelser, and Vasconcellos (1989) said: "The well-being of society depends on the well-being of its citizenry. . . . The more particular proposition that forms our enterprise here is that many, if not most, of the problems plaguing society have roots in the low self-esteem of many of the people who make up society" (p.

1). Perhaps in response to the zeitgeist of the time, or maybe due to the political connections from which this group benefited, or simply because it seemed to make so much sense, this position generated a very broad base of political and social support, meaning that self-esteem suddenly received considerable financial backing. Like never before, self-esteem made its way to other significant parts of society, particularly in the educational setting (Beane, 1991; Damon, 1995). At the same time, the self-help and popular psychology markets capitalized on the topic. The result was a dramatic increase in the number of self-help books on self-esteem in the nation's popular bookstores and a similar rise in programs aimed at enhancing self-esteem in primary school systems across the land. In short, the large but once quiet field of self-esteem became popular and achieved general social significance for the first time in its history through what is now commonly known as the self-esteem movement.

However, popular interest is a double-edged sword. In addition to the obvious benefits, such as more research funding and more people working in the field, bringing a scientific concept to the public forum can also result in negative forms of attention. The most important of these appears to be something of a backlash against the topic, a phenomenon that I find understandable but distressing. Early signs of what we might call an "anti-self-esteem movement" began to appear in social commentaries with eye-catching titles, such as "The Trouble with Self-Esteem," which appeared in *U.S. News and World Report* (Leo, 1990), and *Time* magazine's article "Education: Doing Bad and Feeling Good" (Krauthammer, 1990). Self-esteem bashing still occurs today (Johnson, 1998; Leo, 1998). Such negative commentary is often offered by people with modest scientific credentials, so it may be tempting to simply dismiss such attacks. However, it is also possible to see signs of a similar trend in more professional literature. For example, the psychologist Martin Seligman (1995b) said in a book on child rearing:

> Armies of American teachers, along with American parents, are straining to bolster children's self-esteem. That sounds innocuous enough, but the way they do it often erodes children's sense of worth. By emphasizing how a child *feels*, at the expense of what the child *does*—mastery, persistence, overcoming frustration and boredom, and meeting a challenge—parents and teachers are making this generation of children more vulnerable to depression. (p. 27)

Perhaps one of the most vitriolic attacks on self-esteem is found in William Damon's (1995) work:

In and of itself, self-esteem offers nothing more than a mirage for those who work with children. Like all mirages, it is both appealing and perilously deceptive, luring us away from more rewarding developmental objectives. While capturing the imagination of parents and educators in recent years, the mission of bolstering children's self-esteem has obscured the more promising and productive possibilities of childrearing. (p. 72)

Like all social controversies, of course, the "other side" mounts an equally dramatic defense and counterattack. For instance, James Beane, who has written extensively about self-esteem in the classroom from a positive perspective, took the arguments against making self-esteem a part of the educational curriculum to strenuous task in an article entitled "Sorting Out the Self-Esteem Controversy" (1991). He suggested, for instance, that criticism such as that offered by Seligman is justified in that there is much "fluff" in the self-esteem movement. But Beane also pointed out that there is considerable potential value for the individual and for society in enhancing self-esteem in the educational setting. He went on to say that arguments such as those that resemble Damon's might actually be "reactionary" in nature, reflecting an underlying conservative or "reformist" ideology associated with a right-wing political agenda, instead of scientific thinking. For better or worse, it seems that self-esteem has found its way into our social milieu. The method we use to study this phenomenon *must* be capable of dealing with its psychological and social significance at the academic level, but perhaps it will help us to understand this general social controversy better, too.

Now that studying self-esteem appears to be as important as ever, we can move to the next issue: What is it about self-esteem that promises considerable practical value, generates so much research and theoretical diversity, and lends itself to social as well as scientific discourse? The answer to this question, of course, must reside somewhere in the meaning and structure of self-esteem, which is found in what phenomenological psychologists call the *Lebenswelt* or life-world of everyday experience and activity. After all, it is people who have self-esteem and individuals who suffer the lack of it.

In order to understand this human phenomenon, then, it seems that we must use a method that allows us to do three things. First, it must be capable of accessing the data of human experience, which means researching self-esteem as it is actually lived, describing the nature of this phenomenon accurately, and doing so in a way that is empirical and rigorous enough to be replicable or "scientific." Second, the method must be capable of grappling with a considerable diversity of research techniques, findings, and theoretical points of view that characterize the field today. Ideally, the approach should meet this challenge in a way that integrates the material in a comprehensive fashion. Third, if our work is to have practical value, then the method we use must eventually result in specific techniques for increasing self-esteem that can be applied to, and tested in, real-life settings. Any one of these methodological requirements presents a serious challenge, and finding one method that is capable of dealing with all three factors may involve going beyond those typically used in social science, such as case study, statistical correlations, or even experimental analysis. Indeed, the phenomenological method is the only one I know of that might be able to address all three research needs, so I must present it as the method of choice for this situation. Let me share the reasoning behind this position.

In chapter 2, I will explain what is meant by the "phenomenological method" in detail, because that section deals with methodological issues, but let me introduce it here. In order to do so, however, it is first necessary to differentiate this method of human science research from three "cousins" with which it is often confused. If we did not need a method capable of both broad and deep or "structural" description, then I could do a phenomenology of self-esteem as the word is used in medicine. This use of the term involves a surface, but not necessarily superficial, level of description. For example, one can do a phenomenology of symptoms and create a diagnostic system like the ICD (International Classification of Diseases) or DSM (Diagnostic and Statistical Manual of Mental Disorders) approaches. Describing the obvious, though, often does not reveal that which is hidden, especially the underlying causes that give rise to symptoms in the first place.

Similarly, if we wanted to describe only how self-esteem is experienced or lived by this or that person, then I could do what is more properly called a phenomenalism of self-esteem (Snygg & Combs, 1959). This variation on the word refers to a form of description that is often mistaken for modern phenomenological research, because they both begin with describing a person's experience of a situation, event, or phenomenon. Phenomenal descriptions are limited to a sample of one, however, so their level of generality is minimal. For example, one person may live out his or her anxiety by appearing to be nervous, jumpy, timid, and so forth, but another individual may appear angry, defensive, and aggressive when he or she is worried. Instead of phenomenalism, we need a method that is capable of describing both individual variations in a phenomenon *and* that which they have in common.

The modern phenomenological method is concerned with finding what is called the "general structure" of a phenomenon (Giorgi, 1970).

A general structure is that which defines a particular human phenomenon as such; there is one for each and every human experience. Indeed, the general structure of a human experience, event, or phenomenon is the underlying pattern of meaning that gives rise to these things in the first place, which is why the general structure is definitive. Because we are all unique individuals living in particular cultures and periods of time, the general structure of a phenomenon must manifest itself in a way that is unique and specific to the person experiencing it. Yet, if it is truly a human possibility, and if we are all human beings, then any one of us has potential access to any given experience, although it will be a little different each time. This concern with both the universal and particular dimensions of experience is what differentiates phenomenology from the method known as "content analysis." The latter will tell us what particular elements are involved in an experience, but not *why* they are there or how they are related to one another. Like a blueprint, the general structure may be seen as a kind of map or schematic that is common to all similar buildings, but in a way that also leaves room for individual variation. This combination of universal similarity and individual expression is what distinguishes, for instance, a house from a home, and it is the job of a phenomenology analysis to account for both aspects of a dwelling as well as how they create each other.

Phenomenological psychology, then, is a way of describing both the individual experience and the universal nature of a given human phenomenon as it is lived in real life. As Martin Heidegger, one of the great phenomenological philosophers, said, phenomenological research is letting "that which shows itself be seen from itself in the very way in which it shows itself from itself" (Heidegger, 1962/1927, p. 58). If this is so, then this method should allow us to understand that which shows itself (in this case self-esteem) to be seen from itself (which means describing the general or underlying structure of self-esteem) in the very way in which it shows itself from itself (how self-esteem is lived by any particular person at any specific time). I will present the method in more detail later, but let me say here that it begins with empirical (externally or internally observable) information. These data are then subjected to a systematic process of analysis, which is done in a careful, step-by-step fashion so that the researcher's procedures may be duplicated by others. The final result of this process is the identification of the universal components of an experience and how they may be expressed in any individual instance of the phenomenon.

One way to test the accuracy of a description of a fundamental structure is to use it as a definition, then compare it with other ways of seeing the phenomenon or experience. I call this technique "integrated description" (Mruk, 1994). In other words, the description of the fundamental structure of self-esteem that I wish to develop should result in a definition of self-esteem that is capable of accounting for other ways of defining self-esteem. Also, the more accurate the description of the general structure is, the more comprehensive it should be. So a good general structure should also be able to show how the major research findings of the field support, or at least are consistent with, the definition it offers. Of course, the other and most common way to validate findings in science is to use them to make predictions, then test them for verification. For instance, if the fundamental structure I uncover is valid, then it ought to be possible to build a self-esteem enhancement program around it that can be tested by traditional psychological research methods to see whether or not it produces measurable change. Although phenomenological research itself is usually satisfied with the first approach to evaluating its work, we will use both approaches during the course of this investigation in an attempt to address more traditional requirements for validity.

DEFINING SELF-ESTEEM

In one sense, of course, we all know what self-esteem "really is," because it is a human phenomenon and we are all human beings. But like much commonsense knowledge, there are serious limits to such understandings that become apparent as soon as we examine them closely. As Smelser (1989) observed, "We have a fairly firm grasp of what is meant by self-esteem, as revealed by our own introspection and observation of the behavior of others. But it is hard to put that understanding into precise words" (p. 9). A simple but revealing way to explore this problem is to ask almost any reasonably mature undergraduate psychology class to do the following exercise.

At the beginning of the class or lecture ask each person to write down his or her own definition of self-esteem. Then, invite the students either to read their definitions aloud or to hand them in to be read aloud. As the information comes in, write the key components of each definition on the board so that they can be examined publicly. Let the class know that, at some point, we must develop a single definition at the end of the activity. The typical class sees the point almost immediately: What seems so familiar at the beginning quickly shows itself to be quite difficult. Also, the diversity of definitions tends to be impressive. Often, it is as though there are as many ways to define self-esteem as there are people trying to do so. Last but not least, students notice that each definition appears to have some merit, because they all suggest, capture, or describe an important aspect of the phenomenon. Similarly, the limitations of each given definition become apparent, too.

If the class spends enough time with this exercise, the students will also begin to notice that definitions can be grouped on the basis of key characteristics the various definitions tend to emphasize. One individual will see that some depictions focus on values, such as self-respect. Another person might notice that other definitions center on the feeling or affective dimension of self-esteem. Others will point out that some of the definitions emphasize cognitive factors, such as the attitudinal components of self-esteem, or they might bring attention to the common behavioral aspects of self-esteem, such as being more independent or assertive. If the class is a good one, the students will eventually try to integrate all the components into a comprehensive definition. Typically, they quickly come to see just how difficult it is to define self-esteem. The group's general appreciation for the complexity of the problem deepens when they hold up their own attempts at integration and clarification for others to see and to critique. By the end of this activity, the power of a definition becomes apparent, and so does the need for consensus that Wells and Marwell (1976) discussed.

This exercise is an excellent way to explore the psychology of self-esteem *because it creates a microcosm of what actually happens among researchers.* In fact, by examining existing definitions of self-esteem, Wells and Marwell (1976) did what amounts to an extremely sophisticated version of this activity in their unrivaled review of the research issues facing the field. Smelser (1989) found the same problem existing over a decade later, suggesting that it is both a crucial and a difficult one. Thus, understanding the problems involved in defining self-esteem and presenting a definition with which to work is a central task for any book on the topic.

There are at least two factors that make defining self-esteem so important and yet so problematical. First, a definition opens up a real pathway toward understanding something, in this case self-esteem. In this sense, every major definition is important, because each one may show us some important things about self-esteem that can only be seen from that particular point of view. At the same time, each particular way of seeing self-esteem limits our ability to approach it from a different angle or perspective, much in the same way that every time we look in one direction, it is difficult for us to see in another. Phenomenologists call this limit the problem of perspectivity, meaning that every approach or definition reveals and conceals: We have to stand somewhere if we are to look at something, and each time we turn in one direction, we

close off perception in another. Equally important, there are many definitions of self-esteem to consider. Although we cannot eliminate perspectivity altogether, we must strive to find the most comprehensive
definition (and theory) if we are to reach some degree of consensus.
This task means unraveling what Smelser (1989) called the "definitional
maze" of self-esteem.

There are several ways people go about trying to find a solution to
this problem. One approach is to simply not deal with the issue, a tactic
that is often found in popular literature on self-esteem. After all, dealing
with definitions and their research and theoretical implications is te-
dious work that is often not of interest to the readers or marketers of
such material. (No citation is needed for an example here, because
going to a large chain book store and checking out the self-help section
will demonstrate that this kind of material exists in considerable abundance.) This tactic may be useful for selling books or for writing to
unsophisticated audiences, but it is a poor claim to scholarship. Another
method, and one that is sometimes used even by serious social scientists, is to define self-esteem briefly, then move on. This approach may
be useful if one either agrees with the definition or if one is more
concerned with another issue, such as addressing a topic only peripher-
ally related to self-esteem.

In the long run, such attempts at getting out of the definitional maze
only make it more confusing, not less. The fact is that neither ignoring
the problem nor dismissing it is an adequate solution, if one wants to
describe self-esteem as it is actually lived by real people in real-life
settings or if one is interested in developing a comprehensive theory
of self-esteem. Goals such as these necessitate dealing with the problem
more directly and finding a way of integrating the definitions that do
have some research, theoretical, or practical support. Let us therefore
examine the problem of defining self-esteem in some detail.

Types of Definitions

One of the earliest ways of systematically classifying definitions of self-
esteem was developed by Wells and Marwell (1976). It is based on
two psychological processes: evaluation (which pertains to the role of
cognition) and affection (meaning the role of feelings) as they pertain
to self-esteem:

> In our description, we distinguish between two main underlying pro-
> cesses—evaluation and affection. . . . Like most conceptual distinctions,
> the one between evaluation and affection is not always easy to make consis-

tently and clearly. However, emphasis upon one or the other process leads to different forms of description, explanation, and sometimes, measurement. Self-evaluation generally involves more mechanistic, causal descriptions, while self-affection tends to elicit more "humanistic" conceptualizations of behavior. (p. 62)

The result is a typology of definitions that consists of four ways of defining self-esteem. The basic one is an attitudinal approach, which means treating the self as an object of attention, for we can have positive or negative cognitive, emotional, and behavioral reactions to ourselves just as we do to other objects in the world. The second type of definition developed by social scientists also understands self-esteem in terms of attitudes, but in a more sophisticated way. This time self-esteem is defined as the relation between different sets of attitudes. In this case it is the discrepancy between the self one wishes to be (the "ideal" self) and the self one currently sees (the "real" or "perceived" self) that matters. The closer these two attitudes are, the higher the individual's self-esteem tends to be. The third way to go about defining self-esteem focuses on the psychological responses a person holds toward himself or herself. These responses are usually described as feeling-based or affective in nature, such as positive versus negative or accepting versus rejecting. Finally, Wells and Marwell (1976) maintained that self-esteem may be seen as a function or component of personality. In this case, self-esteem is seen as part of the self-system, usually one that is concerned with motivation and/or self-regulation.

There are other ways to approach making sense out of the definitional maze. Instead of looking at types, for instance, Smelser (1989) attempted to identify the "almost universally accepted components of the concept" (p. 9). He began by presenting three of them:

There is first, a cognitive element; self-esteem means characterizing some parts of the self in descriptive terms: power, confidence, agency. It means asking what kind of person one is. Second, there is an affective element, a valence or degree of positiveness or negativeness attached to those facets identified; we call this high or low self-esteem. Third, and related to the second, there is an evaluative element, an attribution of some level of worthiness according to some ideally held standard. (p. 10)

Smelser went on to note that definitions vary as to whether they focus on self-esteem as more of a global or more of a situational phenomenon. That is, some definitions see self-esteem as being reasonably stable over time, whereas others regard self-esteem as being responsive to situational and contextual influences, which means that it fluctuates over time.

In fact, however, neither developing typologies nor simply identifying common attributes can offer us the one thing that is needed the most: a clear statement concerning what self-esteem is and how it is lived in everyday life. Although typologies of self-esteem reduce the number of definitions we have to contend with, they offer us no criteria for identifying one as more valid than another. And while identifying common elements may be a necessary step toward developing a consensus, it is also necessary to work them into a unified form; otherwise, they simply constitute a list. Clearly, another approach is needed.

Developing a Phenomenological Definition of Self-Esteem

The first thing to ask from a phenomenological perspective is where should we look for a definition, which is to say, what kinds of data are likely to reveal something about the meaning and structure of self-esteem? There are few alternatives. One well-worn path is to create what seems to be a reasonable definition, then employ it operationally. This approach offers maximum freedom in that it allows people to pursue their own vision. In all likelihood, however, such a definition will simply mimic one of those found in the typologies mentioned earlier or add yet another false trail to the definitional maze. While identifying consistencies or doing some sort of a content analysis may help clarify matters somewhat, this tack does not necessarily result in an integration of material, because it does not get at what holds the common elements together. It seems, then, that our best bet for making our way out of the maze is to find a definition that underlies the other definitions, like determining a common denominator for various numerical expressions.

Time can be a helpful factor here, because a kind of a scientific "shake out" occurs as any field matures. Once a definition, finding, theory, or technique is formed, other researchers tend to come along and reexamine such work and either confirm or discount it. Sometimes people make new discoveries that can be compared to the earlier work in such a way that supports or weakens it. In either case, this process repeats itself so that uncertainty is slowly reduced. Information accumulates in this way over time, and eventually some of it achieves a level of credibility in a given area. In a sense, then, time functions as the ultimate test in science: It is an important kind of public scientific "trial" through which all definitions and findings must pass.

One way to gather data that may be helpful in developing a definition of self-esteem, then, is to examine existing ones that seem to have endured for a reasonable period of time. There are two indications that a definition, or any major research finding for that matter, meets this criterion. First, we can consider definitions, depictions, or descriptions of self-esteem to be legitimate data for phenomenological analysis if they were developed by individuals whose work is regarded by other researchers as having made important contributions to the field. We might call this quality the *persistence* of a definition. Such definitions persist because they provide a structure on which research and theory can form. Some of them may even do that because they have some validity. Second, time can be used to signal the viability of a given definition if it continues to occur in the field in a way that is corroborated by others. This kind of confirmation, which may include empirical support, gives a definition *significance*, and that quality makes the material worthy of examination, too. Notice that the same standards can be applied to other material, such as determining which authors in the field are important, which research findings need to be dealt with, which theories require reviewing, and so on. Of course, it is necessary to work with all such information if we are interested in achieving the degree of integration and consensus that was said to be the next step in the development of the field.

The next question is, what are we to do with these data when they are collected, or how do we turn this information into knowledge? One answer is found in analyzing the material phenomenologically, which means describing the underlying structure that gives rise to the data (in this case, the various definitions). In other words, definitions of self-esteem that stand the test of time (persistence and/or significance) may achieve such status because they are grounded in something important, such as self-esteem itself or a way of understanding it that reveals various aspects of the phenomenon. We can subject these descriptions to what Edmund Husserl (1970a/1954) called the "phenomenological reduction," which involves appreciating them from their own perspective. This activity involves suspending our own preconceptions, criticisms, and theoretical perspectives as much as possible while examining the particular datum (definition) under consideration. Then, we can consider what each major definition says about self-esteem and use that information to develop one that is more comprehensive. In other words, we work back from the various insights about self-esteem that have arisen over time and "reduce" this data toward that which gives rise to it in the first place. The eventual return to the thing itself (in this case, self-esteem) is what differentiates this use of the literature from a simple review or content analysis of it. We are *not* just looking at what others did and we are *not* just trying to identify what they found. Rather, we are trying to discover that which gives rise to important insights in the first place.

It was already mentioned that the other way of finding the "real" definition of self-esteem necessary for this project is to see how it is lived by real people in real settings, which means doing some form of life-oriented empirical research. This kind of work is helpful for two reasons. First, self-esteem may not be anything more than a scientific construct. If that is the case, we should not be able to find it in real life. Second, if there is such a thing as self-esteem, then the description of the underlying structure we obtain from researching it in the life-world should match or be compatible with the one we find from doing the phenomenological reduction of key definitions. Such an outcome, of course, increases the validity and value of such a definition. A corol-lary to this position is that the diversity of the field can also serve as a test of validity. If a phenomenological description fails to account for a major definition, research finding, or theory, then we know where it is limited or incomplete.

Now let us turn to the data of existing definitions and analyze them as a necessary first step in this phenomenology of self-esteem.

The Data

At first glance it might seem that identifying major definitions, significant findings, or leading theories of self-esteem is an arbitrary process. After all, how is one to identify that which is appropriate to consider in a stack of information that consists of 7,648 articles and books in English directly relating to the topic? (The PsycINFO search I mentioned earlier arrived at this figure using the "focus" command, which limits the works cited to those that specifically address the keyword as a major theme in the piece. I did not use the "explode" command, which uses less stringent criteria and would yield a much higher number.) This figure does not include the 30,000 or so articles that relate to self-esteem less directly (Kitano, 1989) or the 2,080 self-esteem-related measurement instruments in existence (Wells & Marwell, 1976).

The fact that much of this material is redundant or just not significant makes our task considerably easier. For instance, Wells and Marwell (1976) indicated that the vast majority of these articles and instruments are single studies or tools that are created out of a specific interest or need, then pass into near oblivion. Also, often what is useful in such work can be subsumed under another major idea or finding that has already stood the test of time. Occasionally, however, an author or finding achieves persistence or significance and becomes a beacon in the scientific landscape of self-esteem. This material often becomes a standard against which subsequent work is to be compared. It is important to note that investigating such material in chronological order is helpful, because the flow of time has already been identified as an important part of the scientific method and doing it this way may reveal insights concerning the evolution of how self-esteem is understood.

The first such datum to consider is more than 100 years old and still stands as one of the major landmarks in understanding self-esteem today:

> So our self-feeling in this world depends entirely on what we *back* ourselves to be and do. It is determined by the ratio of our actualities to our supposed potentialities; a fraction of which our pretensions are the denominator and the numerator our success: thus,

$$\text{Self-esteem} = \frac{\text{Successes}}{\text{Pretensions}} .$$

> Such a fraction may be increased as well by diminishing the denominator as by increasing the numerator. (James, 1983/1890, p. 296)

The first thing to notice in William James' definition is that self-esteem is seen as an affective phenomenon: That is, he suggests that it is lived as a feeling or an emotion. This means that, like all affective states, self-esteem is something that we find ourselves as having or lacking, whether we want to or not. A phenomenologist would call this aspect of self-esteem a part of our "facticity," or one of the basic facts of being human.

The second point in what is probably the single most often quoted definition in the literature is also important to note: Self-esteem is depicted as having the character of a ratio. This depiction suggests two important things about self-esteem. One is that a ratio involves a set of identifiable components. The denominator of this existential formula represents our values, goals, and aspirations (pretensions). Our behavior (successes) is the numerator, indicating that what we do about these things has serious consequences for how we know and experience ourselves. The other interesting aspect of this description is that a ratio expresses a dynamic rather than a static relationship: If either component changes, then the expression or outcome changes, too. According to this view, then, self-esteem can be altered, in this case by changing what occurs on either level (modifying a person's aspirations or the frequency of his or her successes). In summarizing James' contribution to defining self-esteem, we can say that it is something that is affective (emphasizes feeling), competence-oriented (it depends on the effectiveness of one's actions), and dynamic (open to change).

The study of self-esteem all but disappeared from mainstream (behaviorally oriented) psychology for about the next 75 years, probably because of the behavioral insistence on observation and measurement that almost banished self-related experience from American psychology during this period. Yet, although Freud never actually used the term *self-esteem*, the psychodynamic perspective always allowed room for such a possibility. For instance, Alfred Adler's (1927) work contains an implicit theory of self-esteem, and Robert White's (1963) work gives explicit psychodynamic attention to this topic:

> Self-esteem, then, has its taproot in the experience of efficacy. It is not built merely on what others do or what the environment provides. From the very start it is based on what one can make the environment provide, even if it is only through more vigorous sucking or more loudly sustained cries. In the infant's actuality, the feeling of efficacy is regulated by the success or failures of *his* efforts, for he has no knowledge of what else may be affecting the environment's response. From this point onward self-esteem is closely tied to feelings of efficacy and, as it develops, to the more general cumulative sense of competence. (p. 134)

White defined self-esteem in a developmental context and ties it to three very important processes: what developmental psychologists often call "mastery," or the biological push for an organism to deal with the tasks of living competently, the emergence of increasingly sophisticated motor and cognitive abilities, and a growing sense of self or identity. He also noted that this process is apparent in the first stirrings of life outside the womb. In addition to being the passive recipient of whatever the environment presents to them, for instance, infants also act upon their surroundings. Each cry, every smile, and any grasping motion can result in the sudden relief of pain, playful exploration, or innocent pleasure if it reaches a sympathetic caregiver or nurturing environment. These early successes (and failures) are more important than they might seem at first because, over time, such efforts become more deliberate and sophisticated. Moreover, the process "speeds up," so to speak, as the infant reaches childhood, when new and increasingly sophisticated abilities and challenges appear, which serve to increase the individual's range of mastery, competence, and feelings of efficacy. According to this view, by the time latency is reached these forces, and the developmental history of how they were manifested in a given individual's life, become the part of a person's identity and experience we call self-esteem.

In tying self-esteem to the biology of mastery and the pleasure of competence to one's identity, White gave self-esteem considerable developmental importance. However, he took great pain to show that this self-feeling is different from mere narcissism because it is tied to reality—in this case, success and failures in the real world. And, although White focused primarily on the latency years as being especially crucial for self-esteem, as that is when we acquire many of the skills necessary for living, he also suggested that self-esteem is a developmental issue that extends far beyond these early years.

Earlier I suggested that the 1960s seemed to be something of a rebirth for the social psychology of self-esteem, an event that has been noticed by others as well (Seligman, 1995b). During this period, for instance, the first three major books explicitly dedicated exclusively to the topic of self-esteem appeared within just 4 years of one another. Each one of them also reflects a major theoretical orientation to the topic in that one of them is sociological in nature, another is learning theory–oriented, and the third is written from a humanistic perspective. This convergence among social scientists at a time when the self and consciousness were returning to the field is too significant to be coincidental.

Morris Rosenberg (1965) was the first of these second-generation leaders in the field, and he made a number of very important contributions, one of which is his definition:

> Self-esteem, as noted, is a positive or negative attitude toward a particular object, namely, the self. . . . High self-esteem, as reflected in our scale items, expresses the feeling that one is "good enough." The individual simply feels that he is a person of worth; he respects himself for what he is, but he does not stand in awe of himself nor does he expect others to stand in awe of him. He does *not* necessarily consider himself superior to others. (pp. 30–31)

One thing to notice about understanding self-esteem as an attitude is that this view casts it in a light where cognition is a key characteristic of self-esteem and how it works. This shift to a more cognitive than affective focus opens up all the perceptual and social factors involved in attitude formation, including various evaluative and judgmental processes that are well known to social scientists. Of course, forming attitudes about the self is more complex than doing so for anything else, largely because the perceiver is also the object of perception (Wylie, 1974). However, social scientists were experienced at measuring and researching attitudes at this time, so that they could start to study self-esteem more empirically than could those working from the psychodynamic perspective.

Another important moment in this definition is that it introduces the concept of personal dignity, or "worthiness," into the field. By doing so, Rosenberg opened the door to the roles that values and standards play in the landscape of self-esteem—after all, values are central to the process of "e-*value*-ation." This view of self-esteem is very different from the more individually oriented psychological work we saw in the other definitions. For example, values, and the acquisition of values, are tied to a number of interpersonal processes, such as culture, which means, among other things, that self-esteem can be studied from a sociological point of view. Concentrating on worthiness and values also forces researchers to deal with a number of strong dichotomies, such as a person's feeling of worth *or* unworthiness, judging himself or herself as being good or bad. Finally, injecting values into the definition opens up the ultimate question of cultural relativism versus transcendental human values. That is, are the values associated with self-esteem merely those that are approved by a culture, social group, or individual preference? Or is self-esteem based on some fundamental human values with which we are all concerned? We will return to this issue later in the book, as it constitutes an important piece of the self-esteem puzzle.

Rosenberg's contributions to this field are enormous. The significance of understanding self-esteem in terms of worthiness parallels James' insight concerning the relationship between self-esteem and success. In fact, the most frequently used definitions of self-esteem today have worthiness as their central feature. Next, characterizing self-esteem as an attitude at a time when social scientists were making considerable advances in measuring and researching such cognitive processes led to the development of a new research paradigm in the field of self-esteem, namely, testing and measuring it. Indeed, Rosenberg's (1965) self-esteem inventory opened the way for literally thousands of empirical studies on self-esteem in both sociology and psychology. Finally, the fact that Rosenberg worked from the sociological point of view in a field previously dominated by psychologists forced it to become a truly interdisciplinary area.

The next significant moment in the field occurred just 2 years later in 1967 with the publication of Stanley Coopersmith's *The Antecedents of Self-Esteem*. This book is especially important because it represents the return of self-esteem to mainstream academic (i.e., behavioral and experimentally oriented) psychology. Coopersmith endeavored to study the "conditions and experiences that enhance or lessen self-esteem"

(1967, p. 1) by using traditional empirical psychological methods, particularly through controlled observation, and defined self-esteem in the following way:

> By self-esteem we refer to the evaluation which the individual makes and customarily maintains with regard to himself: it expresses an attitude of approval or disapproval, and indicates the extent to which the individual believes himself to be capable, significant, successful, and worthy. In short, self-esteem is a *personal* judgment of worthiness that is expressed in the attitudes the individual holds toward himself. It is a subjective experience which the individual conveys to others by verbal reports and other overt expressive behavior. (pp. 4–5)

At first it might appear that Coopersmith's definition offers no additional insights as to what must be included in a phenomenological description of self-esteem. After all, most of what he says is found to reside in the other definitions. Rosenberg (1965), for instance, already depicted the attitudinal and evaluatively oriented aspects of worthiness, and the psychological tradition as exemplified by James (1983/1890) and White (1963) described the affective and success (competence-based) dimensions of self-esteem.

But Coopersmith's definition does offer some new insights. His way of envisioning self-esteem, for instance, invites us to think about just how important it is to a person's identity and awareness. If self-esteem is truly "subject-ive" (meaning "of the subject") in this way, then expressions of that subjectivity (namely, one's behavior) ought to involve and include their self-esteem. If this connection exists, he reasoned, and if behavior can be measured, then it should also be possible to study self-esteem as a variable in human behavior. And being a good behaviorally oriented social learning theorist, Coopersmith did just that. Like Rosenberg, he developed a self-esteem inventory, but this instrument, the Self-Esteem Inventory, or SEI (1975, 1981), became what is probably the most widely used assessment instrument in the history of the field.

In addition, Coopersmith was interested in investigating how high and low self-esteem influenced human behavior in positive and negative ways and outlined a behavioral approach to enhancing self-esteem. Finally, while he was interested in the development of self-esteem, he also insisted that it must be researched more empirically than did his psychological predecessors. For instance, he studied such things as parent-child correlations by using observational and experimental designs; we shall see that much of this work stands today. As a result of this influence, it can be said that the vast majority of studies on self-esteem done since the 1960s have their roots in the research contributions made by Coopersmith and Rosenberg.

The third major figure in the self-esteem revolution of this period is Nathaniel Branden, a humanistically oriented clinician whose book, *The Psychology of Self-Esteem* (1969), may well be the first popular, but still academic, treatment of the topic. Although written primarily in a philosophical tone, his way of defining self-esteem makes two important contributions to the field. First, in addition to explicitly identifying both competence and worthiness as equally important components of self-esteem, he notes that the relationship between them is important:

> Self-esteem has two interrelated aspects: it entails a sense of personal efficacy and a sense of personal worth. It is the integrated sum of self-confidence and self-respect. It is the conviction that one is *competent* to live and *worthy* of living. (p. 110)

In other words, the relationship between competence and worthiness is presented as a third factor to consider in understanding self-esteem. For Branden, then, self-esteem is a function of competence (our own efficacy or abilities), worthiness (our values about right and wrong, good and bad, etc.), *and* the relationship between them (especially whether or not they are integrated and "match up" behaviorally).

The word *conviction* opens up a new element of self-esteem to consider, for it suggests more than beliefs, although beliefs are a part of convictions. Similarly, deep convictions are more than mere attitudinal phenomena, because they have the power to result in very *strong* actions: Sometimes people even die for them. Branden seems to mean conviction in the deepest sense possible, and, although he prefers to couch the term in the context of Ayn Rand's philosophy, the degree of conviction, values, and feelings of which he speaks appears to be akin to what existential psychologists refer to as "authenticity." The implication here is that there are certain fundamental values that are intrinsic to human beings—values so important that people need the feelings associated with them in order to "live," regardless of one's culture or time. Moreover, there is a dynamic quality to such existential convictions: We live by them, through them, and for them according to this view; when we fail to do so, there is a price to pay. This cost involves what Branden calls "pseudo self-esteem," which is akin to the concept of "inauthenticity" among existentialists. Thus, Branden went beyond Rosenberg and Coopersmith in terms of describing the importance of self-esteem as a psychological variable: He saw it as some fundamental human need, perhaps the most fundamental one.

After a series of rather popular material on self-esteem written over the next two decades, Branden developed his original ideas much more fully in his 1994 work, *The Six Pillars of Self-Esteem*. This book probably stands as the most complete statement of his thought, but it is important to realize that this approach to self-esteem does not have the empirical orientation of the other two researchers. Instead, Branden relies on case studies and philosophical argument to support his view.

After the reemergence of self-esteem as a legitimate psychological and sociological topic during the 1960s, the field seemed to turn its collective attention away from defining self-esteem and directed its focus instead to more practical concerns, such as investigating the experiential aspects of self-esteem, understanding the evaluative processes associated with self-esteem, and enhancing self-esteem. Seymour Epstein (1985), for instance, made considerable progress in terms of researching how self-esteem is actually lived by examining what I like to think of as self-esteem "moments," situations and experiences that invoke and involve self-esteem as a crucial element. His definition of self-esteem, however, which is our main concern here, is based on seeing it in terms of worthiness and needs, both of which we have seen before.

> Let us now turn to a consideration of self-esteem, a particularly important descriptive postulate in a person's implicit theory of self. The need for self-esteem, at its most basic level, arises from an internalization of the need of the child to be loved by the parents. . . . Thus, at its most basic level, self-esteem corresponds to a broad assessment of loveworthiness, and constitutes one of the most fundamental postulates in an individual's implicit self-theory. (p. 302)

Similarly, Pope and colleagues (1988), who specialize in enhancing self-esteem with children, based much of their work on the evaluative aspects of self-esteem seen earlier, particularly in regard to the extent to which a child's "perceived self" matches up to their "ideal self." And Bednar and associates (1989) developed a very intensive "cognitive-existential" self-esteem enhancement program based on definitional components we have encountered before.

> Parenthetically, we define self-esteem as a subjective and enduring sense of realistic self-approval. It reflects how the individual views and values the self at the most fundamental levels of psychological experiencing. . . . Fundamentally, then, self-esteem is an enduring and affective sense of personal value based on accurate self-perceptions. (p. 4)

Finally, those who research self-esteem from a social psychological or sociological point of view tend to define it in terms of the attitudinal or evaluative processes introduced by Rosenberg. For example, Roy Baumeister, who emerged as a major force in the self-esteem literature during the 1990s, takes a very straightforward position when he and his colleagues say, "By *self-esteem* we mean simply a favorable global evaluation of oneself" (Baumeister, Smart, & Boden, 1996, p. 5).

This data-gathering activity on the major definitions of self-esteem has, of course, not been exhaustive. However, it does seem clear that we have reached the point of redundance in major psychological and sociological material on the subject. What we have found so far, then, appears to be two things. First, it looks as though there are some foundations for reasonably objective standards against which we can evaluate any definition of self-esteem. For instance, if a definition is going to be complete, it must account for such things as competence, worthiness, attitudes, feelings, and the possibility of maintaining or losing self-esteem. Second, it is clear that the field has accumulated enough definitions for us to begin our work. In other words, consensus is needed, data are available, and the time to do this work is now, providing one uses a method that is up to this descriptive task.

The Fundamental Structure of Self-Esteem

We now know that each major definition of self-esteem seems to suggest something important about this vital human phenomenon. This material can be seen as the raw data that we can analyze in a way that results in articulating the fundamental structure of self-esteem, or that which gives rise to the various definitional possibilities in the first place. These data can be organized in several ways, but three key features clearly stand out: the basic components or elements of self-esteem and how they are connected to each other, the basic qualities of experience involved in self-esteem or how it is lived as a phenomenon, and the basic dynamics of self-esteem, especially how it is both reasonably stable yet open to change over time. Let us examine each of them in turn.

The Basic Components of Self-Esteem

One way to organize the information on what constitutes self-esteem is to examine the various definitions in terms of central themes. Because competence and worthiness were presented earliest in the field, these data can be processed first. Table 1.1 presents the major definitions of self-esteem that we discussed earlier in terms of their inclusion of competence and worthiness.

Competence is the more behavioral and observable component because it involves action, some of which can be seen and even evaluated, for instance, in terms of how effective a given response is to the demands of a particular situation or event. Although worded differently, the definitions offered by James (success) and White (efficacy) are also based on competence as a central characteristic of self-esteem. The insights into self-esteem offered by Rosenberg and Coopersmith emphasize worthiness as a central component. This way of understanding self-esteem seems to involve making a judgment about the actor as well as or instead of the action. Branden's phrase "competent at living" leaves no room for doubt on the place of this component in his definition, but he also gives such an emphasis to worthiness that one cannot be seen as being more important than the other, which means that we must place his understanding on both levels of the array. All of this information is represented in the table, and there is no need to consider other definitions in this analysis because we know them to be redundant in one way or another.

The Lived Qualities of Self-Esteem

Next, all the definitions point to two major experiential or lived dimensions of self-esteem. In some cases, the authors describe these processes in cognitive terms, meaning that self-esteem is lived as some sort of mental evaluation that is expressed as either a positive or a negative perception or attitude. In the other instances, self-esteem is described in affective terms, indicating that it is lived as an emotional state or feeling tone. This information can be organized by arranging it on another array, as shown in Table 1.2.

As before, we find that these self-esteem researchers tend to emphasize one dimension over the other. However, it is necessary to clarify

TABLE 1.1 Major Self-Esteem Definitions in Terms of Competence and Worthiness

	James	White	Rosenberg	Coopersmith	Branden
Competence	X	X			X
Worthiness			X	X	X

TABLE 1.2 Major Self-Esteem Definitions in Terms of Cognition and Affect

	James	White	Rosenberg	Coopersmith	Branden
Cognition			X	X	
Affect	X	X			X

my decision-making process here, because most of the definitions make reference to both possibilities concerning this aspect of the phenomenon. For instance, although Rosenberg clearly leans toward understanding self-esteem more in terms of attitudes than feelings in most of his work, his extended definition quoted earlier refers to both affective and cognitive processes, so it is possible to mark his insight as being concerned with attitudes, or attitudes and affect, but not affect alone. We can say the same of Coopersmith's definition, because it mentions experience even though it focuses on attitudes. Branden's use of the term *conviction* implies attitudes at some level, even though I have marked him as emphasizing the affective dimension, because conviction is such an emotionally powerful term. What I have tried to do here, then, is to show which aspect is most heavily emphasized, unless both seem to be stressed to an equal degree by the author, and I did not see that this time. Of course, there is room for disagreement, but the point remains very clear: The data indicate that a comprehensive definition of self-esteem must account for both processes as a part of the lived dimension of self-esteem.

The Dynamics of Self-Esteem

Finally, we found that all the major perspectives on self-esteem regard it as a dynamic (i.e., embodied, vital, and ongoing) dimension of being human. Indeed, insofar as self-esteem is a developmental phenomenon, we must see it as a dynamic one. Also, self-esteem is like an organic system in that even though it reaches a certain degree of stability by adulthood, it also seems to remain open to change. After all, if this were not the case, how could we say that a person has chronically low self-esteem and that he or she should work on improving it? Therefore, since dynamic processes can be rapid (a very "open" system) or slow (a relatively stable, or "closed," system), the definitions of self-esteem can be analyzed on the basis of whether they emphasize change or stability, as indicated in Table 1.3.

TABLE 1.3 Major Self-Esteem Definitions in Terms of Stability and Openness

	James	White	Rosenberg	Coopersmith	Branden
Stability		X	X	X	
Openness	X				X

Once again, we see a trend toward dichotomies concerning this dimension of self-esteem. James' depiction of it as a ratio, for instance, makes openness to change a central aspect of self-esteem, for as one part of the equation changes, so must the other. White, of course, is very developmentally oriented in his thinking, so his view of self-esteem must contain a degree of openness. However, he is also psychodynamic, which means that most of this openness occurs in childhood and after that intrapsychic processes work to keep self-esteem much more stable than open. Attitudes tend to be more static (consistent, or "customary"), which is why I place Rosenberg and Coopersmith here. And, as Branden suggests, convictions require continual work if they are to be maintained, which means that they are basically open. What seems to be showing itself here is another continuum characteristic: Self-esteem is *both* stable and open. Only a dynamic system can be stable enough to fend off interference in the service of maintaining its integrity, yet still be open enough to be able to adapt to situational variables or repeated exposures to something new.

Let me summarize to this point. So far we have identified criteria for obtaining appropriate data concerning the meaning and structure of self-esteem, collected that information from the major psychological and sociological work on it, and analyzed this information for regularities. In so doing, we find that self-esteem involves at least three essential components, or what some phenomenologists call "constitutive elements" (Giorgi, 1970). First, the very foundation of self-esteem seems to involve some sort of connection between competence and worthiness. Second, self-esteem is lived on both the cognitive and affective levels, as it involves such processes as acquiring values, making comparisons on the basis of them, becoming aware of the results of such comparisons, and feeling the impact of these conclusions in a most personal or meaningful way. Third, self-esteem is a dynamic phenomenon, which means that it can fluctuate more than more stable characteristics like personality and intelligence (Sigelman & Shaffer, 1995). The fundamental structure of self-esteem, then, must capture these findings and show how they are connected to one another to result in this thing we call "self-esteem." Such a definition would be accurate in that its depiction of the underlying structure is based on the thing itself and comprehensive in that it should also be able to show how each major definition can be found in the structure.

The Structure

One description of self-esteem's fundamental structure that does seem to capture the central characteristics shown above may be stated in the following way: *Self-esteem is the lived status of one's competence in dealing with the challenges of living in a worthy way over time.* It is very important to realize that this statement is not just another definition of self-esteem. Remember, a depiction of a phenomenon's fundamental structure is an attempt to describe a particular aspect or possibility of human existence in a way that reveals the essential elements of that phenomenon and that articulates how these components work together to create that particular human process, experience, or behavior in the first place, as well as in any given instance of it. As such, the description provides a skeleton upon which we should be able to organize a body of knowledge concerning what is known about a particular human thing. As I hope we shall see, this organizing power of a phenomenological description makes establishing a meaningful degree of consensus possible in this field.

We may begin by examining the basic components of self-esteem, and how they are connected, as described in the fundamental structure. First, it is important to clarify what kind of competence is involved in self-esteem, what sort of worthiness it entails, and how they interact with one another to create something greater than either one of them alone. Competence is mentioned first because it was identified as the basis for self-esteem earlier than worthiness. James placed competence in relation to aspirations and success, White talked about it in terms of mastering the world around us, and Branden extends the domain of what is to be dealt with competently to include how we live. All three aspects of competence (success, mastery, and authenticity) indicate that self-esteem is tied to how we comport ourselves in the life-world, or how we "act." In other words, competence is the behavioral aspect of self-esteem: It is reflected in and through our individual actions. It is very important to realize, however, that self-esteem cannot be defined on the basis of competence alone. For example, if self-esteem involved only competence, it would mean that a competent liar, a skillful abuser, or an efficient mass murderer would all be individuals who demonstrate high self-esteem. This notion is, of course, absolutely absurd; such thinking violates the entire intent of the concept of self-esteem. Thus, definitions of self-esteem that are based only on competence must be understood as being incomplete.

Instead, self-esteem appears to be structured such that the quality or meaning of what we do (or fail to do) is important, too. The "value" of our actions seems to play a vital role in regard to having (or losing) self-esteem, so in this sense it must be seen as involving standards and perceptions concerning that which is meritorious, good, or "worthy." But worthiness without competence is just as limiting as competence without worthiness. For example, the critics of the self-esteem movement are correct when they point out that simply lavishing praise on a child on a daily basis does not mean that he or she will do well in school (or in life, for that matter), because, ultimately, success is based on performance, and that requires some degree of competence. Although competence and worthiness are factors that affect self-esteem, it turns out, then, that the relationship between these two components is equally important. They are both necessary for self-esteem, because they compliment and balance one another: Worthiness prevents competence from becoming arrogance by keeping the individual focused on basic values, and competence prevents worthiness from becoming narcissism by requiring good feelings to be earned, not given.

Branden began to capture the character of this interactive process through his phrase "*competent* to live and *worthy* of living," but some elaboration is needed, as this description does not tell us what kinds of real-life experiences and situations require competence in a way that leads to worthiness. What I call *challenges of living*, which are certain relatively specific types of situations, are most important in this regard. The prototypical self-esteem challenge is an existential one. These are times when one's status as a competent and worthy person is itself at stake, which means being in a situation where we can demonstrate our worthiness as a person through the competence of our responses, or where we can lose self-esteem through our own failure to respond effectively to what we understand as doing the "right thing." Other kinds of challenges to our competence and worthiness, such as mastering a particular skill, are also important in that they do matter for our self-esteem over time. But facing an "existential" challenge goes directly to the heart of self-esteem much more quickly, and I will give examples of situations at the end of this elaboration.

Our self-esteem, then, is the *lived status* of our individual competence at dealing with the challenges of living in a worthy way. Just as we live our cultural backgrounds, developmental histories, or identities both consciously and unconsciously, self-esteem is also embedded in our perceptions, expressed through our feelings, and embodied in our be-havior—all with varying degrees of awareness. But states of existence, even physical states, must address the issue of existing *over time*, which is the final component of the structure. There are two ways time is active in regard to self-esteem. First, as we mature, the history of our successes and failures at handling the challenges of life eventually brings us to a basic understanding of who we are as persons in this regard, which is referred to as "global self-esteem" in the literature. It is in this way, for instance, that we may talk about a person as having "high" or "low" self-esteem. Maintaining a steady state is itself a challenge, and such things as our history, defense mechanisms, and identity all work very hard to help keep our selves reasonably stable.

Second, states of being require some flexibility if they are to be adapt-able enough to last for any length of time. The lived status of our self-esteem may change temporarily, for instance, when a particular situation speaks to us in terms of worthiness and competence. Winning a coveted award (which would be a positive fluctuation) or being caught engaging in questionable behavior (which would be a negative fluctua-tion) are examples of such experiences. However, it is also possible for the entire system to shift, such as when one experiences a period of prolonged positive personal growth or when one undergoes one of those rare transformative experiences life sometimes offers. Of course, major changes can also move in a negative direction, such as during a period of personal hardship involving depression, addiction, or some other behavioral malady. In any case, the descriptors "lived status" and "over time" attempt to capture the dynamics of stability versus open-ness.

If self-esteem involves one's status as a worthy person in regard to whether or not one faces the challenges of living competently over time, then we ought to be able to find evidence of such processes in self-esteem-related experiences. Remember, this kind of empirically ori-ented research is another way of confirming or disconfirming the general structure. I investigated precisely this type of self-esteem "moment" (which can be defined as an experience that impacts on one's self-esteem) by using a small group of subjects who were reasonably well diversified in terms of age, gender, and socioeconomic status (Mruk, 1983). Participants were asked to describe two experiences in detail: a time when they were pleased with themselves in a biographically crucial way and a time when they were displeased with themselves. The experi-ences spontaneously chosen by all the subjects can be described as encountering a situation that challenged them to deal with what would be called an "approach-avoidance" problem. On the one hand, they wanted very much to do the "right thing." On the other, doing so meant facing a personal limitation or problem that they had worked very hard to avoid facing. We will look at this work in some detail when we develop a phenomenological theory of self-esteem in chapter 5, and, of course, the curious reader can go there now. For now, some brief descriptions of these self-esteem stories may help us understand the fundamental structure of self-esteem in action.

One example involves an older woman with a traditional sense of gender who had to choose between complying with a male supervisor's legitimate work request to give up her current duties for others, or to take a stand and argue vigorously against changing positions based on the fact that she liked her job and did not want the new duties. On the surface, the immediate problem is a relatively simple one of compliance versus risk taking. The analysis revealed, however, that she had a long history of complying with authority figures, particularly males, beginning with her father. In her life, such decisions inevitably led to her giving up what she really wanted, then feeling terrible about doing so. Another example concerns a much younger man who had a clinically significant fear of public speaking. In the past he avoided situations in which speaking publicly would be necessary, sometimes at a cost of considerable psychological pain and missed financial opportunities. However, this individual also had a very strong commitment to his career and work. Then, one day life suddenly challenged him on both levels when his career development required him to either defend his work in public forums or lose any hope of advancement in his field. In these two examples, the individuals faced their particular challenges at living and experienced a concomitant increase in their self-esteem, because they demonstrated competence at living in ways that are worthy of a decent, healthy, functional human being.

Facing such existential dilemmas does not always end on a positive note. One negative example involved a woman who had a life theme of loneliness around the holidays connected with the fact that her entire family died when she was young. One holiday season, she was facing the possibility of terrible isolation yet again, when a fellow worker made advances toward her that she knew she should resist. However, the immediate possibility of comfort seemed too appealing, and the thought of being alone again too overwhelming, so she slept with the colleague (for whom she did not care) in a situation in which she knew fellow workers would know about the event and react poorly to it. Similarly, a young man had a negative biographic theme that involved neglecting his physical well-being in certain situations. He subjected an injured back to continued stress rather than allowing himself the time to rest it, because doing so would have meant thinking about the loss of an important relationship he could not bear to face. Unfortunately, this decision led to the development of an irrevocable illness and many years of pain. In both instances, the person took what at first appeared to be the easy way out, failed to deal with the challenge life presented in a way that demonstrated competence and worthiness, and subsequently suffered negative consequences, such as a loss of self-respect, pain, guilt, and regret. Note that this outcome is consistent with what the general structure would predict when one fails to face the challenges appropriately: Inadequate responses (behavior that is not competent in the situation) can lead to failures at living effectively, and not living up to one's values *ought* to result in negative feelings (a loss of worthiness or sense of unworthiness).

The analysis of this type of self-esteem experience (we shall see that there are others as well) also revealed that there is a six-stage process that the individual goes through when facing major challenges of living. I will present this research, and those steps, in detail when we look at a phenomenological theory of self-esteem later on. The point I am trying to make right now is that the validity of the definition of self-esteem presented here is supported on two levels. First, it seems comprehensive enough to integrate the aspects of self-esteem suggested by the major definitions the field has generated over time. In fact, it is the only definition of which I am aware that does so. Second, in addition to such construct validity, the definition seems to be able to work with the data of real-life experience, which also lends this description of the fundamental structure of self-esteem some empirical credibility.

A Brief Example of the Value of Working With a Fundamental Structure

I would like to take a moment and demonstrate what a phenomenological approach to self-esteem can offer this field by using it to address two problems we have encountered so far. The first one concerns the need for consensus and integration in this area, as mentioned at the outset. Instead of being confused by the fact that there are several "traditional" ways of looking at, researching, and understanding self-esteem, we now can appreciate how such a situation arose and why it has persisted so long. In other words, each definition of self-esteem that has established some degree of significance or persistence in the field seems to have done so because it is partially "real" or "valid" in that it is tied to some aspect of general structure. However, they are all also only partial descriptions, which means that they all leave out important aspects of the phenomenon found in the general structure.

Thus, fragmentation is bound to occur in the field. Those who define self-esteem more on the basis of competence than worthiness develop lines of research and theories that focus more on behavior than on feelings. Similarly, those who emphasize the cognitive dimensions of self-esteem (the attitudinal and evaluative processes) follow one line of activity, whereas those who focus on affective processes (the feelings associated with competence or worthiness) pursue another. We can liken this process to a group of hikers wishing to explore the beauty of a forest. They all may start out in the same area, but soon each one wanders off in a different direction as they are drawn by a particular aspect of the terrain. The consequences of exploring territory this way seem to apply to what happened in our field: Eventually the researchers lose sight of each other, and the lack of a common ground may even turn the forest into a maze.

Indeed, there are those who no longer even consider the search for definitions an important activity and simply accept a particular definition because worthiness is the most commonly used one today. Partial definitions, even common ones, however, only perpetuate the confusion. In fact, they can even lead to some additional problems I will discuss later when we look at work that suggests a positive correlation between high self-esteem and violent behavior. A better approach would be to equip our explorers with a basic map of the forest first, then let them investigate this or that part of it in detail, meet afterward to share information, and thereby reach a higher degree of consensus about what the forest looks like. Unfortunately, it is too late to organize the efforts in this way, but it is still possible to examine the information gathered by individual investigators and see how it fits together in terms of general structure.

Lopsided definitions can also lead to incorrect conclusions, which, in turn, may result in awkward positions. The self-esteem controversy mentioned earlier is an important case in point. There are those in the field who tell us that feelings of worthiness are related to self-esteem, which is certainly consistent with our work on its fundamental structure. But strong advocates of the self-esteem movement mentioned before seem to forget that these feelings must also be "real," which is to say that they must be earned on the basis of one's behavior in the real world. Therefore, it is perfectly correct for opponents of self-esteem programs in schools, for instance, to point out that focusing on developing "warm fuzzies" instead of competent behaviors is, at best, a waste of time. At worst, such an approach can even be destructive, in that it may be associated with the development of narcissism or antisocial behavior.

Yet the same critics also fail to deal with an important issue raised by working with a fundamental structure. Although it is true that the statistical significance of a causal connection between self-esteem and behavior is weak (Seligman, 1995b; Smelser, 1989), it is important to ask how it could be otherwise, given the failure to describe self-esteem as it is actually lived. In other words, most of the existing research on self-esteem and its enhancement is based on work that uses partial or incomplete definitions, particularly those emphasizing worthiness alone. Attempting to derive meaningful statistics from distorted or disjointed data is doomed to lead to weak results. There are other, perhaps better, ways of understanding the lack of statistical significance than to simply conclude, as some critics do, that self-esteem is an empty concept. For example, it could be that it is possible to demonstrate appropriate cause-and-effect relationships between self-esteem and behavior by doing research that is based on defining self-esteem in terms of both competence and worthiness. However, it may also be the case that statistical methods are inherently limited in their ability to pick up such relationships because of the multiplicity of interacting variables involved in complex personal and social behaviors. Indeed, we will see that some argue that the complexity of phenomena such as self-esteem is simply beyond the power of traditional psychosocial methods to examine properly because complex human behavior hinges on meanings, not measurements. At the very least, those who criticize self-esteem work on the basis of weak statistical findings *must* at least deal with the possibilities I just mentioned before their critique should be taken as anything even approaching the final word. One thing we can do at this point, however, is to examine the research on self-esteem in the light of a definition that is based on its fundamental structure. In order to move to that level of analysis, we must first understand the particular research problems and issues that beset and intrigue this field, which as you might suspect, is the business of chapter 2.

PROBLEMS INHERENT IN THE "SELF" OF SELF-ESTEEM

What is the difference between self-esteem and self-respect, self-love and self-acceptance, self-confidence and self-efficacy, or self-image and self-concept? How does self-concept differ from the concept of the self? Probably the most frustrating difficulty in empirically researching self-esteem is that it is an impure phenomenon. By this I mean that it is very hard to study self-esteem as such because it is always connected to many other self-related phenomena and processes, from consciousness to identity (Coopersmith, 1967; Jackson, 1984; Mecca et al., 1989; Ross, 1992; Wells & Marwell, 1976; Wylie, 1974).

Two forces seem to be most active in generating this group of difficulties. First, the problem of definitions appears to exist in regard to researching *all* self-related phenomena. Indeed, some of them may even exist in a definitional maze much more intricate than the one we encountered earlier. A frustrating by-product of this situation is that it is often difficult to know exactly what aspect of self-esteem a researcher is studying, or what a finding has actually uncovered. Second, all of these phenomena are inextricably related to one another by necessity, and the fact that none of them exists apart from the others makes self-esteem research very slippery. For instance, it is extremely easy to unintentionally shift the focus between related phenomena, just as it is difficult to avoid using terms like *self-esteem* and *self-regard* interchangeably. In short, it would be easier to study self-esteem by separating it from that to which it is related, but that is impossible. As a result of this quandary, some self-esteem experts simply ignore this problem, whereas others seem to despair about dealing with it effectively (Wylie, 1974). Of course, one way to understand this situation is to conclude that it makes achieving a respectable degree of consensus virtually impossible (Diggory, 1966). Another possibility is to see this complexity as a necessary, even vital, aspect of self-esteem research: It simply reflects the fact that self-related phenomena coexist in an intricate, multidimensional, interlocking network of structures that depend on each other for existence. Although this condition is not an excuse for poor research or analysis, it does set the parameters by which we work and therefore limits the kind of certainty we can realistically expect.

With this larger research context in mind, we are prepared to take a deeper look at some of what makes researching self-esteem a particularly challenging activity. One of the largest major sources of difficulty in researching self-related phenomena may be connected to the concept, structure, entity, or process that we call the self. In a nutshell, the problem stems from the fact that self can be understood in two very different ways (Diggory, 1966; Ross, 1992; Wylie, 1974). On the one hand, it can be seen as being some real or existing entity, process, or "thing" (phenomenon). On the other hand, the self can be understood as simply being a construct or idea that we use to explain human behavior. Let us briefly explore what each perspective on the self means for researching self-esteem.

The Self Is "Real"

One position is that the self is "real," that is, actual, existent, or having the character of an object in the world. As such, this use of the term pertains to unique characteristics that distinguish the self as a particular, albeit strictly human, phenomenon. Social scientists who understand the self in this way tend to agree that it is a basic component of being human, as important, for instance, as consciousness. Similarly, this self is usually understood as being something that emerges or unfolds over time, which is to say that it is a developmental phenomenon.

Although there is some consensus in this camp, there is also considerable diversity. For instance, most sociologically oriented versions of this "self is real" school are based on the Cooley-Mead tradition. Briefly stated, this view holds that the self emerges from an interpersonal field created by two sets of forces and a process, which is called symbolic interaction, that links them (Cooley, 1909; Mead, 1934). One set of energies is the individual; the other is the social context (including significant others such as family, society, and culture in general) in which the person exists. The self emerges in response to, and as a result of, exchanges between the two energies or systems. A useful analogy is to liken this version of the self to the way a stable node is formed by intersecting wave patterns in a small tank or pond. A single person coming into being, and the activity of being alive, generates waves in the surrounding social waters. Others around this individual react to his or her presence because it affects the general social field. Over time, these "waves" of action and reaction, which may be seen as reflected appraisals, become patterned or stabilized, and a new identity makes its way into the field. Of course, these processes are much more social than psychological, although every once in a while the individual may exert such a great force on the social fabric that it actually undergoes a modification of its own patterns. Great historical figures such as Julius Caesar, Joan of Arc, and Martin Luther King, Jr., are examples of this phenomenon.

Psychologically oriented theories of this "self is real" school are more diverse. Some are depth-oriented. Psychodynamically oriented work, for example, focuses on the internal dynamics of selfhood, particularly those concerning the unconscious and ego development. Humanistic theories tend to see the self as being intrinsic to the individual and unfolding over time. Cognitive psychology concentrates on understanding the self in terms of brain-based processes and informatics, such as feedback, circularity, and self-fulfilling prophecies. The self is "real" here in the sense that software is real once it is installed to run on hardware. Although these particular psychological perspectives vary greatly in how they conceive of the self, they do have one thing in common: All of them see the self as something that has its own specific, identifiable qualities, such as consciousness and identity.

It should be noted in passing that accepting this position has important consequences. If the self is real, then we must examine it scientifically, which is no mean achievement. For instance, the more acceptable, respected, or "standard" research methods we have available in the social sciences are seriously limited in their ability to deal with such a phenomenon. For one thing, whatever the self is, it is not amenable to direct observation, measurement, or manipulation. For another, even if we can access the phenomenon adequately, it is such a complex and multifaceted one that it becomes extremely difficult to isolate any one component from the rest of those that are involved in the self. This situation means that traditional methods are going to be severely tested in their ability to investigate something like self-esteem.

Of course, it is possible to use more qualitative methods that are designed to access inner experience. However, this alternative faces its own limitations. For instance, self-reports are very subjective and interviews are extremely vulnerable to all kinds of confounding factors. In addition to these issues, the self may involve various dimensions of culture that make it difficult to study from either a quantitative or a qualitative approach. For example, not only may culture influence what is "in" the self, so to speak, but it may also influence how we perceive or understand the self. This is a serious issue, because most of the social and psychological positions mentioned above, as well as the vast majority of research in this field, reflect a Western perspective on social science. What would we find if we looked at the self (and, of course, self-esteem) from a tribal, communal, or Eastern point of view? In fact, there is new and exciting research of this type going on right now (Singelis, Bond, & Lai, 1995).

The Self as a Construct

The other position on the self in social science is to use it as an abstract: a scientific concept or hypothetical construct (Wells & Marwell, 1976).

In fact, some postmodern variants of this approach see the very possibility of a unified, coherent self as being a "dead" concept (Johnson, 1998). In general, this view of the self does not see it as an actual entity or phenomenon. Rather, the concept of the self is simply an intellectual tool or a construct, which allows social scientists to treat people *as though* they are integrated in this fashion. This concept of the self is a very useful one, because it allows us to understand or explain behavior. One obvious advantage of understanding the self in this way is that it frees us from having to prove its existence. If one does not have to answer the question of whether or not there really is a self, for instance, then one can simply define how the concept is being used operationally. Instead of attempting to measure the unmeasurable, such a construction of the person allows the researcher to employ fairly standard techniques for assessing psychological phenomena indirectly, such as surveys and tests.

This approach also has serious problems. The most glaring is that if the self really does exist, then ignoring that fact closes off exploration altogether. This situation would constitute a fatal flaw because it ignores a crucial reality. Similarly, if the self is merely a construct, then we are obliged to extend this line of reasoning to most other "invisible" psychological structures, such as identity and personality. Some research on self-esteem and other related phenomena does, indeed, support the idea of each person as having an organizing process or inner essence. The most common and influential example might be the cognitive concept of "self-schema" based on Piaget's work. In this book I take the position that there is an organizing structure to being human that we call the "self," the processes of which provide the basis for a coherent sense of individual identity and experience. Although its content reflects the influence of such forces as history, culture, and individual experience, this organizing capacity of the human brain may even be *the* fundamental structure of our existence. However, until we can demonstrate its existence to those who require laboratory proof, we must acknowledge with Ross (1992) that there is no "final solution" as to which position concerning the self is correct.

ISSUES EMERGING FROM SELF-ESTEEM AS A PHENOMENON

There are at least five characteristics of self-esteem that create considerable difficulty in this field, in large part because they contradict one another. There are two reasons why it is important to understand these *self-esteem paradoxes* (a term I borrow from Bednar et al., 1989, and modify somewhat). First, these self-esteem puzzles give rise to many of the contradictory findings in the field. Second, if the fundamental structure of self-esteem that I presented in the first chapter is accurate, then at some point I must be able to show how these apparent contradictions can be located and reconciled within that framework.

What Kind of Variable Is Self-Esteem?

The issues that stem from self-esteem as a unique human phenomenon often occur when we try to understand how self-esteem works in everyday life. Kitano (1989) presented the problem clearly when he pointed out that self-esteem is a complex variable:

> From a sociocultural perspective, it is a dependent variable, that is, self-esteem is the result of a person's ethnic, social class, or gender group. . . . Another aspect of self-esteem is self-esteem that is in progress or in process. Individuals are perceived and judge themselves in relation to yet-to-be fulfilled goals and activities. . . . Self-esteem is also used as an independent variable—that is, as the "cause" of behavior. An individual is said to behave in a particular manner because of a high or low level of self-esteem. Through knowledge of this variable, then, we can try to predict and understand behavior. (p. 318)

In other words, one reason that it is difficult to research self-esteem is because there are several ways of hypothesizing how it works. The relationship between self-esteem and academic achievement is a good example, because it is the topic of so much positive and negative attention. On the one hand, there are those who see self-esteem as playing a causal role, meaning that it is the independent variable whereas grades are dependent. If so, then we need to study self-esteem and see what we can do to increase it first, allowing grades to improve naturally. On the other, many people see grades as the independent variable, which means that they affect self-esteem. If this is the case, then grades should be the primary focus, as increasing them should boost self-esteem. There are those who maintain that self-esteem is a mediating variable, which only makes the problem of deciding what to do about the relationship between self-esteem and academic achievement even more puzzling. No wonder there is so much controversy regarding self-esteem in the educational setting! What is needed is not a way of proving which view is "right," because that depends on the researcher's perspective. Rather, if we wish to remain faithful to this phenomenon, then we need a way to describe how self-esteem can show itself as a factor that can both influence behavior and be modified by it.

Is Self-Esteem a Developmental Product or Process?

The next self-esteem paradox to consider can be called the process-product continuum issue. This problem concerns the developmental nature of self-esteem, especially how it seems to manifest itself in two ways. One is that self-esteem looks as if it is a product of development. We can, for instance, talk about the developmental processes and events (tasks, stages, etc.) that lead to positive or negative self-esteem in general, or even in a particular person's life. In this sense, developmental processes work to "produce" a certain level of self-esteem in an individual, which becomes reasonably stable as the person matures, then plays an active role in perception, experience, motivation, and behavior when he or she is an adult. At the same time, it is possible, even necessary, to see self-esteem as an ongoing developmental process. From this point of view, self-esteem is not just a stable influence from the past that, once set, shapes perception and behavior. Rather, this position allows us to see that new situations or events may influence self-esteem or even change it over the course of a lifetime. Once again, each view has its proponents and supporting research. Those who are more concerned with measuring self-esteem tend to favor the product notion because it is more stable. Those who are more concerned with change, such as humanists and clinicians, must give more attention to the unfolding nature of this developmental process. To be sure, the problem is that there is merit in both positions even though they seem to contradict each other.

Is Self-Esteem a Global or a Situational Phenomenon?

Experimental and testing research on self-esteem is constantly plagued by another duality. On the one hand, self-esteem seems to be a global phenomenon. After all, whether self-esteem is considered a product or a process, sooner or later an individual comes to have a certain general or average level of self-esteem that is fairly consistent. This is why we can say, for instance, "So-and-so has high (or low) self-esteem," and this general characteristic is the basis upon which self-esteem tests work. However, it is also true that self-esteem is not just a closed system: Different situations can and often do affect self-esteem in positive or negative ways. Experimental research on self-esteem, for instance, typically involves setting up controlled situations that manipulate self-esteem in this way (Wells & Marwell, 1976). The assessment literature is especially cognizant of the fact that self-esteem can vary. Tests, for example, have difficulty differentiating between how much a score reflects recent events, such as a major failure or success, and how much it reflects one's global self-esteem. Once again, the problem is not to ask if self-esteem is either global or situational, stable or changing. Rather, the question is how the fundamental structure of self-esteem allows this phenomenon to show itself as having both characteristics.

Is Self-Esteem a Motivational Need or a Calling?

Researchers (Bednar et al., 1989; Mecca et al., 1989; Wells & Marwell, 1976) have pointed out the various ways in which self-esteem appears to motivate human beings. For example, it is possible to understand self-esteem as a need, especially one that exists to help protect the integrity of the self or identity. As such, self-esteem serves a certain defensive or shielding function (Coopersmith, 1967; Newman & Newman, 1987) in that it acts to ward off the minor slings and arrows that come with everyday life. More important, this protective function of self-esteem also helps us to endure more serious blows by acting as a buffer against the acute pain of major losses, failures, and other narcissistic injuries. In addition to recognizing this defensive purpose, various humanistic (Branden, 1969), psychodynamic (White, 1959), and cognitive (Epstein, 1980) theorists tend to focus on the other end of the motivational continuum. Here the need for self-esteem is more of a "calling" toward mastery and growth. This kind of motivation pushes the individual to face a challenge rather than avoid it, to keep plugging away at an obstacle instead of just giving up, or to "be all one can be" in an existential sense. Once again, however, the question of whether self-esteem is a need (a requirement for living, or a "deficiency" motive) or a calling (a growth tendency, or a "transcendent" motive) is somewhat misleading, because it oversimplifies matters. It is not even possible to use the rather tame analogy of a continuum to describe this self-esteem paradox because, as we saw with the examples of people facing challenges of living presented in the first chapter, both motivations can occur at the same time.

Is Self-Esteem a Psychological or a Social Phenomenon?

The fifth self-esteem paradox emerges out of the condition that self-esteem can be seen as being a personal or an interpersonal phenomenon. As Bhatti, Derezotes, Kim, and Specht (1989) pointed out,

We have also noted that there are many different conceptions of self-esteem—some primarily psychological and others primarily sociological—all dealing with different dimensions of the phenomenon . . . various perspectives on self-esteem lead us to emphasize one or another policy direction. The sociological perspective tends to support policies and programs that will increase self-esteem by reducing environmental pressures on vulnerable persons (e.g., provision of child care for single teenage parents); the psychological perspective tends to support policies and programs that will increase self-esteem by changing individuals (e.g., counseling and psychotherapy). (p. 60)

If we look at the more psychologically oriented definitions, such as those of James (1983/1890), White (1959), and Branden (1969), we see that they have two things in common. First, they emphasize the individual's side of the self-esteem coin in that personal aspirations, goals, and achievements are involved in self-esteem. Second, they give great attention to competence as the central factor in determining self-esteem. Because an individual's actions can often be observed, this behavioral side of self-esteem is more amenable to traditional psychological methods such as observation and experimentation.

More sociologically oriented work tends to emphasize two other, very interpersonal, factors. First, the larger context of individual behavior must always be considered as a crucial variable, which means attending to such things as the role that family, gender, socioeconomic status, and culture play in the formation and expression of self-esteem. Second, this perspective tends to make worthiness more important than competence, which means that the focus is on such things as values and attitudes rather than on behavior. Yet, if we are to take the next step and build the kind of consensus that it requires, we can no longer have a simple preference as to which emphasis we would like to adopt. Instead, we must find a way of integrating both sides of this paradox, especially if we want to design effective programs to enhance self-esteem in the real world.

In closing this section, it is important to realize that I have not been just listing the research issues involved in investigating self-esteem scientifically, although there is value in that, too. Rather, I have tried to describe another research problem any comprehensive theory of self-esteem must face. In this case, it is the character or nature of self-esteem itself, which presents a challenge because it shows itself as having five important characteristics, all of which are contradictory. In doing a phenomenology of self-esteem, we cannot afford the luxury more traditional approaches seem to have when facing this aspect of self-esteem: Instead of simply choosing one side of the paradox over the other, we must find a way of understanding how self-esteem can give rise to each side, sometimes simultaneously.

PROBLEMS GENERATED BY USING THE SCIENTIFIC METHOD

The next group of problems faced by self-esteem researchers occurs when we try to investigate this phenomenon scientifically. Proponents of pop psych (self-help) and metaphysical (self-esteem as a function of spiritual beliefs) approaches do not have to deal with these knotty issues. For the rest of us, there are at least four such difficulties to consider: issues that stem from the fact that self-esteem is investigated by two different social sciences, certain methodological problems that invariably arise in self-esteem research and assessment, the presence of two scientific paradigms (one quantitative, the other qualitative), and the question of validity.

Problems With Self-Esteem as a "Boundary Phenomenon"

There is no avoiding the fact that self-esteem is investigated by two social sciences: It is necessary. That psychology and sociology both lay claim to this phenomenon is important for at least two reasons. First, it means that we must deal with research methods and findings from two disciplines (the latter will be the subject of the next chapter). Second, we must consider the fact that self-esteem is what Norbert Wiener calls a "boundary" phenomenon (Conlan, 1986, p. 10). Wiener, who is sometimes credited with starting the information revolution because of his concepts of feedback and circularity, is of interest to us because he encouraged the exploration of the interface between disciplines, or where they seem to intersect. Conlan (1986) described how Wiener used to host special dinner parties, where guests, who were experts in different areas, would be asked to reflect on the boundaries of their fields. After dinner was completed, they would then present their thoughts to the other guests, who would react to the possibilities. The hope was that open and free discussion among equals would generate considerable creativity—or at least grand entertainment. The point is that the exploration of such scientific no-man's- (or woman's) land from different points of view can lead to insights and creative possibilities that no one orientation might see from its more discipline-bound perspective. I would add that any phenomenon that can be studied by psychology and sociology probably cannot be fully understood from either one alone. Therefore, a proper study of self-esteem involves seeing it as a psychosocial phenomenon and doing interdisciplinary work.

Kurt Back (1984) depicted the interface between the psychological and the social in the following way: "The whole psychological-social complex can be visualized as a network, psychology being concerned with the nodes of the network, and sociology with the links" (p. 207). His analogy is useful because its three parts correspond nicely to our concerns. First, a network has in it definite points of reasonable stability that can be isolated and focused upon. Individual people can be seen in this way, because they are a more visible and discrete part of the human picture, and psychology is best suited to studying behavior from this vantage point. Second, a network is more than just a set of points or individuals: It includes the relationships among them. Sociology is geared toward studying relationships and their patterns, so it focuses on this dimension. Third, neither element of a network is more important than the other: The nodes and links coexist, which means we must study them both if we are to develop an accurate, comprehensive understanding.

Back (1984) went on to talk about the differences between psychology and sociology. One difference concerns their "level of discourse," or what each one tends to regard as the basic unit of study. He pointed out that in physics, for instance, the atom is seen as the classical unit of study. Chemistry tends toward groups of atoms or molecules. Biology adds life to its level of discourse and makes the living cell primary. Psychology brings life up to the level of consciousness, which means the individual is the central unit of study. Sociology expands the level of discourse to groups of people, with the family being the most basic. Back added that as one moves up to higher levels of discourse, one's view becomes larger (each increasingly complex domain or reality encompasses those below it), but does so at the cost of becoming less specific (it is more difficult to test, for instance, social factors than neurological ones), which is to say less "valid" in the traditional sense of the term. Put simply, psychology can be more "exact" than sociology, but sociology can deal with the larger "facts" of human existence. Thus, neither type of research is inherently better than the other, and we need to work with both to understand self-esteem.

These differences in orientation create similar distinctions in much of the research on self-esteem. Psychological research tends to focus on the person. Thus, case studies, in-depth interviews, and experimental designs, all of which focus on one individual or situation, are the most common types of psychological research on self-esteem. Sociological research shows a historical preference working with larger groups. Hence, surveys or social class comparisons are the most common research techniques and the focus is often on the social and cultural factors affecting self-esteem. As might be expected, sociologically oriented programs typically strive to increase self-esteem by creating a more positive social environment. This self-esteem research problem can be seen as a blessing disguised as a curse, because, although it results in a messy body of research, it also allows us to understand self-esteem better. The problem of defining self-esteem is a good case in point. It will be recalled that the definition is based on two components: competence and worthiness. Note that the competence or behavioral component of self-esteem is more amenable to the methods of psychology (observation, experimentation, etc.), whereas the worthiness or value component is more open to sociological methods (surveys, attitudes, social influences, etc.). Therefore, if we really want to understand self-esteem and its literature, then we must do what can only be understood as a social psychology of it.

Problems With Assessing Self-Esteem

The next issues are connected to those mentioned above, but they are of a more practical nature: It is difficult to develop a good (i.e., reliable, valid, and useful) instrument to measure self-esteem, but such tools are indispensable in this field. Indeed, much, if not most, of the empirical work on self-esteem involves testing, surveying, measuring, or assessing an individual's self-esteem and drawing conclusions from such information.

Measuring the Right Things

The first group of design factors to consider in creating, using, or evaluating a self-esteem test is to make sure that the instrument measures the phenomenon it is intended to measure, and not something else. This takes us back to the importance of definitions, because we know that self-esteem is associated with a number of other things of interest to social scientists, such as the self-concept, self-image, self-ideals and values, and so forth, not to mention the fact that not all definitions of self-esteem are equal. With or without the developer's intent, then, some self-esteem tests focus mainly on assessing an individual's competence, whereas others center on worthiness. Fortunately, there are instruments that seem to include both components in their design, such as Coopersmith's Self-Esteem Inventory (SEI, 1981). Most of them, including the SEI, however, fail to differentiate between competence and worthiness in their scoring and, instead, only yield a composite score. Because people are likely to vary in terms of competence or worthiness, a more desirable self-esteem test would be one that both assesses these two major dimensions of self-esteem and provides information on how an individual rates in these two areas. We shall see that this capability is especially important for working with self-esteem in a clinical setting.

Dealing With Dynamic Factors

The dynamic nature of self-esteem is another issue with which test designers must contend. It should be recalled that self-esteem is a phenomenon that is always both global and situational: We live out a certain basic level of self-esteem, but it also has the potential to fluctuate or change with time. The simplest example of how this factor affects a testing situation is where the subject has experienced a recent loss, gain, failure, or success, any of which can affect self-esteem test scores. Moreover, the assessor may or may not know about recent events in the subject's life. A similar problem is that too many self-esteem tests fail to tell us about the particular situations or specific areas of life in which a subject lives with high or low self-esteem. This testing challenge is a difficult one. For instance, a good instrument must be sensitive to the various areas of life where competence, worthiness, and challenges are likely to be involved, contain questions that access them adequately, and be normatized concerning what is typical and what is not. In short, a good self-esteem test should be multifaceted, or capable of capturing such information in a meaningful way (O'Brien, 1985; Wells & Marwell, 1976).

The Development of Norms

There does appear to be some consensus that a good instrument has at least three normative characteristics. First, the selection processes for finding subjects from which to obtain norms must be random so that the test does not reflect a bias for or against any group. Second, the subject pool must be stratified so that the normative sample is genuinely representative of the general population of those who will be examined by the test once it is developed. Third, the size of the normative sample must be large enough so that the test can be used with a wide range of individuals and backgrounds: If we are interested in assessing self-esteem for the general population, then the normative samples must also be sensitive to gender, cultural, and other differences.

Unfortunately, most self-esteem tests are developed by individual researchers for specific purposes rather than by major research facilities or large grant programs (Wells & Marwell, 1976). This usually means that resources are tight, so while it is possible to randomize samples, stratifying them is difficult because time is limited and numbers are small. Even some well-known self-esteem tests are normatized against no more than a thousand subjects, and the vast majority use many less. Yet a small number of subjects cannot hope to provide good norms for the major social, ethnic, economic, or other socially based variables that affect self-esteem. Similarly, developmental factors affecting self-esteem pose a normative challenge. Pope and colleagues (1988) pointed out that developmental age may be a factor that needs to be included in normatizing a self-esteem test, at least for children. It is likely that a 6-year-old, for instance, has different self-esteem issues and norms than a 10-year-old. The problem of normatization is compounded by the fact that many such tests do not even report how or whether they were standardized (Sappington, 1989). The result is that most of the tests are nearly useless, especially for clinical purposes.

Facing Self-Report Problems

The problem with most psychological tests is that they are subjective, in that we must use an individual's report of his or her own experience, behavior, or characteristics in order to draw conclusions about that person. The responses of even the most well-meaning subjects are going to be filtered by all kinds of factors usually involved in self-perception, not to mention the additional problems that may occur when an individual is anxious, angry, suspicious, or mentally ill. Even under the best circumstances, self-esteem tests are vulnerable to the "ceiling effect," or the tendency to see oneself in a positive light when reporting about oneself. The most obvious problem that results concerns the fact that most people tend to rate themselves more favorably on positive qualities and less unfavorably on negative ones than they are likely to actually merit when compared to external standards (Wells & Marwell, 1976). Apparently, most of us prefer a more positive view of ourselves than we actually deserve. Also, the degree of this effect may vary at any given time depending on the circumstances of one's life. Some self-esteem researchers view this in terms of attribution theory (Bednar et al., 1989), but stress or even simple willful deception can exaggerate this effect. Therefore, a good self-esteem test should have some way of detecting this phenomenon, even if it is simply to identify unusually high scores or unusual patterns.

Defensiveness

The last major self-report problem to consider concerns the relationship between psychological defensiveness and self-esteem. Actually, there are two aspects to this problem, because it is tied to one of the self-esteem paradoxes mentioned earlier. The first is that self-esteem is a protective structure, in that it is supposed to help shield us from the stresses and strains of life, so a certain amount of resistance to reporting on one's negative qualities is unconscious, normal, even healthy, and certainly to be expected. In addition, self-esteem can be protective in very subtle ways. For instance, some authors (Bednar et al., 1989; Blaine & Crocker, 1993; Wells & Marwell, 1976) reported research indicating that maintaining chronically low self-esteem can be protective, albeit in a very costly way. In other words, individuals who greatly fear loss or failure may unwittingly maintain low self-esteem so that they are not as disappointed with the outcomes of their performance as they might be if their expectations were high. The psychologic of this self-esteem dynamic seems to be something like, "If I already feel bad about myself, then I don't have to worry about losing self-esteem as much as if I really tried to do my best," which is often called a self-handicapping strategy (Snyder, 1989), or the idea that one can protect onself from pain or loss if one anticipates failure or doing less than one could do in a given situation.

The second aspect is that some people perceive themselves as being worthy and competent who are not. The problem is that this so-called discrepant (Wells & Marwell, 1976), defensive (Coopersmith, 1967), or pseudo (Branden, 1969) type of self-esteem may present a profile that appears to be very similar to high self-esteem on the surface. It is clear from external measures, such as observations by others, however, that these individuals do not behave in ways usually associated with positive self-esteem. For example, they are overly aggressive or may brag excessively. These individuals can easily fool assessors and may even be told they are in good shape in regard to self-esteem when they are actually suffering from some of the most serious self-esteem problems.

Tests without some means of identifying these complications are sure to miss an entire range of serious self-esteem problems. Probably the best way to deal with the problem is to develop validity scales, such as those of the Minnesota Multiphasic Personality Inventory. Although such an exhaustive approach is not practical, it is reasonable to expect a good self-esteem test to at least alert us to the possibility of excessive deception and defensiveness. Sadly, few tests even come close. However, when we review the self-esteem findings in the next chapter, we shall see that there are at least some promising exceptions to consider.

Test Validity: A Question of Limits

Even if a self-esteem test addresses all of the issues mentioned above, we still have to know whether, and to what extent, a given instrument is valid. Although written over two decades ago, the study by Wells and Marwell (1976) still does an unparalleled job of examining the technical difficulties involved in developing self-esteem tests. The report describes how self-esteem measures can be evaluated against three traditional indicators of test validity.

The highest kind of validity such an instrument can have occurs when test items or tasks predict a particular outcome accurately. This "criterion validity" is unlikely to occur with self-esteem tests, in part because it is such a complex and elusive phenomenon. "Content validity" is another approach and is based on whether or not the test questions are connected to self-esteem in some logical way. For instance, it is possible to define what kinds of behaviors or attitudes are most likely to be associated with high and low self-esteem, then design questions that ask about them. This kind of validity increases with the thoroughness of the questions: The more the test covers the whole range of factors thought to reflect self-esteem, the greater the validity of the instrument. We know that there are a good number of such self-esteem tests, but with the exception of a very few, most of them are so brief that they cannot hope to be considered valid in this sense. For example, many of them focus only on worthiness, which means that half the picture is not assessed. Even when both competence and worthiness are covered by a test, brevity often takes precedence over comprehensiveness, because short tests are easier to administer and score than longer ones.

"Construct validity," or "the degree to which certain explanatory concepts or constructs account for performance on the test" (Wells & Marwell, 1976, p. 153), is another way to achieve a meaningful degree of validity in self-esteem testing. This kind of validity is based on the connections between a particular self-esteem test and the theory or definition of self-esteem that a researcher or clinician is using in his or her work. If the theory is well constructed and if the test questions embody the major components of self-esteem as they are expressed by the theory, then the measure at least has a certain logical integrity or theoretical validity. Unfortunately, such tests are usually very transparent and easily manipulated by the subject. But they can be useful, and this feature may add to the value (if not the validity) of the instruments. It can be argued that the major point of such testing is not so much to find out the "truth" about an individual's self-esteem, as it is to help reduce uncertainty in assessing the range (e.g., high, medium, low) in which he or she falls. This "practical" approach to validity is often favored by clinicians, because the here-and-now concerns of identifying basic self-esteem issues and problems for this or that individual client are more important than measuring self-esteem with academic precision or waiting for researchers to achieve a meaningful degree of consensus on a particular issue.

Methodological Diversity in Researching Self-Esteem

A few major self-esteem researchers and theoreticians grapple with the fact that there is considerable methodological diversity in the social psychology of self-esteem. Again, the most thorough and comprehensive work is that by Wells and Marwell (1976). In fact, their entire book is devoted to the subject. Rather than attempt to duplicate this classic, I will refer to it as the leading authority. *The Social Importance of Self-Esteem* (1989) by Mecca and colleagues updates this information but does not change it. The list of methods used to study self-esteem is fairly typical of the social sciences in general. It has been studied introspectively (Epstein, 1979) via case studies and interviews (Bednar et al., 1989; Branden, 1969; Pope et al., 1988) and by using surveys and tests (Rosenberg, 1965), experimentally (Coopersmith, 1967), and phenomenologically (Jackson, 1984; Mruk, 1983). One fairly common way of understanding methodological diversity in the social sciences is to organize it in terms of increasing degrees of objectivity (measurability), which results in a kind of pyramid, as shown in Figure 2.1.

According to this arrangement, the most subjective (qualitative) methods are placed lowest on the hierarchy, and the most easily measurable or objective (quantitative) are placed at the top, with the experiment standing as the epitome of the scientific method. Let me move quickly through this pyramid in terms of the strengths and weaknesses of the various methods as they are used for researching self-esteem. In the next section, I will examine the range of methods from a different, more revealing angle.

Objective Reality

Experimental   Method

Survey/Testing   Method

Observation   Method

Interview   Method

Case Study   Method

Introspection   Method

FIGURE 2.1   The (traditional) methodological pyramid.

Introspection

This approach was first used by James (1983/1890) to study self-esteem. However, examining one's own experience by simply describing it is rarely used in self-esteem research today, because the method is considered to be extremely weak due to its complete subjectivity. For example, classically introspective research depends on one individual's perception of his or her own experience and is therefore vulnerable to reliability and validity problems associated with having a sample of only one. Nevertheless, I find it instructive to note that some of James' early findings based on this technique turn out to be central today to the definition of self-esteem and its major dynamics. We must conclude that, although introspection is at the bottom of the traditional research hierarchy, it is not without value, at least as a source of insight.

Case Study

This method, especially clinical case study, is another "soft" technique used primarily in the psychology (rather than the sociology) of self-esteem and is also quite low on the standard methodological hierarchy. However, it is important even today because it allows us to investigate problems with self-esteem when looking at individual lives. Case study, for example, helps us explore the relationship between self-esteem and psychological functioning by comparing cases, then noting regularities or variations from regular patterns. Indeed, Branden (1969) built his entire theory on this method, and it is well suited to the applied setting. In fact, we will see that most self-esteem enhancement programs rely on case study evidence as the main source of support for their therapeutic efficacy. We all know that case study is an integral part of good clinical training, but it is important to appreciate the limitations of this method of researching and enhancing self-esteem. Although the subject base is expanded by studying several cases, there is still a problem with subjectivity. Also, the data generated and the procedures for analysis are not often amenable to duplication.

The Interview Method

Interviewing subjects is better for studying self-esteem than introspection or case study in that this method can correct some of the weaknesses of the other approaches. For instance, structuring the interview in advance helps to make it more reliable; additionally, an interview can be recorded and transcribed so that others have access to the data, which reduces some of the subjectivity inherent in this method. The major limitations of doing research this way include the fact that sample sizes are still relatively small and that establishing cause-and-effect relationships is difficult to do: Although a hypothesis can be formed, confirmation is difficult.

Observational Method

Since it is not possible to see self-esteem directly, laboratory-based observational methods are not used very often in researching self-esteem. The study by Coopersmith (1967) may be the best example of such work. However, insofar as surveys and testing are ways of looking at or observing a phenomenon, albeit less directly, we encounter what is by far the most common method used to research self-esteem empirically. Surveys and tests are an especially attractive way to study self-esteem, because once an assessment instrument has been developed, it can be used to establish correlations in all kinds of situations. We can use such measures to assess an individual's self-esteem, for instance, in relation to their behavior, performance, grades, or even personality. We can also set up pre- and posttesting situations for measuring self-esteem under experimental conditions or in relation to therapeutic manipulations. High versus low self-esteem is the most frequent kind of comparison made in this regard, but researchers have focused on behavioral correlates of medium and defensive self-esteem as well.

Observing self-esteem by measuring it is important for research and theoretical reasons. For example, establishing observable relationships reduces some of the subjectivity of the research process. Measurements also have practical value for a clinician or educator in that they can be used to target areas or behaviors in need of assistance. Furthermore, showing statistically significant links between self-esteem and school performance, mental health, or any number of clinical conditions gives the entire field more value and credibility. Unfortunately, this approach is difficult to implement because, as we saw earlier, developing good self-esteem measures means facing some difficult research problems and researchers have been criticized for failing to identify causal links between self-esteem and the behaviors that are supposed to be related to it.

Experimental Research

Finally, we come to the experimental method and the top of the method-ological pyramid. According to Wells and Marwell (1976), there are two basic kinds of experiments used to research self-esteem. Both of them usually involve some pre- and posttest measure of self-esteem, although there is tremendous variation in how carefully researchers go about this activity. The more straightforward format is to set up an experiment so that subjects are engaged in an activity, the outcome (success or failure) of which they believe depends on their efforts. However, it is actually the experimenter who controls the outcome, meaning that success and failure can be manipulated and the effects of each on self-esteem can be observed, at least in theory. The other format differs in that subjects are given information about themselves or their personal-ity either just before or while attempting a task or activity. In this situation, the information is manipulated so that, for instance, a low self-esteem subject hears positive comments or a high self-esteem subject receives negative personal information. Either way, the experimental situation helps the researcher to observe or measure changes in behav-ior that may be linked to self-esteem.

The strength of this method is that it allows us to test for causal links between self-esteem and other phenomena or behavior. In addition to research and theoretical value, such information is very important at the practical level. A self-esteem enhancement program that has this kind of evidence to back it is going to be seen as more valid than those that do not. However, there are some real difficulties in applying this method in self-esteem research. These include the limits of the experi-mental method when it is applied to human behavior: It is time-consuming, labor intensive, expensive, and limited in terms of its level of generality beyond the laboratory situation. According to Scheff, Retzinger, and Ryan (1989),

> The rich diversity of experimental research in this area is impressive, and certainly much is owed to the investigators for their ingenuity and persistence. It is therefore especially disheartening that the experimental studies have tended to be inconclusive, often demonstrating effects that are weak, nonexistent, or sometimes contradictory. Although much has been learned, the parts still fail to add up to a recognizable whole. Furthermore, because these studies are conducted in laboratory settings, the extrapolation of results to real situations is uncertain. Such studies may lack what is called "ecological" validity. (p. 167)

Finally, researching self-esteem places severe demands on the experimental method. Epstein (1979), for example, points out some of those that occur when the researcher wants to examine emotionally significant human phenomena in the lab setting: "How does one investigate love in the laboratory, or threats to an individual's ego that produce such high levels of anxiety as to produce enduring changes in personality? Obviously, for both practical and ethical reasons, such states cannot be studied in the laboratory" (p. 50). The significance of this limitation is very important in regard to self-esteem research, especially when it comes to trying to demonstrate the link between self-esteem and behavior, which seems to be the major criticism against the field these days.

The Problem of Scientific Paradigms and Self-Esteem Research

Examining the methodological diversity in this field suggests that each approach offers a way of finding out valuable information about self-esteem. In fact, every such method has generated an entire stream of self-esteem research and findings. Yet we also saw that each approach also has serious limitations, including the problem of achieving any kind of consensus about the findings generated from such diverse work. Indeed, some self-concept experts suggest that investigating this class of phenomena using the scientific method is essentially a hopeless task (Diggory, 1966). Others regard the methodological difficulties in researching self-esteem as reflecting the limits of our quantitative sophistication and therefore call for "improved" statistical methodologies as the only hope (Smelser, 1989).

There is growing recognition from both sociologists and psychologists studying self-esteem that the field is in a state of methodological crisis. Scheff and colleagues (1989), for instance, examined six major reviews of the methodological issues facing such research. Four reached a negative conclusion about the possibility of resolving the problems effectively, whereas two were hopeful about it. Scheff and associates conclude that

> [e]ven reviewers who are completely sympathetic to the intentions of the quantitative studies acknowledge that these studies have produced no results. In our opinion, the implication of all six of the general reviews is not that the field is healthy but that it is in a state of crisis, and has been for some time.... We do not claim that the quantitative studies have been useless. On the contrary, we believe that they were necessary. Their very lack of success suggests the need for new directions in theory and method that might be more suited to the problem at hand.... Perhaps what is needed is a new paradigm more closely connected with the particular problem of self-esteem. (p. 177)

I agree that the field is in crisis. Indeed, I think the problems have become even more acute over the past few years, which is one of the reasons I decided to write a second edition of this book. Yet a crisis for one methodological paradigm may be an opportunity for another (Kuhn, 1962), and one way to see this is to turn the traditional methodological pyramid on its side. Instead of a simple hierarchy, this shift in perspective results in a continuum of methods, as shown in Figure 2.2.

Figure 2.2 shows us that scientific methods actually have a range of characteristics, at least insofar as we are dealing with human phenomena. To the right of the midpoint, for instance, we encounter the focus on measurement and external realities characteristic of the natural sciences. These methods, which begin with simple observation and end with experimentation, become progressively more "objective" as we move from the midpoint to the right side of the line. Such a progression in quantitative sophistication helps us understand the natural world by observing properties, measuring its characteristics, and discovering cause-and-effect relationships, respectively.

People also exist in this world, so such methods can be applied to us, too. But it is also true that we human beings are unique in that we are conscious, which means we live in a world of experience and meanings as well as physics and space. The methods to the left of the midpoint, or those of the "human science" paradigm, are better able to access such internal realities because here the focus is on the experiencing subject (not just "subjectivity") and lived reality (the fundamental

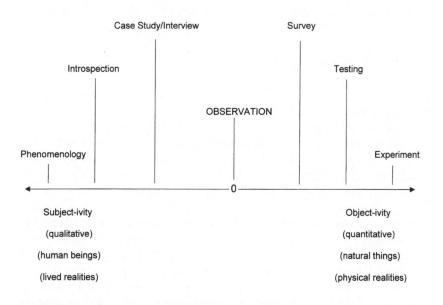

FIGURE 2.2   The methodological continuum.

structures of experience). Note that there is an increase in the descriptive power of these qualitative methods as we move outward from the
left of center, just as there is an increase in methodological power at
the other end of the subjective-objective continuum. (I always find the
use of the descriptors "left" and "right" to be rather suggestive if I think
of these methods as also having the characteristics of "soft" or "hard"
science and the political connotations associated with such positions.)

It is also important to note that neither side of the line should be
seen as good or bad, strong or weak, and so forth. As we have seen,
such simple dichotomies do not work well when trying to understand
the complexities of human behavior. Rather, the important question
concerning scientific paradigms, at least in this field, is whether one is
more suitable to a particular task or not. If we want to know whether
a self-esteem enhancement program is effective, for instance, the methods of psychology practiced in the natural science paradigm make good
sense because in this case it is important to identify and measure
outcomes. If, however, we want to know what self-esteem actually is
and how it is really employed by people in everyday life, then the human
science paradigm is more useful and perhaps more valid. Note also that
scientific rigor and explanatory power of the methods increase as we

move toward the extremes of either side of the methodological continuum.

Phenomenological Methods

We have already investigated traditional methods for researching self-
esteem from the paradigm of psychology practiced as a natural science,
so let us now examine the qualitative paradigm by looking at the methods employed by modern phenomenological psychology. Giorgi (1971,
1984) helps by discussing what phenomenological psychology is not.
He pointed out, for instance, that modern phenomenological psychology
is not introspectionism, because we want to investigate the structure
of a given experience, not just a particular incidence of it. Individual
experience, I like to say to my students, is a good starting place, but
unless we are working in a clinical setting, a sample of one cannot take
us very far in terms of knowledge. What if, for example, the person was
mentally ill, under the influence of a drug like alcohol, or emotionally
upset at the time of the experience or even when writing about it?
Although it is true that investigating a person's experience of something
by having him or her describe it is the beginning of phenomenological
research, that is only the first step. Phenomenological inquiry is interested in understanding both how self-esteem is lived concretely in a
person's life and how a certain experience is possible in the first place.
Instead of merely analyzing components of an experience as we might
with content analysis, phenomenology attempts to describe what gives
rise to and what unites these elements in a way that gives them form
as a particular type of human experience.

Giorgi also pointed out that, contrary to some characterizations, phenomenological methods are not "antiscientific." Quite the contrary, as
we just indicated, phenomenological description and analysis are just
as rooted in the scientific method as naturalistic or traditional psychology, a fact that I try to make throughout this book. Indeed, qualitative
methods can actually be quite formal as we move toward the extreme
left of the continuum.

> If anything, a phenomenological approach is even more rigorous than a
> traditional approach because it tries to account for more of the phenome-
> non.... Traditional psychology has avoided the major psychological issues
> by either ignoring the peculiarly human phenomena or by reducing them
> to such an extent to fit the strict scientific method that they were no
> longer recognizable.... From a phenomenological viewpoint measuring a

> phenomenon is not the same as determining its meaning. These are two separate perspectives that must be balanced in every research. (Giorgi, 1971, p. 14)

Like its natural science counterpart, the phenomenological method involves a step-by-step method of collecting observations of experience, analyzing them, and presenting findings in a way that can be confirmed or challenged by others who replicate the steps.

A related misconception, Giorgi noted, is that phenomenological psychology is sometimes thought to be largely speculative. Although developing theories from one's analysis and findings is always speculative in some sense, phenomenological analysis itself is a disciplined activity bound by identifiable rules. The most important of these is that research must remain faithful to the phenomenon as "it shows itself from itself" (Heidegger, 1962/1927). We cannot simply impose description on a phenomenon as an operational definition might do, because a phenomenological description must arise from the thing itself. This means that phenomenological psychology is not antidata (another misconception). In fact, it may be capable of handling more diverse forms of data than its natural scientific counterpart, a feature that is particularly important for dealing with the diverse methods and findings concerning self-esteem. Similarly, Giorgi (1984) stated that phenomenological psychology is not antitraditional: "Rather, it is willing and able to dialog with traditional psychology" (p. 14), which is a very important part of integrated description. (I should also mention that Giorgi was one of my professors in graduate school and that I first learned how to do phenomenological research using his method.)

Of course, the nature and merits of psychology envisioned as a human versus natural science is a topic that is discussed in great depth. Those who are interested in understanding more of this approach are invited to do so by investigating Giorgi's work already cited, as well as that of Husserl (1970a/1954), Gurwitsch (1964), and Merleau-Ponty (1962/1945). There are even other phenomenologists who have investigated self-esteem (Jackson, 1984). My point is really quite simple but inarguable: There are substantial problems in researching self-esteem that arise from studying it via the traditional methods of psychology practiced as a natural science; therefore, there may be value in trying another paradigm. The good news is that the alternative is not likely to be limited in the same ways as its natural science counterpart. The bad news is that no doubt there are limits to this approach as well. The question becomes, how do we go about studying self-esteem qualitatively?

Qualitative Advances in Researching Self-Esteem

The last decade has seen some genuine advances in applying qualitative methods to studying self-esteem. At least three researchers (Epstein, 1980; Jackson, 1984; Mruk, 1983) have turned to them, in part, in response to the methodological difficulties associated with traditional natural scientific methods. Epstein, for example, took issue with the appropriateness of doing experimental research on self-esteem. His alternative is ecological, which may be done in two ways. One is to manipulate self-esteem in what Epstein (1979) called "natural laboratories," where it is possible to obtain

> measures of behavior in specially selected situations where manipulations could be introduced in a natural manner. Such research can be regarded as using certain events as natural laboratories for the study of behavior. We had previously studied sport parachuting as a natural laboratory for the study of anxiety. . . . Unfortunately, natural laboratories can be found for only limited phenomena. For other events, we turned to self-observation of experiences in everyday life. (p. 51)

Although it is desirable to take advantage of such "natural laboratories," I agree that it is difficult to do so, especially with something like self-esteem. For instance, it is hard to predict when a naturally occurring self-esteem situation is about to present itself, let alone to identify control versus experimental subjects or to repeat it enough times to obtain reliable findings in the ordinary sense. However, the alternative Epstein offers is at least feasible, and having subjects report on their own self-esteem experience in a way that is relatively structured does increase the reliability of such results.

Another version of Epstein's ecological approach is to have students track self-esteem over a period of time. The technique can be used for short periods or longer ones, which means this chronicling of self-esteem can be used for longitudinal studies, which are sorely lacking in this field. If self-esteem is a vital force that is generally present in behavior over time, then what better way to study self-esteem in real life than to have people report on it that way? One advantage of researching self-esteem in this fashion is that the paradoxes mentioned earlier are more likely to show themselves as they are actually lived, which gives us the opportunity to study them better. It is worth noting that Epstein fully recognized the limits of using self-reports as data. However, he also made the important point that they are certainly connected to behavior in some way and may predict behavior at least as reliably as so-called objective indicators do.

Self-report estimates are usually based on impressions gained over repeated observations, whereas laboratory studies usually investigate responses in a single setting on a single occasion. On this basis alone there
is reason to suspect that laboratory findings, as customarily obtained, are
often low in replicability and generality, and cannot therefore establish
strong relationships with findings obtained on other occasions by other
means. (1979, p. 52)

The key to using any method effectively, including this one, lies in
how rigorously the method is executed. Accordingly, Epstein required
subjects to keep a daily record of a given affective or experiential phenomenon like self-esteem (a process that I call keeping a "self-esteem
journal"). He then analyzed these reports in terms of consistent categories, such as type of emotion experienced, stimulus situations that
elicited the affect, impulses experienced at that time, and corresponding
behaviors connected with the event. Note that this approach puts us
in close proximity with the link between self-esteem and behavior as it
actually occurs, something that more traditional work seems to find so
elusive. It should be obvious by now that just because the qualitative
approach is experiential in nature does not mean that it is methodologi-
cally undisciplined: Qualitative work simply has different strengths
and weaknesses.

Phenomenological psychologists also investigate real-life human experiences, such as learning and thinking (Aanstoos, 1984; Colaizzi, 1973;
Costall & Still, 1987; Dreyfus & Dreyfus, 1986; Giorgi, 1970, 1975, 1984;
Wertz, 1984). The basic form of this method involves what can be
thought of as a stepwise process, especially when it is used to investigate
more empirically based data as opposed to the more conceptual information with which we worked when we performed the first phenomenological reduction on the definitions of self-esteem. Typically, the
researcher begins by identifying the phenomenon to be studied, then
finds suitable subjects for its investigation. Data are usually generated
by asking subjects for an initial description of the experience or event,
then expanding on this material, via interview. Each initial description
and its related interview are transcribed as a single body of data. This
narrative or "extended protocol" of behavior is then examined for meaning units, which are in turn used to develop a description of a given
subject's experience as a situated instance of the phenomenon, or how it
is lived by a particular subject at a particular time. Next, these individual
records of the phenomenon are examined for regularities that occur
between subjects. The subsequent recurring themes are then identified
as basic to the phenomenon and are known as its essential, or constitutive, elements. These components, and the relationships between them,

are then worked into a final phenomenological description, usually identified as its fundamental structure, or that which is necessary and sufficient to give rise to the phenomenon for any given individual. Of course,
all the while the researcher attempts to suspend his or her preconceptions as much as possible, which requires considerable attention to the
researcher's own thinking processes each step of the way.

Like their natural science counterparts (Howard, 1985), all human
science researchers recognize that in all cases, the research method
and its design must fit the unique requirements of the phenomena to
be researched. This means that the method must be flexible as well as
rigorous, a condition that results in considerable diversity, just as we
saw with traditional quantitative work. These two characteristics of the
phenomenological method, rigor and flexibility, allow it to be faithful
to the phenomenon, wherever it may lead. Indeed, my work on researching the fundamental structure of self-esteem mentioned earlier
is based on this kind of research. But Jackson's *Self-Esteem and Meaning:
A Life Historical Investigation* (1984) probably represents the most in-
depth and articulate discussion of the value of using the phenomenological method to research self-esteem. In dealing with the problems and
limits encountered when researching it from the natural science paradigm, for instance, Jackson noted that

> [t]he problem seems rather to lie in experimentation itself—or more cor-
> rectly, in the application of the experimental method to the investigation
> of self-esteem. . . . Self-esteem is not a determinate process like the ones
> studied in the physical sciences; its nature lies rather in its subjective
> character and in its ever-changing manifestations and implications. Con-
> fronted by a phenomenon so elusive and so dynamic, the experimental
> method is, as it were, overpowered. (pp. 4–5)

Jackson made it clear that, above all, self-esteem is a meaningful phenomenon—it is literally filled with living implications concerning our
worthiness as individuals facing the vital challenges of living, whether
we do that well or poorly over time. Indeed, he discussed in great detail
the kinds of problems studying such phenomena present for traditional
methods, particularly those involving the experimental design. For example, Jackson pointed out that one of the greatest limitations in approaching human things quantitatively is that this approach tends to
break living wholes down into observable but broken parts. Although
their sum may turn out to be correct in number, it is always less than
the lived realities people experience. Note that Jackson is not saying
there is no value in knowing about the parts. Rather, he concludes that
it is important not to mistake them for the whole, which means, among

other things, that we may benefit most from using a method capable of integrating both quantitative and qualitative findings.

Integrated Description

In all fairness, I must say that phenomenologists sometimes focus so much on meaning that they become just as biased as their natural scientist counterparts in insisting that one approach is better than another. Indeed, much of what passes for phenomenological research today seems to suffer an overemphasis on one of two things. On the one hand, contemporary phenomenologists I have listened to recently at the American Psychological Association annual conventions often tend toward individual or personal experience, so much so that their work leads back to phenomenalism. On the other hand, they sometimes seem so excessively postmodernistic that their work lacks methodological rigor, or may demonstrate so much relativism, that it is difficult to distinguish between psychological research and what might more properly be called literary criticism, or even mere opinion, neither of which is grounded in the scientific method. Rather, if we want to be genuinely phenomenological, then we must stay with the thing itself. Self-esteem seems to be telling us that both scientific paradigms are necessary if we wish to do that faithfully. One way of reaching this goal is to use a form of the phenomenological method I have referred to as "integrated description" (Mruk, 1994). This approach is based on Giorgi's more scientifically rigorous vision of phenomenological psychology in that it is a step-by-step procedure. However, integrated description is also designed to work with the findings of psychology practiced as a natural science, so the result is a more balanced, comprehensive analysis, which may be just what we need to research self-esteem most effectively.

Integrated description is a two-stage research process. First, it is necessary to identify the general structure of a phenomenon in the step-by-step fashion presented earlier. Then, it is necessary to proceed to the integration phase. This part of the process involves identifying what Jackson (1984) might call the "parts" of a phenomenon, which are often best determined quantitatively, then fitting them into their respective places in the general structure. The process might be likened to solving a jigsaw puzzle from the center outward toward the boundaries or to building a house from the foundation to the roof. I actually began this work in chapter 1, when the structure was revealed, and I will continue the process in chapter 3 by identifying the major research findings on self-esteem, specific area by specific area. Later on, I will use the general structure to form a theory of self-esteem and show where the particular findings fit into it in a way that eventually results in practical applications.

Such integrated description can be applied to any number of human phenomena. For instance, if we were doing an integrated description of depression, I would first attempt to find out what it means to be depressed by asking subjects to describe their experience, then develop a general structure of it in a step-by-step fashion. Next, I would examine more traditional research on depression and show where those results fit into the structure. For example, because depression involves bodily sensations and states, I would have to show where and how the biology of depression comes into play in "being depressed." Yet depression also affects perception, so I would elaborate the description further by including findings on thinking patterns typically associated with depression. Furthermore, because depression often affects a person's relationships with others, I would expand the phenomenology to show how the fundamental structure involves the various interpersonal meanings of depression. The result would be a more comprehensive picture of depression than seeing it only as a "chemical imbalance" or a "lack of meaning," although both views would be accounted for in the description.

Using information from both paradigms presents a difficult challenge in two ways. First, it is hard work in that it demands being able to deal with a broad range of material from many points of view. Second, the results are likely to please neither the hard-core empirically oriented, number-crunching social scientist nor the "touchy-feely," literarily inclined, experientially oriented postmodern counterpart. As Giorgi (1971, 1984) pointed out, though, there are a number of ways these two kinds of research can balance each other. For instance, where psychology as a natural science focuses on measuring behavior, a human science approach deals with the meaning of behavior. Similarly, whereas the natural science paradigm looks for determined or causal reactions, the human science approach attempts to account for "free" or intentional ones. Where one method seeks identical repetition of a measure or outcome to reduce uncertainty, the other does so by searching for essential themes that are consistently present in a given phenomenon. In short, human subjects live simultaneously in external and internal worlds: we act as well as react. It is easy to fall prey to methodological tunnel vision if we practice psychology from one perspective and ignore or dismiss the other. Although integrated description may have some limits, at least it avoids this common paradigmatic trap.

THE QUESTION OF VALIDITY AND RESEARCHING SELF-ESTEEM

We now have an idea of what the phenomenological method looks like and how I am using it here, but the issue of whether or not such research is valid must also be addressed. If one accepts the scientific method as being empirical, methodical, theory building, and self-correcting, then there can be no doubt that the human science paradigm qualifies— providing one stays with the procedures outlined by Giorgi (1971, 1984). After all, the word *empirical* implies either observation or experience, and we can even "observe" experience to a certain degree through such techniques as introspection. Both external and internal observations are sources of data, at least in the psychological realm, and they are tied to the underlying structures of human beings. It is true that they are not identical, but this is why we need two paradigms in the first place.

Next, science is a methodological or step-by-step way of knowing, which can be duplicated by others. The research question or hypothesis, how data concerning this idea are generated, what was observed from such activity, and how the material is analyzed to yield regularities are all steps that are identified and recorded. Although we are most familiar with explicating these steps in laboratory notebooks (which can also be seen as quantitative journals), it is important to realize that phenomenological research follows the same rules. Such descriptive or qualitative activities begin with an idea (or hypothesis, if we wish to use traditional scientific language) concerning what gives rise to a given experience. Then, we implement a program of research that includes specifying how relevant data were gathered, revealing how such material was analyzed for regularities, and presenting findings like those concerning fundamental structures. Each step is identified so that the method can be examined by others and be replicated, if desired.

One advantage of science is that it allows us not only to discover information but to organize it into powerful bodies of ideas called models and theories. These scientific creations, in turn, help generate additional questions. Phenomenological researchers are just as active at the theoretical level as are their natural science counterparts. In fact, theory building is something qualitative researchers do rather well. Where quantitative theories lead to predictions and the possibility of controlling various domains of the natural world, phenomenological theories also offer understandings of human behavior that are of practical value. For instance, human science research helps us see how something is lived both in general and in individual terms. Such knowledge can help us to develop clinical interventions that are specifically designed for the unique characteristics of a particular person, group, or culture.

Finally, the scientific method is self-correcting. For example, if a given researcher makes a claim, and if someone else duplicates the steps that lead to it and reaches the same outcome, then the original finding is strengthened or validated to some degree and scientific knowledge is advanced. If the steps are repeated and the same outcome is not obtained, then the step-by-step method forces us to reconsider the claim. For instance, we may reexamine the finding, reconsider the design of the research, or look for alternative explanations. The beauty of the scientific method is that it "wins" no matter what the case, because either outcome creates better understanding over time. In this sense, science can be seen as a great conversation to which anyone can contribute at anytime, regardless of gender, race, culture, or historical period. Although perhaps in a different voice, phenomenologically oriented social scientists are legitimate participants in this great story because they follow the same rules of discourse.

Validity in Self-Esteem Research

The last set of difficulties generated by using the scientific method to study self-esteem, regardless of the paradigm being used, concerns the question of validity. Of course, this issue is a complex one and has been dealt with extensively in regard to self-esteem, especially by Wells and Marwell (1976) and Jackson (1984), who represent the quantitative and qualitative approaches, respectively. They concluded that validity is not so much a matter of absolute truth, but of available proof. In other words, the value of the scientific method is not that it allows us to find hidden answers. Rather, it helps to eliminate possibilities and reduce uncertainty to increasingly manageable levels (Tryon, 1991).

Perhaps a better way of dealing with the concept of validity is to ask, as Jackson (1984) did, validity for what? If the goal of research, for instance, is to measure self-esteem in a person, then the quantitative method is more valid because it is capable of dealing with such a task. If, however, we are interested in investigating aspects of phenomena as they are lived by real people, then qualitative methods are more valid both in principle and in practice. Jackson (1984) talked about this situation in the following way:

> Experimental investigation is based on the criteria of prediction and replication. . . . But this is only one *kind* of criterion, and it establishes only one kind of knowledge. There are other kinds of knowledge that elude the

criteria of prediction and replication; and a specific example is knowledge about self-esteem as a meaningful experience in a person's life. This kind of knowledge resides in a system of relations that is unique and irreducible in each separate instance. Such knowledge cannot be captured by a method that breaks it down into standard components. The experiment, however, is designed to perform exactly this kind of reduction. *It is aimed at washing out the very information which we seek—namely, information about unique and specific constellations of personal meaning.* (pp. 216–217)

If what Jackson says is correct, and I think it is, then we must also add that self-esteem research needs to be concerned with information from both qualitative and quantitative research for two reasons. First, human beings exist in both ways: We are quantitative objects in the world just like any other physical body, and all the laws that apply to such entities also apply to us. But we are also what phenomenologists call "body-subjects" (conscious identities that are always also embodied in physical form), and only qualitative research methods will help us out with this crucial dimension of self-esteem, just as only quantitative methods will help with other tasks. Second, if it is true that the field is in need of consensus, and again I think it is, then we cannot avoid the reality that the social psychology of self-esteem is filled with both kinds of research and findings, which means we cannot dismiss one kind simply because it might be convenient. The question becomes, then, what are the criteria by which qualitative indicators can be said to have validity?

Construct validity applies to qualitative work as much as to quantitative findings, perhaps even more so. This type of validity is based on evaluating whether a finding is consistent with an explicit conceptual framework or theory. Such correspondence is based more on the rules of logic than on numbers, so we should expect to be held accountable in this way. Thus, fidelity (being "true," i.e., descriptively accurate about the phenomenon) is an important criterion used in phenomenological research (Heidegger, 1962/1927; Marcel, 1964). This kind of validity concerns the degree to which a given description of the fundamental structure of a particular phenomenon actually reflects that phenomenon at the empirical (i.e., observed or experienced) level. Although it is assumed that no one description can ever be complete, descriptions can vary in terms of how accurate or faithful they are. This means that it is possible to compare qualitative work and determine which description is more accurate, more complete, or more valid.

The difficulty with this form of validation is, of course, how do we check (validate) a finding or description? To paraphrase Husserl (1970b), for this we must return to the facts themselves. If a particular description leaves out something important about a phenomenon, or if it does not account for a major finding, then the validity of that description is weakened. The reader will note that I used this procedure in defining self-esteem. Most of the definitions were invalid or, more properly, less valid because they left out competence, worthiness, or how they relate to one another. By the same measure, the phenomeno-logical definition had greater validity because all three components were accounted for in that description, and the links between them were described in more detail. We will continue to evaluate the validity of this approach as we examine major research findings and major theories of self-esteem in the next two chapters, as the validity of our description of the fundamental structure of self-esteem depends on its ability to indicate how that which is known about a phenomenon fits into, or is located within, the structure.

In all science, validity is more of a process than an event. In other words, validity is a dialogue between researchers, where convergence (establishing something as being "true" or agreed upon) emerges through what Paul Ricoeur describes as a "logic of uncertainty and of qualitative probability" (Jackson, 1984, p. 219):

> Ricoeur calls this process of validation—this argumentative discipline—"the method of converging indicies." . . . This dialogue is indispensable because it provides the "logic of argumentation" which leads to increasing validity and secure knowledge about a phenomenon. We assume that our dialogue will be fruitful, that we will move toward progressive agreement, because we live in a common world and we study phenomena that spring from common sources—social, economic, biological, and physical. As we observe the ways different subjects organize a psychological phenomenon in this common objective matrix, and as we discuss this phenomenon from a number of theoretical perspectives, we cannot help but converge on its essential structure. (p. 219)

Just as with the natural science paradigm, the results of such efforts (which can be called findings) become material for further investigation by others. Points of convergence arise through dialogue in either para-digm, and essentially that is a qualitative process because it is a social endeavor. Thus, uncertainty is reduced via the same process in both paradigms and is at the core of reaching a scientific consensus.

It would be a serious mistake to think that we are talking about validity as mere consensus—after all, people used to agree that the world was flat, but consensus did not make it so. At the same time, there is a certain way in which all the validity the scientific method can really offer is a process of consensus building, albeit a more demanding one than common sense or mere belief requires. For as Heisenberg (1950) suggested, science does not discover truth; that is the business of religion or philosophy. Instead, empirical work of both the quantitative and the qualitative type continually seeks to refine and expand knowledge through the reduction of uncertainty. As Wells and Marwell (1976) said in regard to a discussion of test validity,

> Validity is not something that an instrument "has," but a qualitative attribution made to it through investigation, negotiation, and persuasion. Nor is validity attributed to the measure in isolation, but within the context of a particular interpretive usage. . . . Very briefly put, validity is a joint property of a measurement or observational technique, an interpretive framework, and a scientific audience. (pp. 155–156)

Validity, then, involves a process, includes reaching a consensus, and is always a matter of degree. Why should it be different with something so complex as self-esteem?

CONCLUSION

Much more could be said about validity and self-esteem research. For example, I could talk about the "plausibility" of a theory, which is the kind of credibility that comes when ideas are useful in an applied or practical setting, whether or not they can be "proven" in the ordinary sense (Wells & Marwell, 1976). However, we are not so much concerned with explicating the scientific method here as with understanding how it can be used to research, understand, and enhance self-esteem. Four things stand out in this regard at this second stop of our journey. First, we know from chapter 1 that qualitative and quantitative methods have been applied to the topic for a long time. Second, it is clear that there is a substantial amount of research currently available on the subject, even though it may vary in terms of such things as validity. Third, the field calls for a greater degree of scientific consensus at the research, theoretical, and practical levels. Fourth, it appears as though reaching this goal will depend on using a method that is capable of integrating both qualitative and quantitative data, as doing otherwise is likely to produce a lopsided social science of self-esteem. The next step, then, is to examine the major research findings about self-esteem as they occur today. Later on we can attempt to integrate them into our description of its fundamental structure.

Self-Esteem Research Findings: Toward a Consensus

As a professor and a clinician who is interested in self-esteem, I constantly encounter enthusiastic but highly oversimplified questions, claims, and even criticisms about self-esteem and its importance. Indeed, I tend to be very cautious when I speak about self-esteem to lay audiences because of what can be called the "self-esteem fallacy." The mistake usually takes the form of something like "Self-esteem is so important. If we could only enhance it, then everything would be so much better." This common yet unfortunate error concerns the fact that people too readily believe self-esteem is somehow a psychological "magic bullet." It is not the intent that is frustrating, for it is well meant. Rather, the research on self-esteem simply paints a different picture. The most important finding to emerge from traditional research concerning self-esteem probably is this: "The news most consistently reported . . . is that the associations between self-esteem and its expected consequences are mixed, insignificant, or absent" (Smelser, 1989, p. 15).

Many social scientists using traditional methods conclude that the solution to the challenge proposed by this self-esteem research finding lies in developing more sophisticated experimental or statistical methods (Scheff et al., 1989). Some even go so far as to say that this finding means that self-esteem is not a very important variable in human behavior (Seligman, 1995b) or even that self-esteem may be strongly linked to negative behavior (Baumeister et al., 1996). Now we know, though, that the phenomenological approach suggests that the problem may actually lie with the methods that are used to research self-esteem and that there is another way of looking at the problem that may take us beyond this limitation. Although it would not be proper to bypass such an important finding altogether, the phenomenological perspective allows us to understand it differently. As discussed in chapter 1, self-esteem is tied to behavior through meaning, and that kind of relationship is not easy to measure statistically. It is more appropriate to examine the vast amount of existing research on self-esteem with a more open mind than it is to simply dismiss it. We can approach the material currently available in a more meaningful way by asking this question: Whether found quantitatively or qualitatively, what does a particular finding show us about self-esteem as it is lived?

This kind of qualitative meta-analysis is similar to the approach I used in defining self-esteem and may bring some clarity to the field, at least in terms of consensus. In other words, providing that we keep in mind the quantitative or statistical weakness of such findings (which may be very different from its qualitative strength or weakness), culling out a body of "standard" findings is useful in a number of ways. For example, it may be possible to identify techniques to increase self-esteem that have been evidenced in some meaningful way. Such a consensus can also help us in evaluating theories and ideas about self-esteem because they can be examined in terms of whether or not they can account for these self-esteem "facts."

Of course, mere consensus cannot be construed as being scientifically valid, otherwise we would still believe that the world is flat or that demons cause schizophrenia. Therefore, I must clarify the criteria by which a given self-esteem research finding is to be considered legitimate material to accept. As with uncovering the fundamental structure of self-esteem, any quantitative or qualitative finding concerning the meaning and structure of self-esteem that passes the test of time is considered to be valid data for our research question. In other words, a finding that is consistently cited by others as a standard in the field meets the criterion of persistence, and one that is corroborated by independent research meets that of significance. Such findings are likely to help us collect the building blocks for consensus.

Note that I am not claiming the following presentation of self-esteem findings is complete. Indeed, since our final goal is to enhance self-esteem, I will focus mostly on research that is of clinical importance. This means that some areas, like self-esteem in the educational or workplace settings (Brockner, Wiesenfeld, & Raskas, 1993), will not be addressed as such. Also, remember that I am not claiming the findings are strong in the statistical sense. This problem has already been discussed, and I will add to that by pointing out that self-esteem findings often contradict one another (Tennen & Affleck, 1993). However, although sometimes such contradiction is a result of conceptual, methodological, or perspectival issues, it can also mean that the phenomenon being studied is simply multifaceted. Finally, as Baumeister (1993, p. iv) noted, even those who think they are familiar with the self-esteem literature are surprised by what they do not know when they attempt to do something comprehensive with it. So, rather than being exhaustive, I have sought to examine the best or most representative work available based on our criteria and on more than 20 years of familiarity with the literature in an attempt to address our clinical and, to a lesser extent, developmental concerns.

PARENTAL FACTORS AFFECTING THE DEVELOPMENT OF SELF-ESTEEM

We begin with family factors for two reasons. First, others precede us in the world and, since standards of worthiness are already present in the cultural and familial contexts into which we are born, worthiness precedes competence in the development of self-esteem. Second, such findings are among the earliest in the field and are still recognized today: "Regardless of the diverse measurement methodologies and the weak evidence for measurement convergence, there is considerable *conceptual overlap* among the various theoretical perspectives on self-esteem. In general, theories stress the importance of the individual's immediate social context—particularly the family—in determining self-esteem" (Schneiderman, Furman, & Weber, 1989, p. 222). It is true that no single family or social factor is overwhelmingly significant, but this can be taken to mean that human development is never simple and that there are no family or parent-child patterns that are common to all children with high or low self-esteem. After all, some children with "great" parents turn out to be quite poor in terms of their self-esteem and behavior, whereas many children with low self-esteeming parents come to be high self-esteeming individuals who demonstrate many desirable behaviors.

This problem of weak statistical correlation is common in developmental literature—even basic texts on developmental psychology point out that the work on linking attachment style to adult relationship formation is weak in this way (Sigelman & Shaffer, 1995). The emerging research on resilience shows that even when there are strong correlations between negative developmental environments and negative adult behavioral patterns, there are plenty of exceptions (Vaillant, 1995; Werner & Smith, 1992). As Tatiana Panas, a colleague of mine, is fond of saying, "Development is just like that," mainly because of the large number of variables involved in determining behavior over any length of time. Such factors are, then, more descriptively understood as being predisposing and interactive rather than causal or deterministic. They are among those conditions that increase (or, by their absence, decrease) the likelihood of self-esteem, but no one factor is enough to create high or low self-esteem. Instead of being dismayed by the weakness of the correlation between self-esteem and family factors, as some researchers lament, perhaps we ought to be thankful for it. The indeterminate nature of these variables means that the absence or diminishment of any one of them does not necessarily doom people to a lifetime of low self-esteem.

Parental Attitudes

Over the years, certain parental attitudes consistently appear to be conducive or detrimental to self-esteem. Most of them were identified by Stanley Coopersmith, but other work has supported them over time.

Parental Involvement

Healthy, as opposed to intrusive, parental involvement with the child may be the single most important parental or primary caregiver attitude affecting the development of self-esteem in children. For instance, parents who are described as being indifferent toward their children, or parents who are absent frequently or absent for long periods of time, tend to have children with lower levels of self-esteem (Clark, 1994; Coopersmith, 1967; Rosenberg, 1965). Moreover, this effect seems to be particularly important for male children (Miller, 1984).

Parental "Warmth"

Mere involvement does not seem to be enough. Quality counts, and parental warmth or acceptance, which to me means being valued by others for who one is, appears to be crucial to the development of self-esteem as well as to general development (Bednar et al., 1989; Coopersmith, 1967). This finding is frequently mentioned throughout two decades of work, but it tends to be a bit vague as a term. Trying to specify the behavioral components of such an attitude is difficult, but the term *acceptance* is used most often to describe a parent's willingness to see a child's strengths and weaknesses, or to be aware of each child in terms of his or her potentials *and* limitations. This kind of acceptance is "warm" in that it is balanced. By seeing both dimensions of a child in a particular situation, for instance, a parent can encourage him or her to explore the world in a way that is appropriate based on the child's age, preferences, competencies, fears, interests, and so forth.

Clear Parental Expectations

Clearly defined expectations and limits are parental attitudes often associated with developing positive self-esteem in children. Setting high but not impossible expectations, for instance, involves maintaining clear standards of worthiness, as well as maintaining consistent limits. Doing so seems to be conducive to self-esteem in two ways. First, setting goals lets the child know that certain forms of behavior are desirable, good, or "worthy" and to be strived toward. Second, setting and maintaining limits is important because failing to do so is destructive to self-esteem in the long run. For example, a long line of developmental literature shows that parental overpermissiveness is related to negative behaviors such as impulsivity and aggressiveness. The same literature, which can be found in almost any standard text on child development (Newman & Newman, 1987; Sigelman & Shaffer, 1995), indicates that limits that are too severe or too harshly enforced are also problematical. For instance, they may engender the development of anxious and restrictive behavior, rather than spontaneity and engagement with life.

Respect

Respectful treatment, which involves acknowledging the essential humanity of a child when dealing with him or her, is another positive parental attitude. Research on parental styles of discipline, for instance, suggests that rather than being authoritarian or permissive, a democratic (Coopersmith, 1967) or authoritative approach is more conducive to developing self-esteem in children. This means a parental willingness to discuss matters and negotiate conflict, but not at the expense of violating certain basic standards of behavior, such as respecting the rights of other people. Of course, few people are naive enough to believe that one must always be democratic or authoritative. Rather, it is a matter of which discipline style one uses most often, or of being a "good enough" parent (Winnicott, 1953). This attitude of respectfulness extends to other areas, such as honoring agreements, taking the time to explain things, and accepting (within limits) a child's preferences.

Parental Consistency

Parental consistency is a fairly standard positive developmental influence that seems related to the development of self-esteem in that it reinforces the other attitudes, such as being a parent who is involved, who cares, and who holds, encourages, and maintains standards. Once again, the idea is that the prevailing attitudes are those of involvement (but not smothering), acceptance (but not indulgence), firmness (but not rigidity), being democratic (but not simplistically so), and doing so consistently (a "good enough" amount of the time). Being valued enough to be treated in these ways appears to enhance self-esteem across the board—it surely is more pleasant and conducive to positive exchanges and outcomes than the opposite. Note that adults also respond well to such treatment and that it is one of the ingredients of good therapy (Rogers, 1961).

Birth Order

Finally, there is a small degree of consensus that birth order can have an impact on self-esteem. All things considered, being firstborn slightly enhances the possibility of developing positive self-esteem. This finding was noted by Coopersmith in 1967 and continues today. Moreover, this ordinal effect seems to be stronger for males than for females. Similarly, there is some indication that children without siblings tend to have higher self-esteem than those with siblings. Although there is no simple causal relationship between birth order and self-esteem, the general understanding is that first or only arrivals receive more attention from, and interaction with, parents than those who arrive later, which means that more direct or focused parental involvement occurs here than with other ordinal positions.

Modeling

Coopersmith (1967) first noticed a positive relationship between self-esteem levels in mothers and their children. But Bednar and colleagues

(1989) made considerable use of this factor by pointing out that parents actually show (i.e., live out, demonstrate, present by example) their children the route to self-esteem (or the lack of it) by how they handle their own challenges, conflicts, and issues: "The impact of parents' behavior upon the child's self-esteem is undeniable; given the immaturity of children, however, parents' expression of their own resolution of the self-esteem question is far more influential than what they teach verbally" (Bednar et al., 1989, p. 257). Parents who face life's challenges honestly and openly and who attempt to cope with difficulties instead of avoiding them thereby expose their children to a pro-self-esteem problem-solving strategy very early. Those who avoid dealing with difficulties reveal a very different route for handling the challenges and problems of life. The important thing about this finding is that we know that children imitate those who are closest and most important to them. Therefore, seeing how their benefactors handle the challenges of living tells children something about what is possible when those challenges come up for them. Once again, different variables intervene over time to shape children's final coping styles, but we cannot deny the importance of early models just because such findings seem "statistically weak."

SOCIAL FACTORS AFFECTING THE DEVELOPMENT OF SELF-ESTEEM

In addition to family factors, there are at least three other social factors affecting worthiness and therefore the development of self-esteem.

Self-Esteem and Values

Basic Values

Because self-esteem involves worthiness, it also involves questions concerning values, otherwise, how would we know what is "worthy" or important to aspire to in the first place? But researching values is very difficult. For one thing, values are hard to define, observe, or measure. For another, there is the problem of cultural relativity. Although learning theory and postmodernism (Gergen, 1991) tempt us to say that all values are culturally relative, it is dangerous to maintain that culture alone determines that which is worthy. If we did that, then we would also have to say that people could be worthy (i.e., "good," "conscientious," etc.) Nazis, racists, or sexists, and so forth, as long as their primary social group promoted such values. Such a position, of course, is ludicrous. The best way out of this dilemma would be to say that somehow certain fundamental pro-self-esteem values are universal, but proving the existence of such basic human values is a daunting task. Thus, the values dimension of self-esteem is always going to be controversial at some level. All I can do here is point out the problem and suggest three things to consider. First, most people in most cultures seem to be able to distinguish between what is deeply worthy of emulating and what is not. Second, certain values seem to have widespread (cross-cultural) recognition, such as courage, self-discipline, honor, and selfless care. Third, the values involved in acquiring and maintaining self-esteem appear to be more connected to these "deep structures" than to those that are more relative to time, place, and culture.

The research seems to indicate that we cannot escape dealing with a relationship between values and self-esteem if we want to understand either self-esteem or its link to behavior. It is clear that although people exhibiting high and low self-esteem may differ in certain key ways, such as in how likely they are to gain that which is valued, what they actually value is quite the same: As the expectancy literature on self-esteem would have it, "Both groups want to feel good about themselves" (Brockner et al., 1993, p. 200). The difference seems to be in what each of these groups tends to expect about their respective chances of really attaining that which is admired. For example, both groups value being successful, but the two groups hold different expectations of how likely they are to be successful, so their strategies for filling in this part of the self-esteem picture differ markedly. The individuals with high self-esteem usually feel competent enough to take the risk and worthy enough to sustain a failure, should it occur, so they may set their sights high to begin with. The latter, in contrast, are often just as concerned with avoiding the loss of worthiness as with gaining more, so they may employ a "self-handicapping strategy" even as they go about trying to be successful, which will help cushion the blow if they fail (Snyder, 1989). In either case, worthiness is at the heart of the matter.

Social Values

The next set of findings concerns the way in which socially derived values affect self-esteem. One pathway could be through what Rosenberg (1965) termed the "stratification hypothesis," which is the idea that there is an association between the self-esteem of a particular social group and the self-esteem level of an individual within that group.

In other words, if an individual belongs to a social group held in high (or low) self-esteem, then the individual's self-esteem will correspond in a significant way. The other possible link between self-esteem and primary social groups is called the "subculture hypothesis," or the idea that the values toward which we aspire are influenced more greatly by those closer to us than by general social or cultural values (Rosenberg, 1965). In this case, shared interests and opportunities, a similarity of attitudes and values being rewarded over time, and common lifestyles are instrumental in determining that which we understand as being worthy of aspiring toward. According to this hypothesis, subcultural forces may even be strong enough to offset other factors, such as a lack of esteem a particular group may hold in a particular society.

Like many debates in the social sciences, the answer to the question of which view is right is yes, because both sets of factors are active. Researchers recognize a consistent, albeit weak, link between self-esteem and general social class in the expected direction (Coopersmith, 1967; Mack, 1987; Rosenberg, 1965; Schneiderman et al., 1989). At the same time, there is agreement among most of the same authors that social factors within a subcultural group to which an individual belongs are more influential in determining his or her particular self-experience than the general social values of the larger society: These "local" values are formed earlier, experienced more directly, and reinforced more frequently, so they tend to have a stronger influence. For instance, the family is seen as being a particularly powerful source of self-esteem-related values; this social organization can certainly have a greater impact than general forces like those associated with social class. Likewise, the aspirations endorsed by one's primary reference group as an older child, adolescent, or even adult are likely to be very active in determining how one perceives and regards oneself in terms of competence and worthiness than are more remote and less direct social influences, even though such general society expectations play a role, too.

Self-Values

Although values are certainly set in a social context, the individual also plays a role in the relationship between self-esteem and values. Thus, the second area that researchers focus on most consistently in regard to self-esteem and values concerns what are called "self-values" (Pope et al., 1988; Rosenberg, 1965). Self-values, which are "the conceptions of the desirable which represent the individual's criteria for self-judgment" (Rosenberg, 1965, p. 15), are important for self-esteem because they connect it to one's identity, which, in turn, creates a link between self-esteem and behavior. Yet these values concerning that which is good and desirable are based more on direct, meaningful, and personal experience than are social or even subcultural values. Self-values are therefore more personal and help to give us an internal sense of selfsameness, which is important for our experience of ourselves as unique individuals rather than as merely members of a social group or class.

Research also shows that certain types of experiences can change self-values in ways that affect identity, self-esteem, and behavior. For example, Epstein's research suggests that "[t]here are certain experiences that can be a turning point in an individual's existence" (1979, p. 73). In this case some 270 subjects were asked to fill out forms that required them to describe such an experience and rate it according to various scales. This information was then analyzed to develop a typology of experiences, leading Epstein to conclude that "[s]ignificant changes in self-concept are produced by three broad kinds of experience, namely exposure to a new environment, being required to make new responses, and establishment or loss of significant relationships" (p. 79). Similarly, self-esteem seems to be affected by value conflicts within the self (Jackson 1984; Mruk, 1983). This happens in situations where people hold one basic self-value to be important but also find that it is simultaneously opposed by another deeply held belief. For instance, an individual may hold independence as a self-value worthy of aspiration, but he or she may also value security so much that he or she actually becomes very dependent in relationships. The history of how such value conflicts both express and affect identity can create lively self-esteem stories, which Jackson (1984) calls "central conflicts" and which I call "self-esteem themes."

Gender and Self-Esteem

Rosenberg noticed a possible interaction between gender and self-esteem as early as 1965, and more recent findings support it. For example, Epstein (1979) found that when female subjects were asked to report on experiences related to self-esteem, they "reported more experiences involving acceptance and rejection, particularly acceptance, than males, and males reported slightly more experiences involving success and failure than females" (p. 62). O'Brien and Epstein (1983, 1988) extended this work into the area of testing and measuring self-esteem and found differences in responses based on gender to be significant enough to require separate norms for males and females. The consensus is that, even in childhood (Pallas, Entwisle, Alexander, & Weinstein, 1990), gender is capable of influencing self-esteem to a small but measurable degree and that this influence occurs in a reasonably predictable direction. Note here that the widely cited study conducted by the American Association of University Women (1991) reported a large difference, but the methods of this study seem highly controversial. In terms of the general structure, however, we can say that women in our society seem to gravitate toward the worthiness component of self-esteem (being valued by others in terms of acceptance or rejection) and that men tend to be pulled slightly more by the competence dimension (success or failure).

Of course, there are plenty of exceptions in either direction, and the question of whether this is a function of nature (biology) or nurture (culture and learning) is still unanswered, although at this point the evidence suggests that social forces are primarily responsible for these differences (Sanford & Donovan, 1984). It should also be said that insofar as a society is sexist in these ways, it prevents or discourages women from pursuing competence, thereby making them more dependent on worthiness, which could risk making them more vulnerable to others and less confident in themselves (Sanford & Donovan, 1984). It must be pointed out that the other side is just as sexist and negative. Pushing men toward competence also limits their access to the other component and this event may be associated with self-esteem problems, particularly those that involve feeling worthy. Being too "macho" or adopting a lifestyle that ignores the importance of being connected to others interpersonally could be an example of this phenomenon. I should also point out that the degree of this difference seems to be much less today than was reported in the research of the early 1980s (O'Brien, Leitzel, & Mensky, 1996), perhaps reflecting some cultural shifts in this area.

Racial, Ethnic, and Economic Factors Affecting Self-Esteem

The questions of whether and how racial, ethnic, and economic forces affect self-esteem are part of another stream of research activity. The issue seemed resolved by Rosenberg and Simmons (1971), who did a large research project involving 1,917 students in urban schools, many of whom were African-Americans. They reported that, contrary to popular assumptions, African-American children do not have lower self-esteem than Caucasian children. Indeed, they examined 12 other studies done on this topic from 1963 to 1970 and concluded, "Our general assessment of these findings is as follows: while the results probably do not justify the conclusion that blacks have higher self-esteem than whites, the weight of the evidence certainly does not seem to support the general conclusion that their self-esteem is lower" (p. 8). But common sense is often hard to defeat, even when evidence contradicts it, and the belief that African-Americans suffer low self-esteem as a group persists even today, despite the fact that more recent research supports Rosenberg and Simmons' original findings (Crocker & Major, 1989; Rosenberg, 1979). The real question is how are we to understand this reasonably well-substantiated finding in light of the view that racial, ethnic, or economic factors such as discrimination or lack of opportunity are detrimental to the self-esteem of various groups. At least four possible explanations for the phenomenon seem to be available today. The first one is, of course, that this research is simply flawed. However, while the commonsense explanation is still common, the field really does seem to have accepted the finding as a legitimate one—at least no major studies contradict the body of evidence.

The second possibility is that, although the overall indication is that such social factors do not affect self-esteem, the studies that do find a difference tend to do so under a certain condition (Kaplan, Martin, & Johnson, 1986). When minority and majority children from greatly different sociocultural backgrounds interacted frequently (e.g., attended the same school), self-esteem was somewhat lower for disadvantaged minorities. This may mean that when a disadvantaged group of people share the same environment with a dominant majority group *and* when discriminatory social factors limit the former in the pursuit of similar goals, then their self-esteem suffers. In this case, the major factor would be the fact that the minority group receives less support to succeed, has additional obstacles to overcome in order to succeed, or a combination of both.

The third possibility is that the finding may be correct as it is. If so, then it is possible to understand the material in terms of the subcultural hypothesis mentioned earlier. In other words, although racial, ethnic (including religious background), and economic discrimination can impact negatively on self-esteem, their influence is mitigated by identification with the primary reference group and its values. Therefore, as long as an individual meets the criteria for success within the primary or subcultural group, then self-esteem can exist and even flourish. This may be one reason that we see many individuals coming from incredibly impoverished backgrounds who achieve and maintain high self-esteem. The same factors seem to be at play in terms of poverty and self-esteem (Schneiderman et al., 1989). Once again, meeting aspirations that are deemed worthy by family, church affiliation, neighborhood, and/or peers may be a stronger influence on self-esteem than are larger, more general external forces. Of course, it may even be that child-rearing practices in various ethnic groups are simply more self-esteem enhancing than those of the white middle-class culture.

The fourth explanation is more psychological than social, although both factors are involved. It is the idea that a social stigma of any type (racial, ethnic, physical, etc.) is a very powerful social and psychological force that affects identity and self-esteem, but in a way that is much more complex than those which meet the eye. For instance, Crocker and Major (1989) suggested that there is a "self-protective" dimension to such stigmatization or prejudice. In other words, a person from such a disadvantaged group may avoid a loss of self-esteem by understanding things that detract from it as a function of prejudice, ignorance, or some other external factor. This self-protective psychological device would allow the person to see such events as not having to do with himself or herself as a person, but with discrimination by others. For example, an individual with average self-esteem who fails to solve a problem, achieve a goal, or be accepted by others may suffer a temporary diminishment of self-esteem. However, if such an event takes place for a stigmatized individual, and if it is seen as involving those who typically discriminate against people "like us," then it is psychologically economical (self-saving) to understand the failure (or loss or rejection) as a function of prejudice rather than of personal shortcoming. Self-esteem is not lowered in this case because it is protected by externalizing the causes. We all tend to use this self-protective strategy in life, and the idea that it is adaptive to use it more often for a disadvantaged individual or group is consistent with the findings.

Self-Esteem and Culture

In the last chapter of the first edition of this book, I mentioned the need for cross-cultural research on self-esteem. My hypothesis was that culture could influence which component of self-esteem received the most emphasis, but that both competence and worthiness would be important for self-esteem regardless of cultural context. It seemed to me that comparing extremely divergent cultures would be the best approach to examine these two possibilities, so I set up a design comparing Eastern cultures with Western ones and attempted to make arrangements to do such work through the East-West Center in Honolulu, Hawaii. Unfortunately, research grants were being severely cut back at the time, so this work was not possible. But the institute did alert me to related research, most of which concerns what is called "self-construal," or how a culture helps people to define the normal, healthy self within its own context.

The classical research on the self in this area involves comparing what are called the "independent," or individualistic, and "interdependent," or communal, viewpoints on the self (Pettijohn, 1998, p. 67). Although there is very little research on cross-cultural comparisons of self-esteem in this regard, the existing work seems to fail to find any particular relationship associated with culture alone. According to Singelis and colleagues (1995), who have done such work with Far Eastern cultures, there are three hypotheses as to why no relationship has been found so far. One is that there is so much scatter between independence (which I would think is linked more strongly to competence) and interdependence (which is perhaps more closely associated with worthiness) within a given culture that it is difficult to make cultural comparisons without using large-scale studies. Another is that self-esteem is universally constructed, suggesting that competence and worthiness are always closely balanced in the development of self-esteem, no matter how the self is construed in a given culture. The third is that the instruments used to do such measurements simply have too strong of a Western bias to be useful in cross-cultural research of this type. We will simply have to wait until enough research accumulates in this area before establishing a meaningful degree of consensus.

THE RELATIONSHIP BETWEEN SELF-ESTEEM AND SUCCESS

James (1983/1890) appears to have been quite correct when he said that self-esteem involves success. Modern researchers are also concerned with this relationship (Harter, 1993; Pope et al., 1988). However, it is important to realize that not all forms of success are the same. An individual, for instance, can be very successful in a career but still be the victim of low self-esteem. In fact, outward or material success can even result from an attempt to substitute or compensate for low self-esteem, as in the case of a person who is driven toward success because of a fear of failure, as a "workaholic" overachiever might be. Also, although success is important for self-esteem because of an obvious connection to one of its basic components, it is competence at meeting the challenges of life that is especially relevant to self-esteem, and not merely being successful or doing something effectively.

Coopersmith (1967) went further in understanding the importance of success when he identified four ways in which it can be positive for self-esteem. They are power (the ability to influence or control others), significance (being valued by others as shown by their acceptance of our characteristics), virtue (the adherence to moral standards), and competence (a successful performance in regard to a goal). Epstein (1979) pointed out that if success is involved in self-esteem, then the possibility of failure must be active, too. Hence, he described four sources of self-esteem more dynamically: Achievement is balanced by loss, power is offset by powerlessness, acceptance is coupled with the possibility of rejection, and moral self-acceptance must also include the possibility of guilt. It is easy to see how similar these two sets of concepts are, so let me offer a framework that includes both of them.

Acceptance vs. Rejection

We saw the role of acceptance as one of the earliest and most consistent findings in the psychology of self-esteem. I prefer the term *being valued* instead of either *acceptance* or *significance*, because being valued seems more descriptive to me. However, to avoid adding more terms to the field, I will simply stay with the word *acceptance* to describe this source of self-esteem, because it is such a standard term in the developmental and clinical literature. In regard to self-esteem, being accepted means that significant others value us as worthy of their time and attention, whereas the absence or loss of being valued in these ways is what is meant by rejection. It is important to realize that there are many ways that acceptance and rejection may be alive in relation to the development and maintenance of self-esteem. For instance, care, nurturance, and attraction are important features of acceptance, but respect, fondness, and admiration are more appropriate in a work or professional relationship. Similarly, there are several modes of being rejected, such as being ignored, devalued, used, mistreated, or abandoned, and such deficiencies may impact negatively on self-esteem. In all these cases, we are dealing with interpersonal events concerning whether or not one is valued by others. Even as adults, who of us has not experienced the increase in self-esteem that comes with a new love or the loss of love, which is associated with rejection, betrayal, or abandonment? Being accepted must be understood as a source of self-esteem that is grounded in its worthiness component.

Virtue vs. Guilt

Coopersmith's (1967) definition of virtue, which is the adherence to moral and ethical standards, is very close to O'Brien and Epstein's (1983, 1988) notion of moral self-approval. I tend to use the term *acting on beliefs*, but, once again, I do not wish to just add terms to the field when plenty of good ones are already available. We will use Coopersmith's term *virtue* because it implies that there are higher standards of behavior to which to adhere than just measuring up to some culturally relativistic or postmodernistically convenient code of conduct. Similarly, guilt, particularly what the existentialists call "authentic guilt," can be understood as the failure to live up to more than just personal standards or those of a particular reference group, although either one of those is sufficient to produce it. The connection between being virtuous and self-esteem was stated earlier when I discussed the consensus about the importance of affirming values. Each time we act virtuously, or in a way that embodies that which we aspire to as being good and desirable, we find ourselves being worthy. Of course, each time we fail to do so affects self-esteem in a negative way: We feel some form of guilt about our lack of being virtuous and a loss of worthiness or even unworthiness.

Influence vs. Powerlessness

Power is the term that both Coopersmith (1967) and Epstein (1979) used to describe one's ability to manage or direct one's environment. However, I will use the word *influence* to describe this source of self-esteem and break with tradition for two reasons. First, power over one's environment may capture something of how this kind of behavior is actually lived, but other people can be a part of one's environment, too. Although power can certainly be used to describe a way of relating to others, it may be too strong a word to describe the more subtle aspects of interacting with others effectively. For example, forcing people to do what we want is not the only way to persuade them, and it certainly does not fit with our understanding of virtue and self-esteem.

Second, there may be a gender-based problem with the term *power*—it may be too "masculine" to be genuinely descriptive. For instance, I have found in working with both academic and clinical self-esteem enhancement groups that women often object to this term. When asked why, the most commonly offered response is that, for them, power carries too much of a negative connotation, as in power over someone or as in the abuse of power. When I ask what term they would prefer, the word *influence* is recommended most often because it is more gender-free. In any event, the ability to interact with the environment and/or others in a way that shapes or directs events is a form of competence in dealing with the challenges of living. Success in this area leads to a sense of having some say in life, which means that this kind of power helps us deal with events more effectively. Conversely, too many failures tend to engender a sense of interpersonal incompetence, learned helplessness, and perhaps even hopelessness, depending on how frequent and how severe the failures happen to be.

Achievements vs. Failures

Achievement is chosen to represent the kind of success Coopersmith (1967) had in mind when he used the word *competence* instead of that term, because his choice of word is too easily confused with the basic components of self-esteem revealed by the general structure. Epstein's (1979) term, *success*, is not employed because it is too general. For example, we can say that it is good for a person's self-esteem to be "successful" at any of the other three sources. I chose the word *achievement* primarily to avoid confusion; it is also more accurate in describing this source of self-esteem, because the successes involved must have personal meaning in terms of facing a life challenge if they are to matter for self-esteem. For example, brushing one's teeth is not a particularly significant act for most of us, but it may be a great personal achievement for an intellectually or physically challenged individual. There appears to be a set of extraordinary personal achievements that affect self-esteem in an extremely powerful way. The research by Epstein (1979), Jackson (1984), and Mruk (1983) referred to earlier indicates that when we reach a goal that requires dealing effectively with problems or obstacles that also have personal significance, then we demonstrate a higher level of competence at dealing with the challenges of living than we have known before. Such successes represent a developmental achievement in the person's own maturation.

Variability Concerning Self-Esteem and Success

There is one more important point of consensus to note about self-esteem and success. There seems to be a good deal of variability in how individuals can use these four sources to obtain self-esteem, no matter which nomenclature we use. Coopersmith (1967) found that

individuals may develop healthy levels of self-esteem by being successful in just one or two areas, particularly if these domains of life are
approved of by their primary reference group: "We should note that it
may be possible for an individual to attain high self-esteem by notable
attainment in any of the four areas. This might occur even where attainment in the other areas was mediocre or even poor" (p. 38). Bradshaw
(1981) offered an analogy which shows this dynamic aspect of the
relationship between self-esteem and success. He placed all the potential experiences that enhance self-esteem in life as a reservoir of possibility. This pool can be accessed by the individual through achievements,
power and influence, being valued, and acting on beliefs to result in a
"self-esteem income flow" (p. 7). The amount of self-esteem that flows
into our selves determines the degree or level of our self-esteem. The
model is also arranged to show that the four routes to self-esteem can
operate alone or in concert with one another. Failures can be seen as
detracting from self-esteem, but blocking any one route is not necessarily a problem because others can be used to compensate for it.

Unfortunately, Bradshaw failed to indicate why these four sources
bring self-esteem and offered virtually no research evidence to support
his model. Even citations are absent. However, the phenomenological
approach allows us to see how each one of the four majors sources is
connected to self-esteem and why behaving in these ways enhances it.
Personally significant achievements and power or influence are firmly
rooted in the competence dimension of self-esteem, even though achieving a goal or demonstrating influence must be done in ways that are
worthy in order to enhance self-esteem. Furthermore, acceptance (being
valued) by others and being virtuous (acting on one's beliefs) are clearly
grounded in worthiness, even though they often involve some form of
competent behavior.

PERSONALITY CHARACTERISTICS ASSOCIATED WITH SELF-ESTEEM

The fourth general area of self-esteem findings concerns an association
between self-esteem and personality.

Positive Characteristics of High Self-Esteem

Positive Affect

Keeping the statistical limits of self-esteem research in mind, there is
evidence supporting a link between high self-esteem and several desir-

able personality characteristics associated with mental health and well-being. First, high self-esteem seems to correlate with positive affect. Some authors point to this characteristic conversely by indicating that there is a relationship between low self-esteem and negative affect, such as depression and joylessness (Battle, 1982). Others note that self-esteem is hedonically preferred (Wells & Marwell, 1976), which means that high self-esteem simply feels better and makes life seem better than does low self-esteem. Another way to talk about this phenomenon is to describe self-esteem as a positive or benign "illusion" about one's characteristics and abilities (Baumeister, 1993; Campbell & Lavallee, 1993), which allows us to see ourselves or our life in a slightly rosier light than either may actually deserve. In short, a positive degree of competence and worthiness is desirable because it makes life more tolerable, spontaneous, and enjoyable.

Positive Outlook

Another general personality characteristic often associated with self-esteem is that of increased openness to experience and possibilities that comes with being effective at dealing with the various tasks and challenges of living successfully. Evidence for this point of consensus comes from studies that show a link between high self-esteem and success in certain areas. For instance, Plummer (1985) found that high self-esteem is related to competent (effective) performance, in that individuals exhibiting high self-esteem were more likely to complete tasks successfully and to do so more often than those with low self-esteem. Sappington (1989) used the phrase *effective functioning* to describe this aspect of having high self-esteem and presented a summary of supporting research pointing to a connection between the two. Behavioral researchers such as Pope and colleagues (1988) used the concept of self-efficacy to describe this connection between self-esteem, being able to take a reasonable degree of risk and dealing with the challenges of life fairly well. Apparently, having too little belief in ourselves means that we are so vulnerable that we have to direct our energy toward protecting what self-esteem we do have, whereas holding positive (but not exaggerated) beliefs about ourselves and how effectively we conduct life allows us to turn our attention and energies to more productive interests and activities.

Autonomy

Individuals with high self-esteem appear to be more independent, self-directed, and autonomous than their counterparts. In terms of concrete behaviors, this aspect of self-esteem was most often noted in regard to being able to maintain unpopular positions in the face of pressures to conform (Bednar et al., 1989; Coopersmith, 1967) and in regard to the ability to be assertive (Pope et al., 1988; Rosenberg, 1965). Certain related perceptual and motivational characteristics also seem to be involved here. For instance, people with high self-esteem seem able to accept both positive and negative feedback about themselves more easily than those with low self-esteem, who tend to focus more on negative feedback and may even discount the positive feedback altogether (Wells & Marwell, 1976). Similarly, people exhibiting high self-esteem tend to focus on self-enhancement or growth-related activities over self-protection as a primary concern, whereas individuals with low self-esteem tend to do the opposite (Campbell & Lavallee, 1993; Tice, 1993), although both groups engage in both activities. Finally, individuals with high self-esteem appear to know themselves better than do those with low self-esteem (Blaine & Crocker, 1993), although this is not always the case.

The Limits of Positive Self-Esteem

For all its value, high self-esteem is not to be confused with enlightenment. Wells and Marwell (1976) pointed out research suggesting a relationship between high self-esteem and some problematical qualities. For one thing, although individuals with high self-esteem may be more open to feedback about themselves, they do seem to have some difficulty seeing their own faults and limitations—it is as though self-esteem protects them too well. For example, the ability to engage in introspection concerning one's own limits and foibles may be hindered by self-esteem that is too high. Some evidence suggests that genuinely high self-esteem may pose certain difficulties in interpersonal relationships, particularly in terms of being sensitive to the needs or limitations of others (Wells & Marwell, 1976). In this case, having high self-esteem may make it difficult to see various issues as being problems, such as being hurt over a small slight or feeling hesitant to try something because one might suffer embarrassment if one does not succeed. Thus, when someone with low or medium self-esteem expresses such a concern, an individual with high self-esteem may inadvertently be insensitive to it. If we use high self-esteem as a positive illusion metaphor, which seems to be very popular in the social psychological literature on self-esteem these days, we might say that self-esteem helps us dismiss minor assaults so we can take risks, but that too much of this good thing is also problematical in that it may mean that we fail to see realistic problems or allow ourselves to get into situations better left alone (Heatherton & Ambady, 1993).

Low Self-Esteem: Three Types of Vulnerability

One important thing self-esteem seems to do that most research agrees upon is to help buffer us from the slings and arrows of everyday life (Epstein, 1980; Newman & Newman, 1987). In this sense, self-esteem is like a shield. Those who have a positive degree of self-esteem are better equipped to face life and tolerate challenge than those who do not. If so, then people with low self-esteem can be likened to soldiers carrying thin or worn shields into the battles of life, which means that they must be more attuned to potential threats, and to threats of a lesser nature, than is otherwise necessary. This deficit is found in the concept of *vulnerability* (Baumeister, 1993; Kernis, 1993; Rosenberg, 1965). It is as though a person suffers from an open wound (Marcel, 1964), which makes him or her both more susceptible to further injury and vigilant for such possibilities, a state of being that requires much energy to maintain and takes this valuable resource away from other possibilities. Note, however, that it is possible to express vulnerability in two very different ways: One can retreat from the possibility of further injury and become ever more cautious (low self-esteem as it is usually understood), or one can respond with denial, bravado, or even aggressiveness. In other words, there are two major types of low self-esteem to consider.

Classical Low Self-Esteem

The classical description of low self-esteem involves a chronic condition of negative affect, pervasive feelings of inferiority, a sense of basic unworthiness, and feelings of loneliness or insecurity. The literature usually characterizes people with low self-esteem as being anxious, depressed, and ineffective. It has also been demonstrated that people who suffer from low self-esteem of this type are often very sensitive to negative feedback or criticism (Bednar et al., 1989). Indeed, it has been shown that those with low self-esteem can be so sensitive to negative information about themselves that they habitually dismiss positive information (Epstein, 1979; Wells & Marwell, 1976). It is easy to see how the tendency to develop and rely on a self-handicapping strategy is adaptive under such circumstances: In some cases, it is better to not raise one's hopes than to have even modest dreams dashed yet once again.

It is important to realize that newer research points out that people with low self-esteem are not as bad off (incapacitated, self-loathing, etc.) as we might think. Rather, they actually think fairly well of themselves in terms of being "a good person," and their caution or general pessimism may actually be a way of maintaining the self-esteem they currently possess. In other words, what we typically mean by low self-esteem may be more of a desire for self-protection than for self-enhancement (Epstein, 1985; Tennen & Affleck, 1993; Tice, 1993; Wood, Giordano-Beech, Taylor, Michela, & Gaus, 1994). This finding may also mean that the fear and loathing of self and life commonly thought to be associated with low self-esteem may only apply to the clinical situation, such as is the case with severe depression or certain kinds of character pathology like the borderline personality disorder.

Defensive Self-Esteem

There is considerable research which suggests that the readiness to perceive and respond to threat or devaluation associated with low self-esteem can be lived out in ways that do not suggest what we normally think of as reflecting low self-esteem. Rather, such individuals may even look like they have "real" or high self-esteem in that they often seem to feel good about themselves, act confidently, look competent, or even behave quite aggressively, none of which is typically invoked by the term *low self-esteem*. Thus, it is necessary to think in terms of two types of low self-esteem (Branden, 1969; Coopersmith, 1967; O'Brien & Epstein, 1983, 1988; Wells & Marwell, 1976) in order to understand it more completely.

This second type of low self-esteem is described in a number of ways, such as "discrepant" self-esteem (Coopersmith, 1967, who also saw it in children), "pseudo" self-esteem (Branden, 1969), "defensiveness" (O'Brien & Epstein, 1983, 1988), and "unstable high" self-esteem (Kernis, 1993). I prefer the term *defensive self-esteem,* because the concept of reacting defensively to a sense of low self-esteem is the one thing that all of these terms and related behaviors have in common. Regardless of what term is used, we all have known people who are overly sensitive to criticism or who are very insecure and live that out by bragging (overcompensating), putting others down (displacing), throwing themselves into their work (sublimating), or even becoming aggressive (discharging), instead of looking cautious, timid, weak, withdrawn, depressed, or anxious, as people with low self-esteem are expected to be. It is very important to recognize the difference between classical low self-esteem and defensive low self-esteem for theoretical and practical reasons, as well as for research purposes. For instance, any comprehensive theory must account for how it is that one individual who suffers from a lack of self-esteem can look and behave in ways that appear very much the opposite from another person who lacks self-esteem. Any enhancement program needs to know about both types of self-esteem if it is to avoid fairly basic mistakes, let alone help people. Think about the potential consequences, for instance, of sending someone to an assertiveness training class who has a defensive self-esteem problem that expresses itself in some form of aggressive behavior. The result of such a mismatch between person and technique could well be any number of negative outcomes, some of which could be disastrous.

Medium Self-Esteem and Personality

Finally, there is a small body of literature on the relationship between what is usually called medium self-esteem and personality (Coopersmith, 1967; O'Brien & Epstein, 1983; Wells & Marwell, 1976). This information is limited but important for three reasons. First, medium self-esteem is found to be associated with certain positive and negative personality characteristics. Second, many if not most of us may be in this range. Third, it is not necessarily a bad place to be.

There are two major lines of research on this type of self-esteem. First, there are those researchers, such as Coopersmith (1959, 1967), who hold that medium self-esteem is simply the result of not having had enough exposure to the developmental factors that lead to high self-esteem, but of also having more than enough exposure to such factors as to avoid having low self-esteem. In this case, medium self-esteem is a midpoint on the continuum of qualities from low to high self-esteem. Higher self-esteem simply means more of it (more confidence, autonomy, spontaneity, etc.) and is always better. Other researchers, such as Block and Thomas (1955), Cole, Oetting, and Hinkle (1967), and Weissman and Ritter (1970), see medium self-esteem as a distinct type. These researchers tend to see the relationship between self-esteem and personality characteristics as *curvilinear* rather than linear. In other words, people with medium self-esteem have the best of both ends of the self-esteem continuum because they avoid either extreme.

We can use the analogy of seeing self-esteem as a positive illusion to help understand this type of behavior. If we think of self-esteem as a kind of benign illusion, then we do not want the extremes, for an illusion that is too weak means that we are so vulnerable that we have to direct our behavior toward protecting what self-esteem we do have, a situation that puts us into a classically low or defensive self-esteem mode. Too much belief in our own worthiness and competence, on the other hand, could actually make us more vulnerable to pitfalls by not recognizing realistic limits or by taking unrealistic risks (Baumeister, 1993). In this sense, a medium degree of benign self-deception about our competence and worthiness may be optimal in that it allows us to be open to life but not stupidly so. Of course, any theory of self-esteem will have to explain how all the major types of self-esteem (high, medium, low, and defensive) are possible in the first place.

THE CONSEQUENCES OF SELF-ESTEEM

Now let us turn to the consequences of self-esteem, which is to say the behavior that is thought to be linked to it.

Self-Esteem and Stress

From the very beginning of modern self-esteem research, an important link between self-esteem and stress, particularly one's ability to deal with it effectively, has been emphasized (Wells & Marwell, 1976). If this is an accurate link, then we must identify how self-esteem is involved in handling stress more effectively. We already noted a relationship between self-esteem and coping skills. Others extend this work to include one's general coping "style" (Bednar et al., 1989; Heatherton & Ambady, 1993). Factors associated with positive self-esteem in this way, such as increased autonomy, greater openness to alternatives, and a higher confidence in one's perceptions and abilities, all predispose one toward favorable outcomes in dealing with problems, challenges, and opportunities in general.

Stress can certainly tax our sense of worthiness as a person, especially if it comes from a negative source and is prolonged. The shielding function of self-esteem seems to help to reduce the negative power of stress by providing some insulation for how we feel about ourselves during such a period. The possible negative effects of stress on our perceptions of self and the world, the meanings we give to what is happening to us, and the actions we select in response to a stressful situation are all influenced by how good this shield happens to be. People with high self-esteem are generally at an advantage in this regard because they are better protected from suffering temporary declines of worthiness associated with failure, loss, or rejection:

> Individuals with high self esteem are protected from extreme fluctuations in self-concept. The effects of minor stresses are easily absorbed. . . .

People with high self esteem are protected by a network of internal and interpersonal resources which shield the self from most traumas. Only in the case of multiple assaults to self esteem (for example sudden unexpected divorce, loss of job) will those with high self esteem be noticeably affected. The lower self esteem is, the more susceptible it is to disruptions from even the mildest life challenges and, conversely, the more highly resistant it is to positive growth and change. (Frey & Carlock, 1989, p. 107)

More experimentally oriented research suggests a link between self-esteem and immunological functioning. For instance, negative self-evaluations appear to be associated with lowered natural killer cell activity in even moderately stressful situations (Strauman, Lemieux, & Coe, 1993). This kind of information supports the idea of a link between self-esteem and physical as well as mental health.

Of course, it is important not to overrate self-esteem. Even those with high self-esteem can tolerate only so much stress for so long. The point is that self-esteem plays a role in determining how one characteristically responds to stress and challenge (Bednar et al., 1989). A related matter that deserves at least some mention is the possibility of a relationship between self-esteem, coping style, and religion. There appears to be no such association for what is called "extrinsic" religion, which is characterized by such things as using church to advance one's social status or praying only in times of need. However, there is also what is known as "intrinsic" religion to consider. This form of religiosity, which might be better described as spirituality, includes a sincere commitment to a spiritual belief system as part of one's core values. This type seems to be fairly strongly associated with self-esteem (Masters & Bergin, 1992). Deeply held faith could be linked to self-esteem and handling stress well in a number of ways. For instance, believing in core values of a spiritual nature could help an individual to endure what others might experience as a loss of worthiness because he or she is accepted by a higher power. Acting in virtuous ways could simply help prevent the individual from making responses that would lower his or her sense of competence or worthiness, events that would only compound a stressful period. At the very least, intrinsic religiosity could help an individual hold on longer and suffer less deeply, because such values remind him or her of larger and more important realities than temporary, material ones.

Self-Esteem and Psychosocial Dysfunction

Although the line between simply coping poorly and developing social or psychological dysfunction is sometimes difficult to draw, there is another class of behaviors and characteristics that involve low or defensive self-esteem: those that have clinical significance. As an aside, note that I am aware of a large group of self-esteem-related phenomenon concerning such things as the negative impact of physical, sexual, or emotional abuse on self-esteem (McCann & Pearlman, 1990). However, instead of creating a special category for these situations, I will follow the pattern established in the fourth edition of the American Psychiatric Association's *Diagnostic and Statistical Manual of Mental Disorders* (DSM-IV, 1994), which focuses on the clinical manifestations of trauma rather than on the type of traumatic event. Even so, I must say that the worst thing about such events, particularly child abuse, is what they do to an individual's sense of competence and worthiness as a developing person, not just the pain involved when the events are happening. Not only can being treated by others in such a way inhibit the development of healthy self-esteem, but it can also facilitate the development of negative self-esteem themes and thereby plague a person long after the event, perhaps for a lifetime. I will return to this topic when I attempt to show in chapter 5 how a phenomenological theory of self-esteem is more effective at integrating research findings than are other approaches.

Self-Esteem and Anxiety

Virtually every major study on self-esteem discusses a link between low self-esteem and anxiety. Indeed, this link is so significant that Skager and Kerst (1989) said in a major review of self-esteem work, "There is no doubt that self-esteem is central in the consciousness of troubled human beings. Psychotherapists report that those who seek help typically suffer from low self-esteem" (p. 250). More recent research continues to evidence the relationship between self-esteem and anxiety (Heatherton & Ambady, 1993).

There are two ways that self-esteem and anxiety seem to be related. First, self-esteem buffers or shields us from stress. At this level, having a self-esteem problem means that an individual is more vulnerable to life itself and is therefore more likely to experience feelings of inadequacy, unworthiness, or what Alfred Adler (1927) called "inferiority." Second, the interaction between self-esteem and anxiety can be associated with more severe forms of psychopathology. Most clinically oriented self-esteem researchers (Bednar et al., 1989; Branden, 1969) point out such a relationship between self-esteem and anxiety, but it is a complex one because many other factors, such as personality, childhood reinforcement history, and biology, contribute to the development of a clinical condition. Battle (1982), for instance, noted work indicating a link between low self-esteem and the compulsive individual. Raskin, Novacek, and Hogan (1991) discussed self-esteem and narcissism. Samenow (1984, 1989) suggested a connection between low self-esteem and the antisocial personality disorder. Dependent or avoidant individuals are thought to suffer a lack of worthiness and competence associated with low self-esteem, as noted in the DSM-IV (American Psychiatric Association, 1994).

Self-Esteem and Depression

Depression is another frequently cited connection between low self-esteem and psychopathology (Coopersmith, 1967; Harter, 1993). One line of evidence for this connection is that there appear to be certain cognitive similarities between people who are depressed and people who suffer low self-esteem. For instance, a number of clinicians (Burns, 1980; Ellis & Harper, 1977) find that certain cognitive distortions are common in depression. There is agreement, for example, that depressed individuals often engage in irrational thinking patterns, or hold beliefs about themselves or situations that do not correspond to the facts. By calling oneself "stupid" for making a simple mistake, for instance, one closes off other possible interpretations, such as the value of learning through mistakes. This act reinforces negative cognitive and behavioral patterns, which, in turn, become more likely to be evidenced in the future. Once a pattern develops, problems with low self-esteem and depression become more likely and more severe. Several studies on clinical populations confirm this relationship (Battle, 1982; Tennen & Affleck, 1993; Truscott, 1985), although the question of which occurs first can be argued (Seligman, 1990, 1995b).

The link between self-esteem and depression can be followed even further. Suicidologists often note that low self-esteem can play a role in that phenomenon. One way that self-esteem and depression seem to be connected is that, insofar as self-esteem protects the individual against setbacks, cracks in this shield allow depression to take hold more easily. The individual then becomes more vulnerable to stressors. Increased vulnerability means less capacity for problem solving and coping effectively, which leads to an erosion of worthiness and hope. The resulting sense of hopelessness is understood as a strong risk for suicide (Durand & Barlow, 1997). In this sense, we can see self-esteem as a life-and-death issue. Other authors focus on a possible link between low self-esteem and certain forms of psychosis, especially mania (Epstein, 1980). Such a link makes good theoretical sense: If one fears an absolute loss of competence or worth, then what better way to feel powerful or important than to develop delusions of grandeur?

Self-Esteem and Substance Abuse

In his review of the literature on the relationship between self-esteem and substance abuse, Kitano (1989) noted, "The most comprehensive view concerning the relationship between self-esteem and drug and alcohol use is put forward by Steffenhagen and Burns . . . who contend that low levels of self-esteem are the cause, not the result, of deviant behavior" (p. 319). Other clinicians also have found that many patients being treated for depression and alcohol problems evidence low self-esteem. Some studies, for example, involved administering O'Brien and Epstein's Multidimensional Self-Esteem Inventory (1983, 1988) early in treatment and then at its end. In both administrations, self-esteem was found to be lower for people who have problems with substance use than for the "normal" population. Scores did improve with treatment, as would be expected if there is a link between self-esteem and substance abuse (Hakim-Larson & Mruk, 1997; Jung, 1994; Truscott, 1985). After all, the negative behaviors often associated with addictions, such as lying (being unworthy) and losing control (a lack of competence), must certainly affect self-esteem.

Self-Esteem and Antisocial Behavior

Kaplan and colleagues (1986) offered longitudinal studies linking self-esteem and certain kinds of juvenile delinquency, establishing the connection as a function of both the individual and his or her social circumstances. The basic idea is that people, especially adolescents, almost always strive to achieve some degree of self-esteem. They typically do so through peer acceptance (being worthy enough to be accepted by a group) and by demonstrating some degree of success (being competent at some valued activity, such as academics, student government, or sports). When the environment denies or limits socially acceptable avenues that would ordinarily lead to positive ways of finding self-esteem, the need for self-esteem remains a constant, which means that the individual becomes more open to alternative routes, even if they are not socially sanctioned.

The rest appears to be fairly mechanical. If such a deviant pathway is explored behaviorally, and if such activity receives some degree of reinforcing recognition or success, then the move toward more problematical social deviance is under way. These behaviors can range from getting away with a petty crime (a display of a negative skill, but some form of competent ability nonetheless) to becoming initiated into a gang (being worthy of group acceptance). If such reinforcement continues, or if little in the way of alternatives is available, then delinquency (and, perhaps, crime) becomes the pathway to self-esteem. What is especially interesting about the work of Kaplan and associates is that their longitudinal studies support this particular link between self-esteem and behavior. Although perhaps modest in terms of yielding statistically significant results, longitudinal studies are rare in the social psychology of self-esteem and therefore should be taken quite seriously.

Other evidence connecting self-esteem to antisocial behavior exists. In studying and treating criminal behavior from a cognitive view, Samenow (1984, 1989) suggested that one of the major problems in treating certain types of hard-core criminals is that their self-esteem is especially vulnerable. Ordinary stresses and strains, such as working at a menial job or having to take orders, can be catastrophically threatening to individuals with a weak self-esteem shield. Unfortunately, these conditions are often part of the world of those who are on parole or are starting over. Instead of focusing on trying to move ahead, or even demonstrating classical symptoms of low self-esteem (which would certainly be understandable), such individuals express their lack of self-esteem defensively through denial, grandiosity, or aggression. A small personal slight or minor demand may thus trigger compensatory reactions, such as quitting (denial), keeping an erratic work schedule in order to satisfy personal desires (narcissism), or being angry (displacement). One fast track to "being somebody" is to cheat, lie, and break the law—a commonly chosen option, which often means more failure and recidivism. Although there are other factors involved in the development of an antisocial personality, a disturbed search for self-esteem seems to be a common thread for people exhibiting antisocial behavior.

Self-Esteem and Violence

Recent research on self-esteem concerns a fairly strong relationship between self-esteem and violence. This line of work links self-esteem, ego threat, and physical aggression. Earlier research of this type noted a peculiar event that seemed to occur under certain circumstances with individuals with high self-esteem. Although high self-esteem is usually associated with more effective self-regulation, it sometimes leads to inflated assessment. Apparently, when expectations are not realized, some individuals, who otherwise appear to have high self-esteem, compensate in ways that are more risky than realistic for the situation, which results in lower performance than is necessary (Tice, 1993). In other words, under certain conditions high self-esteem is associated with less, rather than more, effective behavior. However, I think it is important to realize that the kinds of experimental situations in which this effect is usually observed are not particularly meaningful ones. They typically involve merely playing relatively insignificant games on a voluntary basis and it is unlikely that one's self-esteem is at stake in such situations. This difference, which may be a crucial one, is not typically addressed in such research on self-esteem.

More recent research by Baumeister and colleagues (1996), which has received a high degree of attention in the field and popular press, pursues the relationship between high self-esteem, ego threat, and risk taking and the phenomenon of violence. The findings indicate that people who appear to have high self-esteem, particularly those who have unrealistic, inflated beliefs about themselves or their abilities, may resort to the use of aggression to ward off threats to these perceptions and beliefs when they are in danger of being contradicted by reality. Although it is unclear whether what is going on here involves genuinely high, positive self-esteem or some form of defensive self-esteem (I will argue the latter), it is clear that aggression and violence are related to self-esteem problems in ways that we do not ordinarily think about. Baumeister and colleagues (1996) noted that it is assumed that violence is associated with low self-esteem; this may well be the case for aggression turned inward, as in depression, substance abuse, or suicide. Indeed, classically low self-esteem seems to weigh against the demonstration of aggression toward others, except perhaps in the case of murder-suicide involving some form of loss or rejection. However, there is good reason to think that many gang members, abusers, and criminals—all of whom are prone to violence in one way or another—do indeed think very highly of themselves and their abilities, whether such an opinion is warranted or not.

THE LINK BETWEEN SELF-ESTEEM AND BEHAVIOR

In the past the link between self-esteem and behavior was so widely assumed that it was enough to simply mention it and then move on to a discussion of how to improve self-esteem. Now, however, this task has become more difficult for at least two reasons. First, there is the finding that the statistical evidence linking self-esteem and any given behavior is weak at best. Second, some research suggests that when self-esteem is compared to other factors associated with behavior, such as "explanatory style," or how one characteristically understands what causes things to happen in one's life, self-esteem appears to be more a result of events than a cause of them (Seligman, 1990, 1995b). Let me briefly address each of these criticisms, review the traditional approach to understanding the link between self-esteem and behavior, then present the foundation for a phenomenological understanding of the relationship between self-esteem and behavior, which will be unfolded more thoroughly in the next chapter.

We have already dealt with the first point at some length. Even critics of self-esteem research admit that there are many correlations between self-esteem and behavior. The dispute is over the possibility of a causal connection between self-esteem and behavior, for which there is only weak statistical evidence. However, the phenomenological tradition points out that one very important reason for this situation is that it is the *meaning* of events that affect behavior, and assessing this causal force may be beyond the capacity of traditional methodologies. If this is true, not only is the lack of statistical evidence understandable, but it is also predictable. The inability of a method to assess that which it is incapable of assessing should not be taken as proof that there is no connection between self-esteem and behavior. Rather, this event can just as easily be understood as reflecting a fundamental limitation of the approach, especially when methods that are capable of assessing the role of meaning in behavior indicate that there is a connection, albeit a complex one.

Second, those who criticize the link between self-esteem and behavior by saying that self-esteem is more the result of these other conditions than their cause almost always define self-esteem in terms of worthiness rather than competence. This practice results in two serious errors. First, worthiness is the most affective aspect of self-esteem: It is supposed to pertain to feeling good, or in the case of low self-esteem, feeling bad, about oneself. To omit half the definition of self-esteem (competence) and then to condemn the rest of it as a feeling state is like criticizing the night because it lacks light, when, in fact, both are needed to give form and balance to each other. Second, the strongest, or at least most measurable, evidence of a causal connection between self-esteem and behavior occurs in terms of the competence dimension of self-esteem, because that is more behavioral than affective. When, for instance, it is said that "[w]hat California (and every state) needs is not children who are encouraged to feel good, but children who are taught the skills of doing well—how to study, how to avoid pregnancy, drugs, and gangs, and how to get off welfare" (Seligman, 1995b, p. 35), what I hear is someone talking about the role of competence in forming self-esteem. Similarly, when I read that "[t]he concepts of self-esteem and perceived self-efficacy are often used interchangeably as though they represented the same phenomenon. In fact, they refer to entirely different things. Perceived self-efficacy is concerned with judgments of personal capability, whereas self-esteem is concerned with judgments of self-worth" (Bandura, 1997, p. 11), I wonder how defining self-esteem as competence as well as worthiness would change these authors' assessments. Once again, working with a limited definition has to generate limited results. Although I greatly admire the work of Seligman and Bandura, I question their positions on self-esteem. Defining self-esteem in terms of competence and worthiness, as a phenomenological definition of self-esteem requires us to do, forces us to rethink such criticisms because they may be premature.

Whether seen as an independent, dependent, or mediating variable, the most common way to understand the link between self-esteem and behavior in the traditional literature is as a reciprocal relationship. The most articulate way of describing this link is in terms of a self-fulfilling prophecy. Various research approaches use the concept of a self-fulfilling prophecy to explain the connection between self-esteem and behavior. For example, learning theorists focus on the dynamics of reinforcement in their version of the self-fulfilling prophecy. Coopersmith (1967) said, "Although there are undoubtedly variations in the origins of a cycle from self-esteem to anxiety, the model of a cyclical, self-reinforcing, self-propelling sequence seems appropriate once either state has been established" (p. 133). More humanistically oriented practitioners, such as Frey and Carlock (1989) see a self-fulfilling connection between self-esteem and behavior: "Individuals tend to reinforce their self esteem by adjusting perceptions to conform with perceived self esteem. People with high self esteem tend to manifest success, while people with low self esteem tend to manifest failure—the picture of oneself becomes a self fulfilling prophecy which one often feels incapable of reversing" (p. 135).

The most elaborate use of the self-fulfilling prophecy is found in the work of cognitive theorists, who describe the link between self-esteem and behavior in terms of information-processing mechanisms associated with feedback, circularity, and self-regulation. According to these theorists, once we develop a sense of self, an understanding of how the world works, and the role others play in it, self-esteem is useful as "a special type of information that can describe, evaluate, or influence performance: in our case human behavior" (Bednar et al., 1989, p. 91). Over time, such feedback allows us to know ourselves in terms of having a certain level of ability (which I would call competence) and a certain general feeling about ourselves (worthiness). Just like any self-regulating system, the organism seeks to maintain this steady state of inputs and outputs, which results in a level of basic, or "global," self-esteem. From this perspective, the connection between self-esteem and behavior is founded on the need for cognitive consistency, or the idea that people are more likely to accept information from the environment that is consistent with their self-schemas (Campbell & Lavallee, 1993). Self-serving biases (Blaine & Crocker, 1993) allow us to focus on information that is consistent with our basic beliefs and ignore or dismiss that which is not. Although such a system is useful for maintaining the continuity of identity, experience, and behavior, it also makes change difficult.

"GOOD" SELF-ESTEEM ASSESSMENT INSTRUMENTS

Another set of findings to analyze for the possibility of consensus concerns identifying self-esteem tests which are reasonably reliable, useful, and valid. One frequently cited test that meets our criteria (persistence and significance) is the Piers-Harris Self-Concept Scale (Wells & Marwell, 1976). Besides being reasonably well standardized, this instrument has proven itself useful in the clinical setting (Pope et al., 1988). Similar strengths are found in the Tennessee Self-Concept Scale (Fitts, 1988), which is another standard instrument in this field. However, both measures also have some important limits for our work. Technically speaking, these two measures are tests for self-concept rather than self-esteem, so they miss some important things that we need to know, especially information about competence and worthiness. More important, our focus is on self-esteem in adulthood, whereas these instruments were designed for children and adolescents.

The adult version of Coopersmith's Self-Esteem Inventory (SEI, 1975, 1981) is a 25-item forced choice self-report questionnaire on self-esteem. The subject is presented with straightforward questions and is asked to respond by indicating whether the statement is *like* me or *unlike* me. The number of positive and negative self-esteem responses are added up; this score is compared against a good-sized normative sample. The scores are interpreted in terms of range (high, low, and medium self-esteem). The strengths of this instrument include the fact that it is consistent with Coopersmith's (1967) model and research on self-esteem (construct validity); the presence of some content validity in terms of how the questions relate to what we know about self-esteem in regard to competence and worthiness; and the ease of administering, scoring, and interpreting it in both individual or group settings. Indeed, there is a body of independent research using this instrument that supports its credibility. The weaknesses of the test are equally considerable. Perhaps the most glaring problem is that there is no way that the examiner can know whether the subject is distorting his or her responses in a desired direction. Not only is the ceiling effect strong in this test, but it is so transparent that virtually anyone can manipulate his or her score. In addition, there is no provision for identifying defensive self-esteem, nor is there any way to identify how much of what is being assessed reflects global or situational self-esteem.

The Multidimensional Self-Esteem Inventory (MSEI, O'Brien & Epstein, 1983, 1988) involves some 116 questions of a forced answer type that are scored and interpreted according to 11 scales. These are global self-esteem, competence, lovability, likability, personal power, self-control, moral self-approval, body appearance, body functioning, identity integration, and defensive self-esteem enhancement. The disadvantages of this instrument are that it is more expensive, more time consuming, requires more interpretation by a professional, and is normed against much smaller numbers than the SEI. This last weakness is especially a problem when using the instrument with minority populations. There are plans to address this issue, but as yet no work has been published.

The MSEI's strengths are quite remarkable given the difficulties of testing in this area. First, it is grounded in a major theory of self-esteem (Epstein, 1980), meaning that it has a high degree of construct validity. Second, the content validity of the test is very high in that 8 of the 11 scales concern factors related to the competence and worthiness dimensions of self-esteem. Third, the other scales address the global versus situational and defensiveness issues mentioned above. Finally, the usefulness of the MSEI is supported by research using it in clinical settings, as well as with normal populations. Two other instruments, MMPI-2's self-esteem subscale (Hathaway & McKinley, 1989) and Battle's Culture-Free Self-Esteem Inventory (1992), also have scales for defensiveness. However, the former suffers the problems of lengthy administration and the necessity of advanced interpretive skill. Although the latter also suffers from the problem of a small normative sample for the adult use of the test, the revised edition should be identified as a potentially useful device.

EFFECTIVE SELF-ESTEEM ENHANCEMENT TECHNIQUES

I have already discussed the importance of identifying which self-esteem enhancement techniques actually have clinical and/or empirical support. Before moving into these findings, however, I must point out three common strategies to avoid because they lack such evidence. The first concerns what might be described as the sermonistic or motivational approach. As the words suggest, this material is typically found in well-meaning ideologically or religiously based programs, books, and television shows. Typically, the importance of self-esteem is exaggerated, so that users of this strategy conclude that positive self-esteem leads directly to the behavior considered desirable by a given belief system and that low or negative self-esteem invariably results from those behaviors deemed undesirable. A similar, but often more secular, approach is what we call the "warm fuzzy" or "touchy-feely" method. Books, programs, and individuals operating from this position can be identified by an excessive use of emotional appeals and psychological truisms. Many self-help books can be understood in this way. In both cases, understanding the complexity of the relationship between self-esteem and behavior is ignored, and simple formulas for right living are offered instead.

A more sophisticated form of pop psychology starts out by presenting material related to self-esteem that does have some general basis or support in the social sciences. Someone operating from this approach may offer a few case studies or cite a few general standard works in psychology, but then soon wander from the scientific track. This pseudo-scientific approach makes designing self-esteem tests and self-help techniques easy. For instance, Sappington (1989, p. 5) cited work by Glaslow and Rosen done in 1978 indicating that some 20% of the self-help techniques presented in books were never tested before they were printed. In addition, he noted that another 27% of the techniques require some contact with a mental health professional, a fact that is often omitted.

In all fairness, I must point out that enhancing self-esteem clinically is one of the newest areas of work in the field. At least evidence is mounting that self-esteem can change, particularly during major life transitions (Epstein, 1979; Harter, 1993; Jackson, 1984; Mruk, 1983). Because we are still in the early stages of this work, some tolerance is needed. In addition to identifying what appear to be the more effective techniques, I will try to discuss these tools in light of what we know about self-esteem from the previous chapters in a way that allows us to see why and how they may help.

The Importance of Being Accepting and Caring

We saw from the findings concerning parental and social factors affecting self-esteem that how we are treated by others can affect the development of self-esteem. Although such factors may diminish somewhat with age, we never lose this capacity to respond: Parents are replaced by others, such as friends, spouses, coworkers, and bosses, who accept/ reject or care for/neglect us in important ways. Being accepted, then, should be a part of any decent self-esteem enhancement program. Humanistically oriented therapists might couch this part of a program in terms of "unconditional positive regard." Psychodynamic therapists may view this aspect of the helping relationship in terms of a therapeutic or working alliance. Behavioral and cognitive practitioners tend to understand acceptance, care, and trust as rapport building. This technique may be seen as the most basic one because it is tied to the development of self-esteem in the first place and because most systematic attempts to enhance self-esteem include acceptance as a part of the process (Bednar et al., 1989; Coopersmith, 1967; Epstein, 1979; Sappington, 1989).

The fundamental attitudes of nurturance and good will that accompany acceptance and caring foster the kind of environment and interaction that are conducive to human growth and development. Indeed, therapeutic acceptance and care are probably necessary, but not sufficient, for enhancing self-esteem, because any therapist or program that did not use them would probably fail. In addition, treating a person suffering from low self-esteem with such respect and compassion can itself be a powerful therapeutic experience, mainly because the individual is usually more familiar with rejection than with acceptance. The research we examined on being valued as a source of self-esteem supports the use of such methods with both children and adults. However, it is a mistake to think that simple care and unqualified acceptance are all that is needed to enhance self-esteem or to run a successful enhancement program. Acceptance means approving of the individual but not all of his or her behaviors, particularly those that are associated with low self-esteem. And caring for the well-being of another does not mean assuming responsibility for how he or she conducts life—the individual still needs to be the one who is acting in ways that are competent and worthy.

Providing Consistent, Positive (Affirming) Feedback

There are very good reasons, and some supporting evidence, to maintain that consistently providing people with positive (affirming) feedback about themselves or their behavior is another way of building self-esteem (Bednar et al., 1989; Bhatti et al., 1989; Frey & Carlock, 1989).

As Bhatti and colleagues (1989) summed it up, "Many experts suggest focusing on positive rather than negative behavior to begin building self-esteem" (p. 54). Frey and Carlock (1989) pointed to a study that attempted to quantify this practice: "Yamamoto (1972) indicated that a reward to punishment (R-P) ratio of five rewards for every one punishment is optimal in actualizing potential. . . . Low self esteem individuals often experience a one-to-five ratio or worse, or experience an adequate ratio, but do not really integrate it into self" (p. 190). Although this kind of exact relationship between the number of rewards and punishments is not to be taken literally, the consensus is clear: There is value in giving positive feedback to people with low self-esteem.

This principle is compatible with all the major perspectives on self-esteem we have seen. A symbolic interactionalist, for instance, understands that the development of the self depends on feedback from others, called reflected appraisals. Although this process is more influential earlier in life, it continues in adulthood through family, friends, coworkers, bosses, and so on. Therapists who provide positive feedback consistently (but not necessarily constantly) provide pro-self-esteem appraisals, which are fed into the individual self-system. Such positive reflections of a competent and worthy person may be especially therapeutic if they are the only source of such affirmation in an individual's life. Learning theory should have no trouble with this practice, because the motivating power of positive reinforcement is well known and the principle of being consistent in reinforcing behavior is a standard tool for shaping it. Taking the time to compliment a person when he or she spontaneously demonstrates a positive behavior or attitude, for instance, makes good sense in terms of conditioning self-esteem through operant methods.

The humanistically oriented therapist or facilitator, who already sees positive regard as the key to human growth and development, adds one more point to the use of feedback: It must be authentic or real. In other words, positive feedback must be based on a genuine positive perception, or be tied to the reality of the client's behavior, in some identifiable, concrete fashion if it is to be helpful. Of course, the idea of using feedback to alter self-esteem is part of the cognitive approach to change in both theory and practice. Not only is feedback part of how self-esteem develops in the first place, but it also drives the self-fulfilling prophecy that maintains self-esteem over time. Practitioners of the cognitive approach are more sophisticated in this regard because they understand that systems also use feedback to maintain themselves by resisting change. Epstein (1985), for instance, indicated that there are subtleties to be considered in the use of positive feedback. He pointed out, for example, that too much positive feedback can be threatening to some people with low self-esteem, just as large doses of good medicine can upset the balance of the body's system. In this case, we must modify the use of positive feedback so that it comes in small, less threatening, more acceptable doses.

Generating Positive Self-Feedback Through Cognitive Restructuring

In addition to others providing us with feedback that affects our identity and esteem, we provide it to ourselves. This process can be conceived of psychodynamically in terms of narcissistic supplies and ego ideals, or it can be understood behaviorally in terms of a discrepancy between the ideal self we want to be like and the real self we perceive ourselves as actually being. The humanist therapist may understand such a positive flow of experience, feeling, and behavior in terms of congruence or authenticity, while cognitively oriented clinicians may think of this process as an internal feedback system with identifiable patterns of positive or negative information-processing loops, called "self-talk" (Bednar et al., 1989; Burns, 1980; Sappington, 1989). No matter how one expresses it, part of being human appears to involve being aware of the lived status of our worthiness and competence, both in a given situation and in general. Although the degree of such awareness is extremely variable, it does provide us with another route to influencing self-esteem.

Among the traditional views, the cognitive perspective provides the most articulate rationale for intervening at this level. First, it explains how the self-esteem feedback system works, which can be talked about in terms of the computer programmer's acronym GIGO (garbage in, garbage out). In other words, any information-processing system (including the brain) will make use of, or interpret, the data it receives by taking the information through a given set of steps or mental programs (in this case, the "master program" of the self or identity). If this information is confused, negative, or derogatory, then the output will take on a corresponding form. If the information is positive, accurate, and healthy, it will be reflected in perception, behavior, and experience. Second, the cognitive perspective uses techniques referred to as cognitive restructuring to alter basic programming. This is done by identifying what are called irrational thinking patterns and correcting them by developing more realistic understandings of the self, world, and others (Bednar et al., 1989; Burns, 1980; Ellis & Harper, 1977; Frey & Carlock, 1989).

The therapeutic process usually begins by presenting a list of common irrational thinking patterns or cognitive distortions that people can readily identify in themselves or others. Next, the relationship between negative habits of thought, experience, and behavior is usually explained by using the concept of self-fulfilling prophecies. Then, individuals are asked to identify the cognitive errors to which they are most prone and give an example of how they actually happen for them in regard to a real-life experience or situation. Finally, clients are shown relatively standard ways of modifying (restructuring) this dysfunctional pattern. The process involves three basic steps: learning how to identify cognitive distortions, labeling them as such according to some nomenclature of thinking errors, then substituting a more rational or realistic response. These techniques may work on increasing self-esteem in several ways. First, they interrupt the normally smooth-flowing links between thinking, feeling, and acting in negative ways that create and maintain low self-esteem. Second, demonstrating some control over behavior allows the individual to feel competent and worthy, which are connected to self-esteem. Third, with practice, new habits of perceiving, thinking, experiencing, and acting may be acquired, thus breaking the old negative self-fulfilling cycle and allowing a more positive cycle to emerge.

Increasing Self-Esteem by Using Natural Self-Esteem Moments

We saw that some cognitively and phenomenologically oriented self-esteem researchers investigate how self-esteem is lived by people in real life. This work has also indicated that self-esteem can change spontaneously, particularly in periods of transition (Epstein, 1979; Harter, 1993) or at certain crucial turning points (Jackson, 1984; Mruk, 1983). A logical extension of both types of findings is to apply them to the task of enhancing self-esteem (Bednar et al., 1989; Mruk, 1983). In other words, if we could find a way to identify these situations as they are occurring or about to occur, then it might be possible to intervene therapeutically and perhaps even turn them into positive self-esteem moments. The practical question is, of course, how to do so methodically. I will address this issue in chapter 6.

One thing that most clinicians advocate is to help people increase their awareness of the role that self-esteem plays in their life (Branden, 1983; Frey & Carlock, 1989). The basic idea behind such consciousness raising (itself a standard therapeutic and psychoeducational tool) is that once people see what a valuable resource self-esteem is, they will be more appreciative of the need to manage it effectively. Keeping a journal about one's self-esteem and what affects it in one's own life is one technique that can be used to increase such awareness (Epstein, 1979; Frey & Carlock, 1989; Sappington, 1989). Talking about self-esteem with someone, such as a counselor or therapist, is another way of appreciating the ebb and flow of self-esteem over time and helps to make us more mindful of it. It is important to understand, however, that awareness alone is not enough, because self-esteem also requires competence at living. Therefore, it is desirable to couple increased awareness of the importance of self-esteem with actual challenges to it in a way that leads to increased competence and therefore change. Such interventions have been documented using problem-solving behavioral methods (Pope et al., 1988) and certain existential moments (Bednar et al., 1989; Hakim-Larson & Mruk, 1997). It is usually recommended that interventions be done by professionals.

Enhancing Self-Esteem by Assertiveness Training (Empowerment)

Assertiveness training, which is based on knowing one has certain rights as a human being and knowing how to exercise them appropriately, and other forms of empowerment can be used to enhance self-esteem (Bhatti et al., 1989; Frey & Carlock, 1989). For one thing, we know that having the capacity to stand up for oneself and one's self-values, or being virtuous, is connected with a basic source of self-esteem and success. Also, people who have this skill are usually more competent in terms of getting their individual needs met. For another thing, in addition to accessing an important source of self-esteem, standing up for oneself can also limit the impact of factors that lessen self-esteem in one's life. Such assertiveness helps us avoid self-esteem damaging situations, to say no to negative treatment from others, or to leave poor relationships more easily than is otherwise likely. Assertiveness, then, is a double-edged sword that cuts both ways in reaching for self-esteem.

Fortunately, these skills can be acquired at any age (Alberti & Emmons, 1982). However, the process is not simple. Indeed, the research on assertiveness training indicates that a good program involves several weeks of training, mainly because each skill must be practiced as well as demonstrated (Rakos, 1990). Even so, this kind of investment seems well worth the effort, especially for people who consistently end up in self-esteem trouble because of deficiencies in this area. Of course, it is important to note that there are some instances where increasing assertiveness is not necessary and may even be damaging, such as in the case where an individual is already overly aggressive as an expression of defensive self-esteem. Such training should therefore be conducted by professionals.

Increasing Self-Esteem Through Modeling

It has been over a century since William James suggested that successes and failures are crucial factors in determining self-esteem. Psychology has learned a good deal about helping people tip the scale to the favorable side since those early days (Bednar et al., 1989; Pope et al., 1988; Sappington, 1989). Modern learning theorists, for example, talk about self-efficacy (Bandura, 1997), which can be thought of as a person's sense of how he or she is likely to do in a given situation based on a number of variables, such as past performance on similar tasks. The general idea is to help people increase their sense of self-efficacy by learning to become more successful, which, in turn, increases self-esteem. In addition to general research on modeling as a therapeutic tool, the best evidence for increasing self-esteem this way comes from Coopersmith (1967) and Bednar and colleagues (1989). Showing by doing seems to be good for two reasons: Modeling is helpful when trying to learn complex activities, and we human beings model so very well. We cannot help but model our parents, older siblings, peer groups, and teachers, and we learn all kinds of things in doing so. This faculty applies to the clinical situation as well. For example, a good facilitator or therapist will demonstrate techniques for handling conflict or other difficult situations in ways that promote self-esteem, that is, by attempting to do so in ways that are both competent and worthy. Moreover, many clients with low self-esteem have had few opportunities to model a person who is reasonably competent and worthy, so the clinician becomes especially important as a model. Indeed, due to modeling, clients probably learn more from the clinician than the clinician ever realizes.

Enhancing Self-Esteem by Increasing Problem-Solving Skills

Most self-esteem enhancement programs include the idea that self-esteem helps us cope more effectively with life's challenges, both large and small (Bednar et al., 1989; Pope et al., 1988; Sappington, 1989).

Above all, coping well means that a person is able to influence the situations of life, which is to say deal with its problems with a reasonable degree of competence. One way to increase self-esteem, then, is to teach people how to solve problems more effectively and efficiently (Bednar et al., 1989; Pope et al., 1988). This kind of work can be done as a structured activity in the therapeutic setting. For instance, it is possible to break learning this skill into more manageable steps, each one of which can be practiced and evaluated until learning occurs (D'Zurilla & Goldfried, 1971). These steps typically include learning how to recognize that a problem exists, being able to identify possible responses and their likely outcomes, knowing how to select the best alternative given a particular situation, and having the ability to develop a realistic plan to reach that goal. The process of learning these skills is facilitated by a good teacher, a nonthreatening environment, appropriate reinforcement, and supervised practice, all of which are fairly standard practices rather like assertiveness training.

Several positive things can happen for self-esteem once this skill has been acquired. First, knowing how to solve problems better increases the chances of being successful in general, and more frequent successes are an indication of being more competent. Second, even though better planning is no guarantee of success, it certainly reduces the likelihood of failure as compared to planning poorly. Decreasing failures is also good for self-esteem, particularly in relation to projects or activities that are personally significant. Third, the technique is flexible enough to allow us to target a particular area that is especially troublesome to an individual client, then to help the client develop a realistic problem-solving strategy for improvement that takes into account the individual's strengths as well as weaknesses. Indeed, "individualizing" (Fischer, 1986) this technique is the ideal way to address specific individuals with particular self-esteem themes. Finally, increasing competence through better problem-solving skills can be done in ways that are sensitive to age, gender, culture, and so on.

Using Individual and Group Formats to Enhance Self-Esteem

There is consensus about two of what we might call "contextual factors" that are helpful in enhancing self-esteem. The first concerns a program's format and allows us to have some design flexibility (Bednar et al., 1989; Frey & Carlock, 1989). One approach is to build a program around the traditional one-to-one relationship between client and clinician. A key advantage of this intense self-esteem encounter is that it focuses on identifying and understanding a particular individual's self-esteem themes and problems in considerable detail. The therapist and client can even target these issues as central therapeutic activities. Another advantage is that the process can go on for longer periods of time, meaning that it should be possible for both therapist and client to see change, which is always encouraging. Also, more seriously ill patients, or clients with more deeply embedded self-esteem problems, often require more attention. On the negative side, we know that this intensive interpersonal work requires considerable resources in terms of clinical expertise, time, and money.

The other major design format is to enhance self-esteem through the group setting (Bhatti et al., 1989; Burns, 1993a; Frey & Carlock, 1989). There are several ways the group experience can be helpful. For one thing, it can be designed to meet the needs of various populations. For instance, groups can be tailored to meet the needs of specific clinical populations. In this case, most of the general rules for clinical groups apply, such as screening clients carefully before admitting them to such a group (Vinogradov & Yalom, 1989) and using cotherapists of the opposite sex. Groups can also be set up to emphasize growth instead of remediation. In fact, such psychoeducational groups seem to be very common in the field, because they can reach a broader range of people and ages (Frey & Carlock, 1989). The basic structure of this form of group work seems to include a leader who acts as a therapist, facilitator, and teacher and a group size of between 10 and 20 individuals. In both the clinical and educational situation, group activities are organized in a systematic and progressive fashion, usually moving from introductory exercises, to some form of self-assessment, through consciousness-raising activities, then to a number of exercises aimed at the development of self-esteem.

Whether clinically or growth-oriented, the group format offers several interesting advantages. Groups are usually more cost effective, which is important when seen in the light of today's mounting health care costs. Hence, they can be used to address larger numbers of people and people of limited income (Hakim-Larson & Mruk, 1997). Also, groups may seem less threatening to people who are put off by the idea of psychotherapy, or to those who are simply interested in bettering themselves and not having someone "dig around in their heads." Most of all, the group format can do some things better than the individual setting (Vinogradov & Yalom, 1989). The rich mixture of perception, experience, and individual style that comes from being around several different people more closely approximates the conditions of real life than the individual treatment setting. For instance, a group situation usually presents a greater variety of "safe challenges" or here-and-now opportunities to try out new pro-self-esteem behaviors, such as communicating more effectively or being more assertive. Groups also bring in more of the social factors affecting self-esteem, such as offering more opportunities for such helpful processes as positive feedback, acceptance, and healthy modeling. Finally, they can offer a sense of camaraderie and support that are hard to duplicate in individual formats: Seeing how others suffer from low self-esteem, and witnessing their struggle to gain it, can be helpful in many different ways.

Enhancing Self-Esteem Requires Practice

The last contextual factor affects all the rest, so perhaps it is the most important. In spite of popular books to the contrary, the evidence shows that enhancing self-esteem in a lasting way takes considerable time and work. There is no effective "1 minute to self-esteem" program. There are several reasons for this, of course, but they can be summed up most succinctly by pointing out that self-esteem problems take a long time to develop: They usually involve deeply ingrained habits of perception, experience, and behavior, all of which are well sedimented by the time we reach adulthood. These self-esteem habits shape our world in ways that are both subtle and complex, meaning that change requires considerable unlearning as well as new learning, both of which take time. In the final analysis, then, self-esteem is increased through hard work and practice, practice, practice—there is simply no escaping this basic existential fact.

UNDERSTANDING THE PHENOMENOLOGY OF THE TECHNIQUES

It may appear as though these nine tools for enhancing self-esteem that emerge from a phenomenological analysis may not seem like much in the way of results. However, when seen in the proper light, they are clearly valuable because they are the most valid techniques we have available today, suggesting that they can be used with some confidence—at least these methods of helping offer the practitioner or a program the current "best chance" of being clinically credible. Although there is not hard experimental evidence to support the efficacy for some of these techniques, we can mount a credible rationale for using them with our clients.

It is also helpful to consider the connections between these ways of increasing self-esteem and its fundamental structure one final time, because any enhancement program I develop must be founded on this relationship. It should be obvious that some of the methods work because they are ways of facilitating a sense of worthiness, which grounds them in that part of the structure, whereas others work by increasing behavioral skills necessary to become more competent at living. A few techniques seem to involve both worthiness and competence, and the two contextual factors need to be kept in mind. This can be summed up in an information map, such as the one shown in Table 3.1.

In sum, we have four basic groups encompassing nine self-esteem enhancement techniques at our potential disposal, two of which depend primarily on worthiness (acceptance and positive feedback are statements of worthiness from others). Two more techniques stem mainly from the competence dimension of self-esteem (modeling and problem solving involve acquiring new skills or competencies). Three techniques require both competence and worthiness (cognitive restructuring involves becoming more competent at thinking in worthwhile ways, assertiveness training means becoming more skilled at standing up for one's rights as a worthy human being, and natural self-esteem moments challenge self-esteem on both levels). The last two tools are contextual factors that can be useful in helping us tailor programs to specific individual and population characteristics.

In closing this segment of our journey, I want to point out once again that self-esteem research is very difficult and complex. No doubt, some things will become clearer over time and others will change. Yet clinicians are faced with the present and our clients cannot afford the luxury of waiting, so it is time to build on the best of what we know today. We will do that in chapter 6, but first we need to integrate the major self-esteem findings by developing a comprehensive theory of self-esteem based on its fundamental structure.

TABLE 3.1 A Phenomenology of Self-Esteem Enhancement Techniques

Worthiness Based Techniques	Competence Based Techniques
Acceptance	Modeling
Positive Feedback	Problem Solving
Competence and Worthiness Based	**Common Contextual Factors**
Cognitive Restructuring	Therapeutic Format
Assertiveness Training	Practice
Self-Esteem Moments	

4

Major Self-Esteem
Theories and Programs

MAJOR THEORIES OF SELF-ESTEEM

It is reasonable to think that most of the research we just examined reflects various theories about self-esteem, some of which have clinical implications. We need to examine this possibility for two reasons. First, doing a phenomenology of the major theoretical and clinical approaches in the field may reveal valuable information concerning what constitutes a good theory of self-esteem, which can be helpful in building our own theory. Second, identifying the basic elements of existing self-esteem enhancement programs might be helpful in developing a phenomenologically oriented approach. Trusting that by now the reader will not confuse the technique we have been using with mere review or content analysis, I will continue to apply the phenomenological method to the literature by treating each major theory or program as a datum to be examined. In order to proceed, however, it is necessary to define what constitutes a legitimate theory or program for examination.

Fortunately, solid theories can be identified by the fact that they seem to have several key characteristics. First, they tend to focus explicitly on self-esteem and not on a related topic. Next, they seem to maintain a high degree of consistency with a major theoretical perspective or long tradition of thought in the social sciences. In addition, good theories appear to be reasonably systematic in that they move from the abstract to the concrete, or from theorizing about self-esteem to offering some practical suggestions for enhancing it. Finally, good systems pass the test of persistence or significance mentioned earlier. Such criteria exclude popularistic formats, religiously or spiritually oriented approaches (although there are some interesting ones), and what I call self-esteem "fragments." These items consist of sentences, paragraphs, and sometimes even a few pages in an article or book that address self-esteem and that often suggest insights into it. Unfortunately, they are actually only tangential discussions or too incomplete to be treated as data.

In order to save time, I will cover only one major theory from each major social science perspective (the psychodynamic, sociocultural, learning theory, humanistic, and cognitive points of view). Each theory or program, then, will be the one that best meets these criteria among the views available from a particular perspective. Of course, this limit means that some theories or programs will not be mentioned, and if one is a favored approach for a particular reader, he or she may feel disappointed. However, because there are no more than a handful of major self-esteem theories and fully developed enhancement programs to begin with, this approach is at least representative of all the major perspectives.

William James: A Historical View
With Modern Relevance

Most books and many articles on self-esteem mention the contributions this great American psychologist has made to understanding self-esteem. In addition to defining self-esteem first, James tells us some things about its origins. He begins by pointing out that each person is born into a set of possible social roles or identities created by such factors as history, culture, family, and circumstance. Over time, we find ourselves becoming invested in one such "self" more than the others, which makes it central in terms of our self-regard:

> I, who for the time have staked my all on being a psychologist, am mortified if others know much more about psychology than I. But I am contented to wallow in the grossest ignorance of Greek. My deficiencies there give me no sense of personal humiliation at all. Had I "pretensions" to be a linguist, it would have been just the reverse. So we have the paradox of a man shamed to death because he is only the second pugilist or the second oarsman in the world. That he is able to beat the whole population of the

globe minus one is nothing; he has "pitted" himself to beat that one; and as long as he doesn't do that nothing else counts. He is to his own regard as if he were not, indeed, he *is* not.

Yonder puny fellow, however, whom everyone can beat, suffers no chagrin about it, for he has long ago abandoned the attempt to "carry that line," as the merchants say, of self at all. With no attempt there can be no failure; with no failure, no humiliation. So our self-feeling in this world depends entirely on what we *back* ourselves to be and do. It is determined by the ratio of our actualities to our supposed potentialities; a fraction of which our pretensions are the denominator and the numerator our successes. (1983/1890, p. 296)

Note that this section contains elements or precursors of several of the important ideas and findings about self-esteem discussed in the previous chapters. In particular, James notes a connection between self-esteem, values, success, and competence in his wonderful analogy. For example, once an individual settles on a "line" (of identity), he or she is staked (intimately tied) to it and carries (represents) it in the world. To gain or to lose status in this heavily valued, intensely important area involves serious psychological consequences, so the individual becomes concerned with backing up (protecting or defending) this part of his or her identity. Finally, over time the individual manages to carry the line successfully (competently) or not, which leads to a reputation (level of self-esteem) by which the person is known to himself and to others.

The analogy is a dynamic understanding of self-esteem. For the idea of "carrying a line" also suggests managing it, which evokes all kinds of connotations concerning aspirations (the merchant has dreams and priorities for the business) and competence (running a business well or poorly, or showing a profit or loss). The depiction of self-esteem as a fraction or ratio means that although self-esteem may be fairly constant, it is also open, or vulnerable. Change can occur in either what is valued (pretensions or aspirations) or how often it is affirmed (successes), both of which depend on the individual and life circumstance. Although he never went this far, we can see how James implies a way of enhancing self-esteem. For if it is true that success enhances self-esteem, then increasing success in valued areas, as well as decreasing failures there, should improve it. Indeed, we shall see that most therapeutic approaches to increasing self-esteem incorporate this century-old idea into their programs in one way or another.

A danger in appreciating historical contributions is that it is easy to exaggerate their significance. I must point out, then, that James' work is also limited by several factors. First, his insights are often just that—

James' work is based almost entirely on the method of introspection. Second, his concern with self-esteem is limited to a few pages and could well be called a self-esteem fragment if it did not have the effect of launching an entire field. Finally, although it is true that James' basic formulation is a cornerstone for modern-day enhancement approaches, this issue was not a concern for him, or for psychology, at the time.

ROBERT WHITE AND THE PSYCHODYNAMIC APPROACH

Although Sigmund Freud was interested in matters related to self-esteem, the closest he came to dealing with it is found in a discussion of what he called "self-regard" (Freud, 1957/1914). Alfred Adler (1927) addressed the topic more directly, but it is Robert White who is representative of this perspective today. He sums up his psychodynamic predecessors by saying that

> [t]he formula that has most often guided psychoanalytic theory in describing the later vicissitudes of self-esteem is based on the relationship between ego and ego ideal. This presupposes that the ego ideal and superego are at least partly separate institutions of the mind. The ego ideal becomes the repository of the original narcissistic omnipotence, and the ego enjoys self-esteem to the extent that it matches its ideal in actuality. (1963, p. 128)

In large part, White based his developmental view of self-esteem on a crucial problem that traditional behavioral and psychoanalytic theories have with understanding motivation. Behaviorism, he contended, tries to deal with motivation by conceptualizing it in terms of need theory, which has the characteristic of a drive. According to this view, the organism's normal state of physiological balance is disrupted when a state of deprivation arises concerning a basic need. This imbalance creates a tension, which, in turn, gives rise to a drive state that moves the organism's behavior in such a way as to satisfy the need because doing so reduces the discomfort and restores homeostasis. The psychoanalytic view focuses on the same kinds of events but accounts for them differently. In this case, instinctual drives create tensions in the psyche that motivate behavior in ways designed to reduce such pressure through some form of release or discharge. The problem with these views, said White, is that "in both there is persistent pointing to kinds of behavior neglected by orthodoxy: exploration, activity, manipulation, and mastery" (1959, p. 312). In other words, sometimes organisms actually seek to increase stimulation or tension, which seriously contradicts either position.

Experimental support for White's observation has been available since the early 1900s in the Yerks-Dodson law (White, 1959) and continues today in sensory deprivation studies and in animal and human studies concerning play (Rathus, 1996). Concluding that neither behavioral nor traditional psychoanalytic concepts can deal with this contradiction, White suggested that another idea of motivation is necessary. This biologically based desire for positive stimulation manifests itself as a continuous developmental push which shows itself as attempts to master the environment, what White called "competence":

> I now propose that we gather the various kinds of behaviors just mentioned, all of which have to do with effective interaction with the environment, under the general heading of competence. . . . I shall argue that it is necessary to make competence a motivational concept; there is a *competence motivation* as well as competence in its more familiar sense of achieved capacity. (White, 1959, pp. 317–318)

White called the motivational aspect of competence the need for "effectance," but unlike many other needs, this one is seldom experienced acutely. In fact, competence seems to emerge primarily in the spare waking time "between episodes of homeostatic crisis" (1959, p. 321). The power of the effectance motive comes from understanding it as a steady, rather than an urgent, drive—or a consistent interest in dealing with the challenges of life. Likewise, satisfying this need does not lead to clearly identifiable feelings of satiation. Instead, competence results in a "feeling of efficacy," which is pleasurable but often in more subtle ways. It should be noted that satisfying the need also has high reward potential in terms of its survival value: The need for competence motivates the organism to actively master the skills necessary for dealing with the environment and life effectively.

In his 1963 article "Ego and Reality in Psychoanalytic Theory," White took these notions concerning competence and effectance directly to self-esteem. First, he pointed out that "[t]he primary difficulty that has hampered psychoanalytic theory in dealing with self-esteem is, it seems to me, the failure to distinguish between esteem and love. Esteem has more to do with respect than love, and respect for oneself is essential for self-esteem" (p. 129). This respect emerges from the fact that self-esteem is connected to achievements. For example, the infant begins by being helpless in its dependency on the environment and significant others, particularly the mother, to meet its needs. But even in its earliest days, this process is not as passive as it may seem, because the infant also manipulates its environment, and those same significant others, in crude but surprisingly effective ways.

There is a steady growth from being *unable* to being *able* to affect the environment in desired ways. With respect to another part of the environment, especially the mother in her nurturing activities, [the infant] rather quickly reaches a peak in his capacity to command services. This form of efficacy will then go into a contractive phase as the mother becomes less willing to do everything, and renunciation of power will be necessary. But the two lines of development quickly become complimentary: as the child progressively sacrifices his privileges of command over the household, he becomes less needful of these privileges through growing competence to deal with things by his own efforts. (p. 133)

Thus, self-esteem, White concluded, has its "taproot in efficacy." Whether it is as small as having mother respond to a cry or as grand as taking one's first steps, self-esteem is achieved or earned, not just given. Seeing self-esteem as a developmental phenomenon, of course, also means that it is subject to all the other processes and forces of development. For instance, many of the achievements associated with self-esteem are tied to developmental stages. Each one of them is an opportunity for further exploration, and additional successes (or failures) facilitate (or retard) the development of healthy self-respect and esteem.

Finally, White explored the connections between competence, the ego, and self-esteem. Ego strength, or the ability of the individual to deal with anxiety and cope effectively with the demands of reality, is linked to self-esteem because the relationship between anxiety and competence is reciprocal: "A strong ego, let us say, is one which has developed substantial competence in dealing with impulse and with environment. A weak ego is one which, lacking this development, has had to make heavy use of defensive measures of the anticathetic type, thus sacrificing further flexible learning" (White, 1963, pp. 138–139). The ego, then, can respond to the inevitable anxieties of life in two opposing ways: mastery (competence) or defensiveness (rigidity). How an individual comes to characteristically take one alternative over the other, however, is no simple matter, especially since we all use both. For instance, competence and ego strength tend to promote one another and lead to continued learning or development, whereas anxiety and defensiveness tend to go hand in hand and move us in the other direction. Patterns that reflect the cumulative influence of one's particular capacities, favorable or unfavorable environmental factors, and the degree of anxiety present in one's life build up over time. Eventually, the processes of development reach the point at which the individual responds in ways that are characteristic of the person, reflecting a general or global level of self-esteem.

By linking it to competence, White opens up the clinical significance of self-esteem. As he says, the "development of a systematic theory of psychopathology requires a fairly precise knowledge of the chronology of competence" (White, 1963, p. 140). There are several ways that knowledge about the developmental history of an individual's competence or self-esteem is helpful to clinical work. For instance, to fully understand the reasons for the emergence of any given problem, we must know more than just what caused anxiety and therefore defensiveness: It is also important to appreciate how the individual found ways of avoiding even more severe anxiety or more serious problems, so that we know what we have to work with in terms of ego strength and creativity. Similarly, knowing where and how the patient experienced successes and knowing the areas where the client demonstrates what White called "conflict-free functioning" can be useful in helping the individual increase the ability to deal with some kinds of conflicts more competently. White also pointed out that giving therapeutic attention to competence and defensiveness helps with other clinical issues. For example, we can understand how it is that some people may come from very severe environments and do quite well. After all, they must have found effective ways of handling conflict or of creating conflict-free areas in which their development could continue in more positive directions. This aspect of White's work may be something of a precursor to the more recent thinking about psychological resilience, which is examined more empirically in modern work such as that offered by Werner and Smith (1992) and which has become so important today in the literature on trauma.

In addition to being historically significant, White's work is important because it situates self-esteem in the context of human development. Indeed, he suggested that self-esteem is a developmental issue that extends well into adulthood. Also, being psychodynamically oriented, he could not help but open up the clinical implications of self-esteem in regard to the development of psychopathology and its treatment. However, the problem of perspectivity mentioned earlier means that there are some important limits to White's contributions. The most important one is the curse of the psychoanalytic perspective, which is that these insights are based on a theory that cannot be examined empirically. White's contributions are ideas rather than clear findings.

THE SOCIOLOGICAL APPROACH: MORRIS ROSENBERG

As in psychology, sociological work on self-related issues started to appear around the turn of the century, mainly in the Cooley-Mead tradition mentioned earlier. However, the first major work of this type on self-esteem appeared in the mid-1960s when Morris Rosenberg began his monumental investigations involving more than 5,000 subjects. After defining self-esteem as "a positive or negative attitude toward a particular object, namely, the self" (1965, p. 30), he focused his attention on specifying "the bearing of certain social factors on self-esteem and to indicate the influence of self-esteem on socially significant attitudes and behavior" (p. 15).

Rosenberg began by pointing out that understanding such things as self-image or self-esteem as attitudinal phenomenon created by social and cultural forces offers many advantages for social science research. Foremost among them is that social science has ways of measuring various dimensions of attitude formation, which means that it should be possible to apply the same techniques to understanding ourselves. For example, similarities between external and internal attitudes occur in terms of content (what the attitude is about), direction (positive or negative value of the attitude), intensity (its affective strength or how strongly the attitude is held), and stability (how durable or long lasting it is). In his words, "If we can characterize the individual's self-picture in terms of each of these dimensions, then we would have a good, if still incomplete, description of the structure of the self-image. And the same would be true of any other object in the world" (1965, pp. 7–8). However, Rosenberg was also aware that studying self-esteem this way presents its own problems. Chief among them is that self-attitudes do differ from other evaluations of objects in very distinct ways. For one thing, no two selves are the same, which means that making comparisons between individuals is difficult because differences are likely to be as important as similarities. Moreover, self-attitudes involve a certain motivational quality, a bias if you will, not usually found with attitudes toward other things; that is, we are inclined to have a positive attitude toward ourselves. Finally, and perhaps most important, self-related phenomena are reflexive: We are using the self to evaluate itself, which makes research in this area very difficult, rather like a Heisenberg principle of uncertainty applied to social science instead of to physics.

Another important dimension of Rosenberg's view of self-esteem is that this attitude concerning one's worthiness as a person is what is sometimes called a "pivotal variable" (Rosenberg, 1965) in behavior:

> High self-esteem, as reflected in our scale items, expresses the feeling that one is "good enough." The individual simply feels that he is a person of worth; he respects himself for what he is, but does not stand in awe of himself nor expect others to stand in awe of him. He does *not* necessarily

consider himself superior to others. . . . Low self-esteem, on the other hand, implies self-rejection, self-dissatisfaction, self-contempt. The individual lacks respect for the self he observes. The picture is disagreeable, and he wishes it were otherwise. (p. 31)

In short, the presence or absence of such perceived worthiness disposes one toward positive or negative experience and related behaviors. Rosenberg went on to explore the way in which self-esteem (or the lack of it) is created: It results from a process of comparison involving values and discrepancies. According to this view, individuals have self-esteem to the degree they perceive themselves as matching up to a set of central self-values. These core values concern what the individuals have learned, through the process of socialization, to be worthy of emulating or attaining (Rosenberg & Simmons, 1971). The relationship between ideals, perceptions, evaluations, and degrees of self-esteem runs in the expected directions. The smaller the gap between the so-called ideal self and the current, actual, or "real" self, the higher the self-esteem. Conversely, the greater the gap, the lower the self-esteem, even if one is actually viewed by others in a positive way. Of course, tying self-esteem to values to the process of socialization also means that this theory of self-esteem is deeply social. For example, Rosenberg's ideas on selfhood are grounded in the Cooley-Mead position that the self is a social phenomenon. His research pursued social factors affecting self-esteem, such as those concerning the role of subcultural influences like religion and social class.

Identifying the importance of Rosenberg's theory for the study of self-esteem is easy to do. First, his approach can be seen as paradigmatic for what we have called the sociological perspective on self-esteem: It begins with the assumption that the self is a social construction and works on the premise that self-values associated with self-esteem arise from an interplay of cultural, social, familial, and other interpersonal processes. Notice that worthiness is emphasized over competence in this framework, even though both are mentioned by other authors working from this point of view. Next, Rosenberg opened the way for socially oriented theories and practitioners to focus on the possibility of enhancing self-esteem, by addressing external conditions. In other words, if self-esteem is a function of the social environment and if a negative social environment impedes the formation of positive self-esteem or creates low self-esteem, then practitioners from this point of view will see hope in removing such obstacles and creating positive social influences wherever possible. The careful reader will see a connection between this approach and the self-esteem controversy addressed earlier. Both the California self-esteem movement and its educational offshoot approach understanding self-esteem and enhancing it from this perspective, because their definitional focus is on worthiness and their practical focus is on improving social conditions as the main route to enhancing self-esteem.

Rosenberg is a giant in this field, but there are some limitations to this approach to understanding self-esteem. For one thing, sociological work tends to address self-esteem from the outside rather than from the inside. In other words, the personal (psychological) dimensions of self-esteem such as individual motivation are difficult for this view to incorporate. Similarly, the roles that individual choices and responsibilities play in gaining or losing self-esteem are not effectively accessed from this point of view. Finally, changing self-esteem in an individual life can be very difficult to do sociologically: Creating pro-self-esteem environments and attitudes is extremely expensive and time consuming, even when individuals choose to cooperate.

STANLEY COOPERSMITH AND THE BEHAVIORAL PERSPECTIVE

In *The Antecedents of Self-Esteem* (1967) Stanley Coopersmith aimed to develop "a conceptual framework that might serve as a guide in investigating self-esteem, or a tool for altering it" (p. vii). Like many behaviorally oriented theorists, his approach included an explicit concern with addressing practical as well as theoretical matters. After doing some 8 years of empirically oriented research on the subject, Coopersmith concluded that "[f]or both psychologists and laymen, 'self-esteem' has great significance—personally, socially, and psychologically. It is therefore disconcerting that so little is known about the conditions and experiences that enhance or lessen self-esteem" (p. 1). Given the fact that learning often takes place in a social context, there are some important similarities between Coopersmith's and Rosenberg's approaches. For example, they both see self-esteem as an attitude and as an expression of worthiness:

> By self-esteem we refer to the evaluation which the individual makes and customarily maintains with regard to himself: it expresses an attitude of approval or disapproval, and indicates the extent to which the individual believes himself to be capable, significant, successful, and worthy. In short, self-esteem is a *personal* judgment of worthiness that is expressed in the attitudes the individual holds toward himself. It is a subjective experience

which the individual conveys to others by verbal reports and other overt expressive behavior. (Coopersmith, 1967, pp. 4–5)

Similarly, both approaches see a relationship between self-esteem and experience or behavior, such as anxiety and depression. However, the differences between the two theories are more significant. For one thing, Coopersmith's work focuses more on the individual's personal experience than on cognitive or social factors. For another thing, like behaviorists and psychologically oriented social learning theorists in general, Coopersmith based his work on well-established learning principles rather than on general social influences.

For example, Coopersmith found that there are three major antecedents of self-esteem (parental warmth, clearly defined limits, and respectful treatment). Instead of describing them as general social forces, however, he concentrated on the learning mechanisms that connect these factors to self-esteem. Respectively, children *learn* they are worthy because their parents treat them with affection. They develop higher standards because these values are consistently *reinforced* (classically and operantly) over others. Children treat themselves with respect because they see how their parents act toward people and *model* those behaviors themselves. Conversely, if self-esteem can be learned, the lack of it is also learned. Parental neglect, too many or too few limits, and indifferent or demeaning models result in different kinds of self-constructs and behaviors. Likewise, children learn about competence (or incompetence, for that matter) through the various successes and failures that they have over time. In short, this view sees self-esteem (or the lack of it) as an acquired trait.

Coopersmith, and this approach in general, focuses on the relationship between self-esteem, threat, and defensiveness as a primary research and clinical concern. In general, people with low self-esteem seem to be more vulnerable to stress. Therefore, they tend to be more concerned with defending against challenges than resolving them, which, in turn, seems to bring with it feelings of anxiety, inadequacy, and helplessness often associated with low self-esteem (1967, p. 248) and their accompanying behaviors. Coopersmith went on to investigate these dynamics and concluded that there are several types of self-esteem instead of just the "high" and "low" versions seen in earlier work:

The nature and pattern of our findings suggest that low self-esteem (passive acceptance), medium self-esteem (active espousal), and discrepant self-esteem (lessened social effectiveness) are associated with different defensive actions. Defensiveness, in short, is not a single phenomenon associated

with low self-esteem but appears to consist of a variety of reactions reflecting different deficiencies of esteem. (p. 256)

Coopersmith found that self-esteem and defensiveness interact with a
host of environmental, developmental, and learning variables to produce recognizable patterns of behavior called "types" of self-esteem, a
conclusion that seems to stand the test of time as one of the major
findings in this field.

The practical focus of this approach takes it to the clinical level in
that Coopersmith's work ends with the development of the foundations
for behaviorally oriented therapeutic strategies designed to enhance
self-esteem at the individual level. In particular, he offered several general clinical guidelines for enhancing self-esteem and eliminating factors
that detract from it. Although he did not go farther than offering suggestions, three of them have stood the test of time even today. He began
by advocating a form of assessment consistent with his theory and research:

> First, the conceptual analysis (Chapter 2) posed four major bases of esteem:
> competence, significance, virtue, and power. That is, persons come to
> evaluate themselves according to how proficient they are in performing
> tasks, how well they meet ethical or religious standards, how loved and
> accepted they are by others, and how much power they exert. We believe
> that determining the basis or bases a given individual employs in judging
> his worth may well be a crucial step in determining the source of his
> difficulties and in guiding therapeutic efforts. (1967, p. 262)

Next, he built on the findings that children with high self-esteem tend
to have families that set clear limits and expectations. Therefore, Coopersmith suggested that structured therapeutic situations may be more
effective in increasing self-esteem than unstructured techniques. Finally,

> [a] third implication is that the patient may benefit quite markedly by
> modeling his behavior after an effective, assured, and competent individual.
> The exact behavior that an individual may require or seek to follow un-
> doubtably varies with each person, but it may be that the style of response
> is more critical than the particular action. Thus the individual may observe
> how an effective individual deals with anxiety, resolves ambiguity, and
> makes decisions. . . . Providing advantageous behavioral alternatives in
> their specific expression is a more parsimonious procedure than waiting
> for their self-discovery, and even more parsimonious than awaiting their
> recurrent use. (1967, p. 263)

Although Coopersmith did not investigate the efficacy of these modes
of intervention, they are clear extensions of his theory and consistent

with general, proven behavioral principles of treatment, in this case, the principles of modeling.

It is easy to see the significance of Coopersmith's contributions to the field. For one thing, his work has a higher degree of credibility because he used observational methods in controlled situations, as well as case studies, interviews, and surveys. In addition, a number of his original findings stand up to the test of time. For instance, more than 30 years later, Coopersmith's Self-Esteem Inventory (1975, 1981) is still one of the most widely used instruments for assessing self-esteem in children and adults. (In fact, I was invited to consider participating in revising this instrument during the mid-1980s.) His work on a range of self-esteem types broadened our understanding of the relationship between self-esteem and behavior. We shall see that his therapeutic suggestions turn out to have reasonably good empirical support and have been adopted by many workers in the field today.

This is not to say that there are no limitations to Coopersmith's work. In fact, there are at least three. First, the theory is couched in a form of behaviorism that is no longer considered contemporary. (To be current, his entire model should probably be recast in terms of social cognitive learning theory.) Second, his research focuses largely on self-esteem in childhood and adolescence, not to mention that his major subject pools are white middle-class boys. Finally, in keeping with the behavioral preference for dealing with that which is measurable or otherwise observable, this approach to research and practice does not seem to access the internal or experiential dimensions of self-esteem effectively: The roles of meaning, choice, and a sense of ownership (responsibility) for one's behavior all seem inaccessible to this approach.

THE HUMANISTIC VISION OF NATHANIEL BRANDEN

I always find it significant to note that three of the most important books written on self-esteem were published in the 1960s, as though to mark the introduction of self-esteem back into mainstream social science. *The Psychology of Self-Esteem* (1969) by Nathaniel Branden brings to the field the so-called third force (after the psychoanalytic and behavioral influences). It will be recalled that Branden was the first to define self-esteem in terms of worthiness and competence in equal measure. He also saw self-esteem as an existential need: "Man experiences his desire for self-esteem as an urgent imperative, as a basic need. Whether he identifies the issue explicitly or not, he cannot escape the feeling that his estimate of himself is of life-and-death importance. No one can be indifferent to the question of how he judges himself; his nature does not allow man this option" (p. 110).

This need drives human behavior in two ways. First, we are not born with the knowledge of what fills this need, so we must find out about it through trial and error: "Man's need of self-esteem is inherent in his nature. But he is not born with the knowledge of what will satisfy that need, or of the standard by which self-esteem is to be gauged; he must discover it" (Branden, 1969, p. 110). In other words, we learn about competence and worthiness through our most human faculties: reason, choice, and responsibility. This process, as Branden described it, involves exercising one's conscious abilities to assess situations realistically and to respond to them in a way that is consistent with basic or fundamental human values. Living rationally like this brings with it certain powerfully positive feelings that are right "in principle" (p. 110). Happiness, joy, pleasure, and self-acceptance are seen as natural responses to living authentically in this way.

Second, in addition to motivating us in such a positive, rational, and humanistic direction, Branden pointed out that the need for self-esteem is so strong that the lack of it motivates us in very adverse ways.

> So intensely does a man feel the need of a positive view of himself, that he may evade, repress, distort his judgment, disintegrate his mind—in order to avoid coming face to face with facts that would affect his self-appraisal adversely. . . . If and to the extent that men lack self-esteem, they feel driven to *fake* it, to create the *illusion* of self-esteem—condemning themselves to psychological fraud—moved by the desperate sense that to face the universe without self-esteem is to stand naked, disarmed, delivered to destruction. (1969, p. 110)

If one is cut off from (or, more properly, if one cuts oneself off from) legitimate sources of self-esteem, then one searches for substitutes. Branden called the result of this deficiency "pseudo self-esteem." Of course, such self-deception and inauthenticity do not go unpunished in a humanistic framework. As Branden said, "Conversely, one of the most disastrous consequences of an impaired or deficient self-esteem is that it tends to hamper and undercut the efficiency of a man's thinking process—depriving him of the full strength and benefit of his own intelligence" (p. 140). Although using a substitute (pseudo self-esteem) may temporarily satisfy this need, doing so over time exacts a terrible psychological cost.

In a later book entitled *Honoring the Self* (1983), Branden clarified the dynamic nature of self-esteem, particularly that which is associated with pseudo self-esteem, by adding two components. First, he identified four basic pillars of positive self-esteem: the degree of an individual's conscious awareness, one's integrity as a person, the willingness to accept responsibility for one's decisions, and self-acceptance, or being honest about the kind of choices one makes. Second, he emphasized that we all must struggle to honor the self because it can be challenged at any time. Thus, living authentically "is often a struggle of heroic proportions" (p. 19). We can see how each "pillar" supports the others by looking at what happens when one is missing. For instance, the lack of awareness of the need for self-esteem makes it more difficult to understand how important it is for us to make choices that affirm our self-esteem. A low degree of integrity means that our actions may become incongruent and will lessen our ability to engage in honest struggle. Failing to take responsibility is a self-deception of the greatest kind because that limits our ability to see and correct our self-esteem mistakes. Ultimately, the inability to accept the value of being ourselves leads to the possibility of self-neglect or even self-hatred:

> A man's pseudo-self-esteem is maintained by two means, essentially: by evading, repressing, rationalizing, and otherwise denying ideas and feelings that could affect his self-appraisal adversely; and by seeking to derive his sense of efficacy and worth by something *other than* rationality, some *alternative* value or virtue which he experiences as less demanding or more easily attainable, such as "doing one's duty," or being stoical or altruistic or financially successful or sexually attractive. (1969, pp. 144–145)

Thus, the dynamics of self-esteem are related to those of lifestyle, or how one goes about the process of living. Real self-esteem, which is powered by need and fed by authentic decisions, is a healthy, optimal style, whereas pseudo self-esteem, which is powered by the same need but feeds on inauthenticity and the avoidance of reality, is a vicious, deficient style. In this case, the person faces two problems: a lack of real self-esteem and a lack of the ability to see that clearly. The result is a perfect situation for the development of neuroses or worse. Indeed, so great is the need for self-esteem in this theory that extremely low levels of it can lead to self-destructive behaviors and even death. In this sense certain existential difficulties, such as dependence on drugs or alcohol, neglecting one's health, staying in abusive relationships, and suicide can be connected to a lack of self-esteem.

Nathaniel Branden may be the most prolific and widely read author among the major self-esteem theorists. In addition to bringing the humanistic perspective to bear on self-esteem in the first place, he offers one of the most articulate renditions of this approach in his 1994 work,

The Six Pillars of Self-Esteem. There are at least two major contributions that Branden's theory and the humanistic perspective it represents make to the field. First, self-esteem is identified as an existential issue, which means that it is more than a developmental process, social concern, or personal problem. From this point of view, self-esteem is at the center of life's stage and that makes it a vital psychological issue. Second, the humanistic emphasis on individual freedom, choice, and responsibility means that self-esteem is just as important in adulthood as it is in childhood. Such a focus requires us to appreciate that whether we have positive or negative self-esteem means something to us; in particular, that it is an important part of human existence and that it must be managed throughout the life cycle. However, there are also two main weaknesses to consider. First, the research humanistic psychologists usually offer to support their view of self-esteem is generally limited to case studies. Second, this perspective is often more philosophical than psychological. For example, the evidence Branden provides seems to come mainly from informal clinical case studies and the objectivistic philosophy of Ayn Rand.

SEYMOUR EPSTEIN'S COGNITIVE-EXPERIENTIAL VIEW

The last major theory of self-esteem is situated within the context of the information-processing approach more commonly known as cognitive psychology. Seymour Epstein's view is based on the cognitive notions of information (experience), organization (concept formation), representation (a system of concepts arranged hierarchically), and the process of development. This view finds that human beings organize information and experience of the world, self, and others into what Epstein has called "personal theories of reality."

A major assumption of the theory is that the human mind is so constituted that it tends to organize experience into conceptual systems. Human brains make connections between events, and, having made connections, they connect the connections, and so on, until they have developed an organized system of higher- and lower-order constructs that is both differentiated and integrated. Whether we like it or not, each of us, because he has a human brain, forms a theory of reality that brings order into what would otherwise be a chaotic world of experience. We need a theory to make sense out of the world, just as a scientist needs a theory to make sense out of the limited body of information he or she wishes to understand. (1980, p. 102)

In other words, over time individuals come to develop sophisticated cognitive maps. These personal theories of reality include both an understanding of the world and others (what Epstein called a "world theory") and an understanding of who we are in relation to them (a "self-theory"). Like all theories, personal theories make sense out of data, only in this case it is the information given to us through our experience, family, culture, and so forth, in addition to that which is more sensory in nature. As with any theory, we generalize from a set of concepts in a way that helps us to understand past, present, and future events. Finally, such personal theories are practical in that they are "prescriptive," which is Epstein's way of saying that they help us to survive and grow. These cognitive tools help us to identify our needs and ways of satisfying them that are likely to be successful given the particular time, culture, family, and circumstances in which we live. Such theories are "a conceptual tool for fulfilling life's most basic psychological functions, namely, to maintain a favorable pleasure/pain balance over the foreseeable future, to maintain a favorable level of self-esteem, to assimilate the data of reality within a stable, coherent, conceptual system, and to maintain favorable relationships with significant others" (Epstein, 1985, p. 286).

Epstein went on to define self-esteem as a basic human need to be "loveworthy" (1985, p. 302). As a basic need, self-esteem occupies a central role in our lives as a motivational force, both consciously and otherwise. If one's level of self-esteem is altered, Epstein said, "it has widespread effects on the entire self-system" (1980, p. 106). A crucial aspect of the relation between self-esteem and our theories of the self, world, and others involves a powerful conflict. On the one hand, the primary function of these theories is to make sense out of the chaos of life. Once the self and world theories become established, they create a basis for stability, so the individual works hard to maintain them. Change is resisted because it can be destabilizing. Indeed, altering one part of a system affects many other parts, which can lead to disrupting one's ability to function in general. Thus, feelings, especially painful ones like the loss of self-esteem, become very important in this system: They constitute a powerful feedback mechanism that helps to minimize potential disruption by warning us to avoid it. The anxiety that accompanies a threat to self-esteem, for instance, motivates us to avoid or fight the danger in order to maintain our sense of worthiness.

On the other hand, a good theory must be able to expand over time in order to accommodate new information. As our theory of the world expands in a positive way, such growth is pleasurable in that it makes us feel good or worthy. This pleasure is reinforcing, which means that the individual seeks to change even further. Therefore, instead of just holding things steady and protecting us from disruption, self-esteem drives us toward, of all things, change. The result of these two natural but opposing forces is a basic self-esteem conflict or paradox with which we all must deal:

> As a fundamental preconscious postulate, self-esteem has profound effects on behavior and emotions. Accordingly, the regulation of self-esteem is of critical importance to the individual. However, a person's reaction to events that have the potential to influence self-esteem is determined not only by the person's need for enhancement but also by the person's need to maintain the stability of his or her conceptual system. That is, the combined effects of both variables must be taken into account. (Epstein, 1985, p. 303)

Next, we find that Epstein sees self-esteem as being structured hierarchically. According to his theory, there are three interacting levels in the self-system. Like the base of a pyramid, basic self-esteem is the most stable and influential level once it has solidified developmentally. Next, there is an intermediate level of self-esteem. This can be thought of as the degree of self-esteem one has in particular domains of experience or activity, including such things as skill levels or competence, lovability, likability, self-control, personal power, moral approval, bodily appearance, and bodily functioning (O'Brien & Epstein, 1983, 1988). Although each of us is concerned with all of these areas, the degree of interest or concern given to any one of them varies with each individual, which means there is plenty of diversity in self-esteem. The third level of the hierarchy is the most visible because it is situation-specific. These everyday manifestations of self-esteem come and go very rapidly as we move through our day and week. However, except under unusual circumstances, this level of self-esteem is relatively weak in terms of its ability to affect or modify the other two levels. Instead, they both readily influence this more transitory manifestation of self-esteem so that things "get back to normal" fairly quickly.

I selected Epstein's work to be representative of the cognitive perspective for four reasons. First, it is one of the earliest yet most comprehensive attempts to understand self-esteem from this position. Second, he offers a highly organized body of ideas and concepts that are compatible with later cognitive views, such as the one offered by Bednar and colleagues (1989), which we shall examine shortly. Third, the theory seems to be able to address some of the material we saw regarding the research problems and findings associated with self-esteem. For example, it offers a way of understanding the global versus situational issue discussed in chapter 2. Finally, as we shall see in some detail later, this approach to self-esteem has practical implications, especially in terms of finding ways to measure and assess self-esteem. However, there are two serious limits to appreciate. The first is that Epstein's theory is more concerned with personality development than self-esteem per se. Second, and much more important, generally speaking, the cognitive perspective tends to be mechanical, reductionistic, or what phenomenologists call "dehumanizing" (Aanstoos, 1984; Costall & Still, 1987; Dreyfus & Dreyfus, 1986). In other words, as seen from a cognitive perspective, self-esteem is more like the cold lines of a computer code rather than the vital force of life we saw with other positions.

Summary of Findings About Theories

The one question we must ask of these general theories of self-esteem from a phenomenological perspective is, what do they show us about developing a good theory of self-esteem? Several "findings" emerge in this regard. First, with the exception of a strictly biological point of view, each of the major perspectives in the social sciences offers a credible foundation for a substantial theory of self-esteem. The implication is that each major approach reveals something about self-esteem that the others cannot. Second, although each view is unique, they all have some general features in common, suggesting that such regularities should be addressed in a comprehensive theory. For example, we see that definitions are used consistently and that each theory is systematic. Third, there seems to be a fairly consistent set of specific self-esteem themes or issues addressed in these theories. They include understanding self-esteem as a developmental phenomenon, showing how there can be types of self-esteem, appreciating that self-esteem is a motivating factor in behavior, and recognizing the link between self-esteem and behavior, particularly in terms of well-being or the lack of it. Fourth, although each general theory of self-esteem starts out at the abstract level, they all have implications for how to go about enhancing self-esteem at the practical level.

Finally, traditional theories of self-esteem fail to do some important things. In particular, although each view is concerned with being comprehensive, there is very little dialogue between them, not to mention integration. And, although they all talk about practical implications, we see that what is actually offered for enhancing self-esteem is a set of very general guidelines. In sum, a genuinely comprehensive theory must be based on a concise definition of self-esteem that is used consistently from theory to practice, make an effort to address the four standard theoretical issues in the field and integrate them into a theoretically consistent whole, and do so in a way that leads to specific techniques for enhancing self-esteem.

MAJOR SELF-ESTEEM ENHANCEMENT PROGRAMS

Although the major theories of self-esteem presented above do not accomplish much at the practical level, programs aimed specifically at enhancing self-esteem have been developed. One way to appreciate the difference between self-esteem enhancement programs and the general theories is to see the programs as a new development in the field, perhaps as a coming of age. After all, it cannot be completely coincidental that they all began to appear around the same time (the mid-1980s) and only after the development of the major theories. Also, the major self-esteem enhancement programs seem to be long on technique and short on theory, which is the opposite of what we have just seen. This portion of our phenomenology uses the same criteria to select a program for examination as was used with theories, and it proceeds in the same fashion. In gathering the data I looked for approaches that seemed to focus explicitly on enhancing self-esteem instead of more general therapeutic goals, examined them in terms of their significance or persistence as defined earlier, then analyzed them as representing one of the major theoretical orientations just presented. Similarly, I will begin here with a brief presentation of the basic self-esteem ideas upon which a particular program builds, then indicate how the system goes about enhancing self-esteem practically, and end with a statement concerning the strengths and weaknesses of the approach based on what we know about self-esteem so far. The goal of this portion of our phenomenology is to find what is required to make a good, that is, theoretically sound, practically oriented, empirically supported, self-esteem enhancement program, which should help in building one in the next chapter.

Frey and Carlock: Eclectic Variations on a Humanistic Theme

Basic Ideas

Diane Frey and C. Jesse Carlock are two clinicians who introduce their work by saying, "Many books on self esteem focus either on theory or practice. This book takes the theory of self esteem and translates it for the reader into practice. In this way it stands alone among all other books on self esteem" (1989, p. vii). The definition of self-esteem that they develop is remarkably similar to Branden's: "Self esteem has two interrelated components: the feeling that one is competent to live and the feeling that one is worthy of living" (p. 7). The major mechanism for regulating personal experience is found in the humanistic concept of "organismic self-regulation." The main body of this program consists of a large collection of experientially oriented human growth and development activities. Frey and Carlock tend to be very eclectic and use many ideas from other perspectives. For instance, the development of the self-concept is presented in terms of social learning factors, particularly negative environmental influences (or "psychological pathogens," as they say) that contribute to self-esteem problems. Also, they use the cognitive concepts of "self-talk" and self-fulfilling prophecies as central routes to changing self-esteem, both of which are very cognitive.

System and Techniques

The most outstanding characteristic of this approach to enhancing self-esteem may be that the program is very systematic. Although Frey and Carlock bring an incredibly divergent mix of theoretical concepts and experiential exercises into play in their approach to enhancing self-esteem, all of these ideas and activities are organized into a clear four-stage process or framework. Moreover, the authors stress that while each phase is a distinct step on the path to enhancing self-esteem, they actually constitute a system in which the whole process is greater than the sum of its parts: Following it sequentially provides maximum benefit.

This process of enhancing self-esteem begins with the "identity phase." This one is the least well defined of the steps, probably because it involves the question of identity, which, as we saw in chapter 2, is a much larger one than self-esteem. However, the authors do offer a clear rationale for beginning here: "Initially in intervention, an individual with low self esteem needs to discover his/her own identity. Because of distorted perceptions, such persons rarely have a clear understanding of who they really are" (Frey & Carlock, 1989, p. 181). In addition to learning about oneself in some very basic ways, this step allows for the fact that there are often obstacles that block awareness or self-experience that have to be worked through in order to know about ourselves and our self-esteem. Accordingly, Frey and Carlock offer several standard exercises to help individuals engage in self-discovery, such as values clarification activities and the like.

Although the search for identity can probably be expanded indefinitely, at some point it is necessary to shift into the second stage, which focuses on developing an "awareness of strengths and weaknesses." This stage concerns helping clients to develop an appreciation of their assets and liabilities as persons. These activities generally focus on identifying strengths in a way that makes them meaningful to participants, although weaknesses are looked at, too. This part of the work is necessary because individuals with low self-esteem are usually very practiced at ignoring their assets and are good at focusing on their liabilities. Indeed, such resistance is a constant problem in moving to higher levels of self-esteem, especially in the beginning. Two kinds of work characterize this stage. First, the facilitator consistently offers positive feedback—each time such an opportunity presents itself. Of course, this feedback must be done on the basis of sincerity (it must be true) and concreteness (it should be clear and specific). The second kind of intervention involves altering how people filter information to help them take in information more accurately. This means they must begin to acknowledge the positive as well as the negative and not exaggerate the significance of the latter or minimize the importance of the former. Several activities are offered to assist in this process, especially providing a supportive group environment and offering positive feedback experiences.

The third stage, called the "nurturance phase," is the most complex. Whereas the preceding step is said to have the effect of developing a more positive sense of self-esteem by focusing on strengths rather than weaknesses, it actually only plants the seeds for lasting change. The analogy is quite appropriate, because it implies a beginning, but one that is fragile and in need of further attention:

> The first two phases in themselves are not sufficient as newly acquired positive self esteem can be lost if it is not nurtured. Teaching nurturing helps the person to enhance strengths and use them to minimize weaknesses. As a person moves from one part of their environment to another, the praise/criticism ratio may change, especially when one is in more toxic environments. (Frey & Carlock, 1989, p. 197)

The aim of the nurturing phase, then, is to help the new pro-self-esteem behaviors to take root, so to speak. It is especially important to foster the ability to help people transfer their newly developed awareness of the importance of positive self-esteem to environments outside the supportive but limited atmosphere of the therapist's office or group room. Moreover, Frey and Carlock recognize that this project is difficult under even the best of situations. For instance, they point out that some people suffer home or work environments that are "toxic" (a richly descriptive term) to self-esteem. The deepest or most intensive work of the program is done during this phase.

The major thrust of the activities involves dealing with the self-fulfilling dynamics that Frey and Carlock feel are at the heart of perpetuating low self-esteem. In particular, the negative thinking and behaving patterns that sustain low self-esteem must be overcome and replaced with more positive ones. Accordingly, they offer a number of exercises and activities to facilitate this development. For instance, teaching individuals to identify their self-esteem needs and to get them met in appropriate ways are steps in the right direction. Similarly, participants are asked to affirm their own positive qualities, as well as those of others, in a supportive group setting. Likewise, the importance of individuals in developing their own self-esteem support systems is stressed.

In the final stage, this approach focuses on the importance of maintaining self-esteem after the program is over. In this fourth or "maintenance" phase, "[o]ne needs to learn how to maintain adequate self esteem just as it is necessary to maintain a car, house, or an interpersonal relationship if it is to grow and flourish" (Frey & Carlock, 1989, p. 205). There are several very important reasons for building such a step into a self-esteem enhancement program. First, Frey and Carlock see increasing self-esteem as an evolving process, so the work that goes on in therapy is just the beginning. As people or their circumstances change, the ways in which they get their self-esteem needs met may change, too; therefore, "[d]uring the maintenance phase, individuals are taught to turn experiences into learning situations, practice facilitative risk taking, set appropriate goals, forecast desired personal outcomes, and publicly affirm goals" (p. 206). The exercises and activities used to further these aims include learning how to set realistic goals and how to develop appropriate risk-taking strategies.

In addition to developing a systematic approach to enhancing self-esteem, Frey and Carlock note that there are at least three significant practical issues that are almost always present to consider. The first is called resistance, and it concerns dealing with the usual technical problems associated with change in general, as well as those explicitly associated with changing self-esteem. Next, Frey and Carlock point out the role of and need for assessment in changing self-esteem. They note, for instance, that self-esteem issues vary considerably from person to person, which means the clinician must become attuned to differences in participants and make appropriate adjustments, a process that is facilitated by accurate assessment. Finally, they recognize that changing self-esteem is a difficult, long-term project: "The change process, like much of human learning, is erratic. Improvement can be followed by a slight regression, which is in turn followed by improvement. This process repeats itself until some stabilization of changed behavior occurs" (p. 213). Ultimately, then, the entire system is based on persistence and hard work.

Evaluation

There is much praise for this approach to enhancing self-esteem, especially the fact that the original edition of this program was probably the first systematic approach specifically designed to increase self-esteem. In addition to being based on an identifiable set of psychosocial ideas, the program is broken into clearly defined steps, each one of which includes specific objectives and concrete activities. Moreover, these steps progress in a logical fashion, and the exercises are based on fairly common therapeutic or growth-oriented activities. Finally, the authors point to some 11 years of case study support for their program. This program seems to be fairly flexible and can be applied in a number of clinical settings.

Because this approach is based in large part on the human growth and development tradition of the humanistic perspective, it suffers from some limitations. The most important one is that many humanistic assumptions are not open to observational or experimental validation. More specifically, most of the exercises advocated by Frey and Carlock are very "soft" in the way that was so popular during the 1960s and 1970s. While these techniques are easy to implement and may result in increased awareness, there is not a large body of supporting research on whether or not they actually increase self-esteem. Indeed, some of the Gestalt techniques can be very problematical for disturbed populations (Rathus, 1996). However, I must point out that more recently there has been some published research done on using this program with various populations and it does seem to be helpful (Frey, Kelbley, Thomas, Durham, & James, 1992).

Although there is a background of humanistic thinking that is relatively consistent, at times the authors invoke so many psychological and sociological ideas that the work may be more of a conglomeration of ideas than an integrated body of them. Finally, there are some technical points that need to be strengthened. For instance, the assessment activity Frey and Carlock mention is usually just a clinical judgment instead of the result of a more rigorous assessment process such as one involving the use of psychological tests. In addition to better tailoring activities to individual needs, testing may help in spotting potential difficulties of which the clinician must be aware in this kind of work, such as knowing who is likely to be experiencing problems with depression, character disorders, and so on. This issue becomes especially important for an approach that is to be used with a wide variety of clients.

Increasing Self-Esteem Behaviorally: Pope, McHale, and Craighead

Basic Ideas

Pope, McHale, and Craighead's approach focuses on working with children and adolescents, even those who excel academically but still have low self-esteem. It also addresses the needs of various challenged populations. However, the learning principles on which it is based apply to all ages:

> The model from which we derived procedures to enhance self-esteem is labeled a social learning model. . . . At the most basic level, behavior is changed according to some principles from the area of psychology called *learning theory*. Since the focus is on social development, the utilization of these principles in applied settings such as home and school is called *social learning*. These basic principles have been known for some time. . . . (Pope et al., 1988, pp. 7–8)

Self-esteem is defined as "an *evaluation* of the information contained in the self-concept, and is derived from a child's feelings about *all* the things he is" (p. 2). Like most social and learning approaches to self-esteem, this way of understanding it is based on a discrepancy notion: the difference between the individuals' ideal self-concept (what one thinks one should be) and the perceived or actual self-concept (how one currently sees oneself). Self-esteem problems are seen as resulting from a significant difference between these perceptions, which creates the possibility of two basic self-esteem problems. The first one occurs when the ideal self-concept is too high or unrealistic given the individual or his or her circumstances. The resulting gap between what is desired and what is actually seen creates low self-esteem; the greater the difference, the greater the self-esteem problems. This type of low self-esteem is associated, for instance, with overachieving children who do well in school or elsewhere but who still feel unworthy because they fail to meet their expectations, however unrealistic they may be. The second type of self-esteem problem occurs when the ideals and expectations are appropriate for a particular person, but they fail to live up to them in realistic ways. For instance, an underachieving individual may suffer a sense of worthlessness that comes with failing to meet reasonable expectations of performance or behavior given their actual abilities.

In either case, this enhancement program focuses on working with five domains affected by self-esteem: global (overall) self-esteem, social self-esteem (which concerns how the child evaluates himself or herself in relation to others), academic self-esteem (or the child's school performance and abilities), how the child sees himself or herself as a valued (or unvalued) family member, and the quality of the child's body image (or how a child sees his or her physical appearance and abilities). The goal is to identify areas where self-esteem problems are especially strong, then design cognitive-behavioral activities to either increase skills to bring performance up to reasonable standards or to reduce exaggerated standards to allow a reasonable degree of skill or success to be and feel satisfactory.

Because learning is the engine that powers this approach, it is not surprising to find that general learning principles are used, especially positive reinforcement and modeling, to effect change. Indeed, even the role of the therapist is couched in a learning framework. For instance, the authors indicate that the clinician must be a warm and caring *teacher* as well as a skilled practitioner. Modern social learning theory also recognizes the importance of certain cognitive processes as crucial components of behavior and behavioral change. One of them, problem solving, is a pivotal element in this approach: "One of the basic findings of cognitive psychology is that humans possess problem solving skills. The potential discrepancy between our ideal and perceived self-concepts can be viewed as a problem to be solved" (Pope et al., 1988, p. 11). In addition to presenting a general strategy for change based on such an orientation, Pope and colleagues are concerned with the developmental context of self-esteem. Their program recognizes that there are relatively specific, age-related, developmental factors in the five areas mentioned above that affect self-esteem. This realization means that it is necessary to tailor intervention strategies toward the cognitive and behavioral skill level of the client. At the same time, it is recognized that each individual is unique. Children and adolescents (as well as adults) have personal preferences, different environments, and individual talents or deficits that must be considered in creating an effective self-esteem enhancement program. In other words, the program depends very heavily on rigorous psychological assessment.

System and Techniques

The program begins with a rigorous assessment process aimed at identifying an individual's particular self-esteem problems, needs, and potentials. Interviews with the child and significant others, actual observations of the client in his or her natural environments while engaged in everyday activities, and psychological tests are all methods of gathering information that are recommended by the authors. The assessment process aims at identifying which basic type of self-esteem problem appears to be present and determining how serious it is, both of which involve a person's global self-esteem. The other four areas (social esteem, academic esteem, how one is esteemed as a family member, and one's feelings about body image) are evaluated as well, making the assessment comprehensive.

The authors recommend using standard tests, such as the Piers-Harris (1969), to assess general self-esteem problems and issues. They also recognize that assessing specific areas like those mentioned above is more difficult, mainly because that involves creating specific age-based norms for each domain and because human development may vary considerably in any one of them. The authors are sensitive to such factors as gender and self-esteem, as well as cultural diversity (although that term is not used) and self-esteem. Hence, they strongly recommend talking to others involved in the child's life: Such sources of information, especially that which is obtained from family and schoolteachers, can reveal important things about how a child lives out academic, social, familial, and physical issues that may not be apparent in the therapy hour.

In addition to identifying self-esteem problems, a good assessment includes understanding the individual's particular strengths (Fischer, 1986). This part of the process is important because it is easier to design activities or experiences that are more likely to be successful and rewarding if we work with existing skills. Finally, the authors suggest that the clinician should assess and understand the individual's cognitive and self-evaluative styles. In other words, the therapist should develop a sense of the subject's "private speech" or habitual thinking patterns, especially those that concern the standards by which the person judges his or her behavior. In short, the assessment process is a crucial one for this enhancement approach. Not only does it let the therapist know with whom he or she is dealing so that the program can be individualized for the client, but it also gives ideas about what is realistically possible.

This enhancement program aims to increase self-esteem by teaching the individual new age-appropriate skills to help him or her handle the demands and problems of life more effectively. Pope and colleagues recommend that the clinician share this intent with the client in words the client will understand so he or she can be a partner in this process. The clinician and client contract to meet together on a regular basis to do this kind of learning. One or two 30-minute sessions per week are recommended for younger children, and one or two 60-minute sessions per week for older clients. The authors also point out that the program can be done in group or individual settings. In either case, the therapeutic activity is structured in two ways. First, the process is broken up into 8 segments, each of which focuses on a certain kind of behavioral, cognitive, or social skill related to self-esteem. These skill areas are learning to solve social problems, developing positive self-statements, using a realistic attributional style, increasing self-control, setting appropriate standards, developing social understanding and social skills, increasing communication skills, and improving body image. The authors make it clear that the eight skill areas are arranged in a particular order and that following this sequence is a crucial part of the program (Pope et al., 1988, p. 41). So important is this point that it is stressed in the introduction to the program, then again as the single point of the book's afterword.

Second, the format for all the activities associated with any of the areas is structured in a consistent way. In other words, each area becomes a program module. These modules always begin with an assessment of the individual's skills, abilities, and potential in each particular area so that the therapist knows what is needed and what is possible. Once the particular skills that are needed to cope with a given domain are identified, they are taught by following specific exercises. Then, "homework" is assigned to the client, a technique that reinforces the new material and helps transfer it to the real world. Although all the modules are structured in the same way, an individual may need less time in one area and more in another until a satisfactory degree of progress occurs, so it is still "individualized" (Fischer, 1986). Note that this program relies heavily on what behavioral therapists call "homework," which means that problems are identified, clients are given new alternatives to try, clients receive feedback about their attempts, and clients apply the new alternatives to real life until the new skills become habitual. Such techniques make good theoretical and practical sense in a learning-based program because skill acquisition takes time and practice. Including real-life experiences into treatment means that learning may occur even after the program ends. In fact, "booster" sessions are recommended to "meet with the child to reassess his ability to use his new skills in a way that enhances his self-esteem" (Pope et al., 1988, p. 139).

Evaluation

There is much to be said for this self-esteem enhancement system. First and foremost is what computer programmers call its "transparency." A computer program is transparent to the extent that its steps are easy to see, logically progressive, and very efficient in regard to carrying out its purpose. In this sense, the program is genuinely transparent, even elegant. The steps and procedures are extraordinarily systematic in that there is a clear, logical connection between the recommended exercises or activities and the well-respected cognitive-behavioral therapeutic techniques, such as using positive reinforcement, teaching problem solving, and modifying self-talk. Finally, the program is structured in a stepwise fashion. This makes it possible to track progress by comparing initial base ratings with final outcomes.

The chief limitation of this approach for our purposes is that it focuses on children and adolescents in ways that are difficult to apply to adults. Children, for instance, have relatively little control over their lives, which makes it easier to create a supportive environment and monitor compliance than is possible for adults. Children also are more similar to each other than are adults. This means, among other things, that it is much easier to identify what is appropriate and what is not for a child of a given age than for adults, who are more diverse. Similarly, children are more malleable than adults: They are more open to change and positive influence. In other words, the program may suffer a lack of practicality in regard to using it with adults. Another limitation is that the kind of thorough assessment recommended is both time consuming and expensive. Although the program can be implemented in group format, it is unlikely that many institutions have the resources to offer this opportunity to large numbers of people. Unfortunately, there is little follow-up information or outside documentation supporting the efficacy of the program beyond that which is presented in the book.

Bednar, Wells, and Peterson: Enhancing Self-Esteem Cognitively

Basic Ideas

The self-esteem enhancement system found in *Self-Esteem: Paradoxes and Innovations in Clinical Theory and Practice* (1989) by Bednar, Wells, and Peterson is based on two perspectives. The first consists of concepts found in modern information-processing psychology, which makes it a cognitive approach. The second set of ideas concerns a theory of psychopathology and its treatment based on a combination of cognitive and existential thought.

After defining self-esteem as a feeling of self-approval, Bednar and colleagues go on to say that it is a dynamic phenomenon that develops as a result of the cognitive processes of feedback, circularity, and self-regulation: "Our model of self-esteem is based on four underlying assumptions, each of which involves *feedback* about personal and interpersonal acceptability.... In brief, feedback is a special type of information that can describe, evaluate, or influence performance: in our case, human behavior" (1989, p. 91). Two kinds of feedback seem to be most important in relation to the development of self-esteem. Information about our behavior and selves that comes from others (or the social environment in general) is called external, or interpersonal, feedback. This kind of information includes many of the social factors affecting self-esteem we found in reviewing the research, such as gender and cultural influences. The other form, called internal feedback, comes from our own experience, especially the evaluations we make of our own behavior and of ourselves. Both kinds of information play a role in regulating our actions, but internal feedback is more important because it is affective, which is to say stronger, more direct, and difficult to dismiss. Bednar and colleagues also maintain that reality is such that most of us face more negative sources of feedback about ourselves than positive sources. Because it is less frequent, they conclude, positive feedback is more important than negative. This internal/external, positive/negative feedback system is constantly operating and continually provides information to us about ourselves and what we are like. At some point in the developmental process, however, these feedback systems become self-regulating and therefore relatively stable. At that point, we achieve a degree of positive or negative self-esteem and seek to maintain it, much as Epstein described earlier.

The other major process affecting the development of self-esteem is the individual's "response style," or how a person characteristically responds to psychological threat or conflict. According to this view, such stress (or what other theories call anxiety) is an inevitable part of life. Although they can vary in terms of intensity and frequency, there are two opposing ways to deal with stressors: People can respond to psychological threat by attempting either to avoid or to cope with it, and each alternative has powerful consequences for self-esteem. Avoidance, for instance, is a form of denial, which makes it an immature, defensive response when compared to coping, which is mature and realistic. Probably because it seems to promise less pain initially, avoidance is the path of least resistance in dealing with threat and anxiety. But avoiding conflict is more costly in the long run because doing so cuts us off from valuable information concerning ourselves and situations.

> It is as though we try to say to ourselves that this is too unpleasant to be true and then proceed to act as though it were not. However, there must be some recognition of the possibility of truth; otherwise there would be no threat that would mobilize the defenses. . . . Obviously the prospects for personal growth are virtually nonexistent when the individual's response to threat is *to deny that which it has already glimpsed to be true.* (Bednar et al., 1989, p. 74)

Avoidance makes it very difficult to make realistic and effective decisions about what needs to be done, not to mention that important possibilities for growth are missed.

Moreover, excessive avoidance leads to chronic defensiveness, which creates its own burden: In turning away from the truth, we are trapped by it, because now we must manage both the conflict and the false solution we offer it. Ultimately, avoidance results in a phenomenon the authors call "impression management," which means having to maintain a facade as well as continuing to avoid the threat that gave rise to it. This stance toward the world and others requires a massive expenditure of perceptual, psychological, and behavioral energies. The more we choose avoiding over coping, the more likely serious distortions and unrealistic behaviors are to occur. The development of positive self-esteem becomes extremely difficult under such conditions. If impression management continues long enough, then low self-esteem develops— and with it an increased sensitivity to threat or even the possibility of threat. Eventually, this self-fulfilling prophecy leads to more serious difficulties, including the development of abnormal or pathological behavior.

Of course, the healthy way to deal with conflict is to cope with it, which, according to Bednar and colleagues, requires considerable effort, even courage. For coping means facing the problem honestly, tolerating discomfort and uncertainty while doing so, taking psychological risks associated with being open to self-awareness about shortcomings, and, above all, accepting responsibility for one's actions. These are the existential components of self-esteem. The authors maintain that although human beings both cope with and avoid conflict, they tend to develop a "response style" that favors one or the other over time through the process of "reciprocal determinism" (a version of the concept of a self-fulfilling prophecy).

From this position, changing self-esteem must be based on the laws governing feedback, circularity, and self-regulation. The authors point out, for instance, that in order to survive, systems can never really be completely closed; they must always maintain the ability to adapt to changes in the environment, because change is an environmental fact. Hence, new kinds of feedback can affect old patterns. If this influence becomes strong enough, relatively significant changes may occur. It is even possible for new homeostatic balance to be reached. In regard to self-esteem, then, if we can change the coping versus avoiding ratio in a favorable direction, there should be a corresponding change in the quality of self-evaluations. If this new and positive information occurs frequently or powerfully enough, then the self-fulfilling nature of the system should lead to higher levels of self-esteem, which, in turn, should lead to healthier, more rewarding functioning. Instead of a vicious cycle, the same dynamics of feedback, circularity, and self-regulation set up a virtuous one.

System and Techniques

It is interesting to note that although this approach understands self-esteem largely in cognitive terms, the techniques of change lean toward existential practices. Of course, these two perspectives are inherently at odds with each other philosophically, because the concept of free will is essential to the humanistic position but strongly opposed by cognitive psychology. Even so, the central task is to reduce the degree to which a person engages in behavior (including thoughts and feelings) that promotes avoiding problems and to simultaneously strengthen the individual's capacity to cope with them. Because Bednar and colleagues recognize that there are affective, behavioral, and cognitive factors that make up experience, they structure clinical activities so that they intervene on all three levels: "The easiest way to do this is to deal with psychological events as they occur in the 'here-and-now,' which allows immediate access to the thoughts and feelings that accompany behavior as it occurs" (Bednar et al., 1989, p. 173). This present-centered focus is characteristic of existential encounter.

In short, the therapeutic methods used to enhance self-esteem in this approach emphasize "experiential" learning, which means that the therapy focuses on how the client actually avoids conflicts and problems, especially as they arise in the actual therapy session:

Experiential learning, then, is the crucial consideration in helping clients come to a fuller realization of their self-defeating patterns of avoidance. We are continually looking for opportunities during the therapy hour to "catch" the client fully engaged in a "Catch-22," or paradox. Our assumption is that when personal learning takes place simultaneously at a cognitive, behavioral, and affective level, it has more psychological impact than when these domains are insulated from each other. (Bednar et al., 1989, p. 174)

The process of change this program offers involves mastering four reasonably specific, indispensable steps. First, it is necessary to identify the client's dominant avoidance patterns of dealing with conflict, anxiety, or psychological threat. The therapist attempts to do so by observing how the client engages in avoidance here-and-now in the sessions. The aim is to have the client come to see these patterns for what they are, so after the initial confrontation, which involves pointing out the avoidant pattern of behavior, the therapist asks the client to name or label the way he or she closes off dealing with conflict honestly. Each such pattern is identified and named in this way so that the client develops a sense of ownership for his or her own ways of avoiding dealing with conflict. Second, the therapist moves the client toward identifying and labeling all the thoughts and feelings that accompany these avoidance patterns. This is done by having the client describe, in as great detail as possible, such things as the actual behavior involved in a particular way of avoiding, what he or she feels when engaging in avoiding, and the kind of thinking that goes on at these times. Even though painful, this step is also best done in the here-and-now with the therapist because the material is psychologically fresh.

The third and critical phase is to help the person face the avoidance patterns he or she characteristically employs and confront the negative self-evaluations that accompany them. In other words, the client is asked to face underlying fear, cowardice, or self-loathing head on. Once again, this is done most effectively in vivo or with real conflicts that emerge in the actual sessions. The aim is for the client to encounter his or her own modes of avoidance as they are actually being lived. The act of making this realization and accepting responsibility for it often occurs as a painful event, but this pain is seen as a necessary first step toward coping. This new and honest behavioral response is also pointed out and focused on. The client must describe in as great detail as possible what it is like to finally face the problem and to try and cope with it. The therapist takes care to have the individual identify, explore, and label positive responses and self-evaluations, because doing so is reinforcing and because it helps break old cognitive and behavioral patterns. The final step is one of continued learning, or "gradually learning to cope with personal conflicts" (Bednar et al., 1989, p. 140). This step can be done in vivo and by using events from life outside the session. It involves continuing to identify, label, and experience the positive nature of coping over avoiding whenever it occurs, until coping becomes the primary response style. The authors conclude by pointing out that such learning is a process and takes time.

Bednar and colleagues offer specific technical suggestions concerning timing and methods of facilitating this process at each step of the way. In addition, they divide therapeutic work into two basic kinds of activity. The first, called remediation, constitutes the bulk of the program and is aimed at breaking the negative avoiding patterns. The other work involves strengthening what they call the client's "disposition to cope," a process that is "different from, and more pleasant for, the client than describing avoidance behaviors because it does not involve attempts to alter the personality in such fundamental ways. It does not call for the acquisition of brand-new behavior patterns or profound increases in the client's level of personal risk and responsibility" (1989, p. 209). Thus, self-esteem can be enhanced by conflict-free learning as well as by intensive work on problematical areas. In fact, sometimes it is necessary to focus on positive behaviors in order to balance the hard work of dealing with negative material.

It is important to appreciate that Bednar and colleagues specify that their program requires skilled assessment and that they identify two types of essential assessment activities. The first is called "process evaluation," which aims at determining "the client's capacity for a candid and realistic conversation about the meaning and significance of personal problems with a nonpunitive, reasonably astute professional person" (1989, p. 188). Because the therapist is looking for limits as well as ability, he or she is very active in this assessment. For instance, the therapist makes it clear that it may be necessary to actually push the client toward sensitive or painful material. The focus is on what makes *this* particular person defensive, how ingrained the patterns of avoidance are, and how well this individual can tolerate looking honestly at himself or herself. Process evaluation, which involves assessing how well the client is able to take advantage of the therapeutic process, is done throughout the program. It is especially important to pay attention to this dimension of the work at its beginning, lest the program move too fast or too slow for an individual. The other form of assessment focuses on what the authors refer to as an evaluation of "content and substance." This kind of evaluation focuses more on understanding the specific patterns of coping and avoiding that a person characteristically uses. For instance, it includes assessing what specific issues trigger these responses in a given individual's unique personality and life, and which behaviors he or she uses to avoid facing the conflicts involved in his or her responses.

Finally, Bednar and colleagues unequivocally indicate that the role of the therapist and the abilities of the person in that role are vital to this self-esteem enhancement program. In fact, it can be said that the entire process hinges on the ability of the therapist because he or she actively seeks to "make things happen" in the therapeutic encounter. Such an orientation also means that the responsibility of making sure that things do not happen too quickly or too intensely also falls to the therapist because either of these two possibilities could be harmful to the client. This approach to enhancing self-esteem depends on an intense personal encounter right in the office—and on client risk taking both in and out of the session—for it to work, so it is not a "soft" path to self-esteem. Indeed, the authors say that "[p]sychological anguish induced in treatment is the first sign of personal change in the direction of coping" (1989, p. 134). Experiencing the full impact of one's own negative self-evaluations is a necessary, but tricky, part of treatment:

> Intense personal distress can become a powerful incentive for personal growth and change if clients clearly understand that their distress is a result of their own avoidance patterns, which they have already discussed, defined, and labeled. For this reason, successful therapy requires clients not only to have a clear understanding of their own patterns of avoidance, but also to fully experience the negative self-evaluative thoughts and feelings that accompany these behavior patterns. This is usually the most distressing point in therapy. . . . This entire process is based on a high level of emotional arousal and intensity for clients. . . (p. 134)

The authors take great pain to show the need for such intensity in treatment. In fact, they list nine qualities of both the therapy and the therapist that characterize this approach, and some of them are very active processes, indeed. Therefore, they strenuously advise against moving too fast or too hard, because doing so can be genuinely harmful to the client. Bednar and colleagues clearly emphasize the need for the program to be offered by a highly skilled, experienced therapist.

Evaluation

There are some very good things to say about this approach. Its most important and distinguishing feature is probably that it is an explicitly clinical program: More than any other, it requires professional assessment and intervention by a highly trained individual who is capable of handling the vicissitudes of an intensive treatment process that involves risk taking both in and out of sessions. Another advantage the program offers is that it is capable of addressing the more serious self-esteem problems: The combination of intensive individual work coupled with a high degree of clinician expertise allows other conditions, such as clinically significant depression and character pathology, to be treated at the same time as work is done on self-esteem. Also, multiple authorship means that more than one perspective is brought to bear on developing the approach: The authors point out that their theory has been supported by some 30 years of combined clinical experience.

The weaknesses or limits of this clinical approach are largely practical. For one thing, it can be difficult to tell how much of what is offered is designed to enhance self-esteem and how much of what Bednar and colleagues describe is directed at developing the general theory of abnormal behavior advanced in the book. There is nothing inherently wrong with a combined program or purpose, but it is a complicating factor for our purposes, which is to concentrate on self-esteem. Another and more important issue to consider is that the very thing that makes this approach so powerful also limits its usefulness: The program is very clinical. One problem related to this characteristic of the approach is that such a program requires and relies on a highly trained and experienced clinician. Of course, this means that it is likely to be expensive, which is a severe limit for many agencies and individuals. Even though the authors point out that some low-level general workshops are possible, the approach cannot be readily offered to large numbers of people. Similarly, it is a long-term program, which means that it takes time and commitment to complete, and not all clients and mental health centers have the resources to respond to these needs. Finally, the program's intensive, individualized, and psychotherapeutic structure makes it difficult to do follow-up research and/or independent corroboration. Although significant, these limits are relatively easy to see. I must point out in all fairness that at least some of these weaknesses may be addressed in the second edition of the book, which was written by two of the original authors (Bednar & Peterson, 1995) and which is not being examined here.

A Note on Burns' "10 Days to Self-Esteem"

There is one more self-esteem enhancement program that I feel I must at least mention, although it may not fit the criteria I have been using. There are two reasons David Burns' cognitively oriented *Ten Days to*

Self-Esteem (1993a) and its companion, *Ten Days to Self-Esteem: The Leader's Manual* (1993b), deserve attention. First, the program is a systematic approach to dealing with problems related to self-esteem, like excessive anxiety and depression. Burns defines self-esteem in terms of worthiness, then presents 10 sessions or steps aimed at enhancing self-esteem or removing obstacles that interfere with it. These steps are arranged in a sequential order and are worked in a self-help or a group setting. They are "The Price of Happiness" (which involves introducing the program, assessing problem areas, and finding out what one has to do to change), "You FEEL the Way You THINK" (an introduction to cognitive principles of behavior and changing it), "You Can CHANGE the Way You FEEL" (which emphasizes learning about the difference between healthy and unhealthy feelings and emotional responses), "How to Break Out of a Bad Mood" (cognitive techniques to alter negative feelings and moods), "The Acceptance Paradox" (contrasting Western and Eastern approaches to and techniques of change), "Getting Down to Root Causes" (identifying one's own self-defeating attitudes and beliefs), "Self-Esteem—What Is It? How Do I Get It?" (understanding and developing conditional and unconditional self-esteem), "The Perfectionist's Script for Self-Defeat" (ways of dealing with a major set of self-esteem problems common in our society today), "A Prescription for Procrastinators" (how to increase personal responsibility), and "Practice, Practice, Practice!" (the need to work the steps in order to benefit from them). Each step involves a number of specific activities, including assessment and enhancement techniques, that help prepare the individual for the next level. Also, Burns offers explicit guidelines to practitioners, such as assessing individuals for group work, running the programs in inpatient and outpatient settings, and handling various problems (or problems involving difficult people) that frequently arise. The program even includes workbooks and manuals.

The second reason for including this approach is that Burns offers considerable evidence for it as being helpful to people. He is a credible author, having popularized cognitive techniques pioneered by Albert Ellis and Aaron Beck (Burns, 1993a, p. 6). Also, his program seems to be more thoroughly tested than others: It has been used with various populations, including those who are severely mentally ill, and is the subject of an ongoing research project (1993a, 1993b).

Although I have little doubt that the program will be successful clinically, there are two difficulties with it. First, Burns makes no bones about the fact that the program is a self-help approach. Although there is some evidence supporting this kind of work under certain conditions, it conflicts with the more scientific approach with which we have been concerned. For instance, he largely avoids dealing with many of the research problems and issues involved in self-esteem work that we saw in chapter 2. Second, there are some admittedly religious or philosophical aspects to the approach that, although interesting, make it difficult to accept in a more scientific framework. For instance, Burns says, "The aims of *Ten Days to Self-Esteem* are both practical and spiritual" (1993a, p. 10) in the introduction to the program. Later, it becomes clear that his ideas of self-esteem as a phenomenon appear to be a blend of scientific and spiritual concepts:

> I like to think about the process of gaining self-esteem as climbing up a ladder. If you feel worthless and inferior, you may start out on the ground because you have very little self-esteem. On the first rung of the ladder you develop conditional self-esteem. . . . Once you have conditional self-esteem, you can climb up to the next rung on the ladder. On this step you develop unconditional self-esteem. You realize that self-esteem is a gift that you and all human beings receive at birth. . . . On the next step, you can adopt the even more radical position that there is no such thing as self-esteem, just as there is no such thing as a worthwhile person or a worthless person. . . . This solution to the problem of self-esteem is in the Buddhist tradition because self-esteem is rejected as a useless illusion. . . . [T]he death of your pride and your ego can lead to new life and to a more profound vision. When you discover that you are nothing, you have nothing to lose, and you inherit the world. (1993a, pp. 186–188)

Because we saw that there is a connection between self-esteem and spirituality in the research on "intrinsic" religious practice, we can accept these ideas at that level. Yet it is difficult for us to follow them further in the format we are using to look at self-esteem if we wish to maintain a more scientific focus.

Summary of Findings About Enhancement Programs

Now the phenomenologically significant question becomes, what do these major self-esteem programs show us about how to design a good program? In other words, is there a kind of general structure that underlies scientific approaches to increasing self-esteem? Knowing about the essential components of such a process is important in two ways: This kind of information may be helpful in developing a phenomenological program and such findings may help us to evaluate the quality of a program with regard to existing standards of practice.

First, the data indicate that there is *theoretical consistency* between the major approaches to enhancing self-esteem and the general theories of self-esteem that they represent (or upon which they are founded). For example, Frey and Carlock's approach is based on a definition of self-esteem that is nearly identical to Branden's, and most of their growth-oriented techniques are humanistic. Pope and colleagues clearly build on social learning theory and practice, which are also seen in Rosenberg's and Coopersmith's theories. Bednar and associates identify their program as being cognitive and existential, and the techniques they suggest for enhancing self-esteem seem to be compatible with Epstein's cognitive-experiential theory. The point is that, with the possible exception of Burns' work, major self-esteem enhancement programs tend to have logical, identifiable ties to general theories of self-esteem, which, in turn, are connected to even larger theoretical perspectives in social science. A good self-esteem enhancement program, then, is set within the context of a general theory of human behavior.

Second, an examination of the data presented in this chapter suggest that *self-esteem enhancement programs are systematic*. Good programs seem to be structured in a programmatic or stepwise fashion. In each case, the program is organized according to clearly defined stages. Further, these steps are always arranged sequentially so as to produce a cumulative effect when executed properly. Moreover, each phase is itself organized in a particular way. Any given step in any particular program aims at a reasonably clear goal and includes a specific set of therapeutic activities designed to help the client reach that aim. Additionally, programs involve common goals or practices. The more notable ones include increasing awareness of the importance of self-esteem, dealing with defensiveness and resistance to change, changing self-defeating behaviors, and acquiring new competencies. When seen phenomenologically, each program stands as a path toward self-esteem which, if followed properly, will eventually lead people to higher levels of competence or worthiness. Among other things, this means that enhancing self-esteem can be a specific, perhaps even specialized, therapeutic enterprise.

Third, each major self-esteem enhancement program recognizes the *importance of assessment*. This component can be included as an informal process, as in Frey and Carlock, or a formal one, as in Pope and colleagues. Assessment usually works hand in hand with therapeutic work, so that they strengthen each other. Identifying how great a person's self-esteem issues are, knowing what type of self-esteem problems are being presented, and being able to adjust the pace and intensity of techniques to the needs of a particular person, all involve assessment procedures and skills. In short, assessment is an important part of enhancing self-esteem in two ways: It tells us what is needed for a given individual and helps to prevent us from harming people through any number of forms of misdiagnosis.

Fourth, self-esteem enhancement programs do not rely on theory and technique alone. They all recognize the *importance of the role of the therapist or facilitator and his or her presence as a person* in enhancing self-esteem. I doubt that any of the programs can be run successfully by just walking through the steps mechanically. Moreover, much of the process and outcome depends on the usual therapeutic intangibles, such as being reasonably caring, providing a certain degree of nurturing or warmth and acceptance, and being able to listen well. However, each program seems to require learning various skills, so the role of the clinician or facilitator in enhancing self-esteem is also that of teacher, coach, and champion, as the case may be. This means setting clear goals, providing workable steps to reach them, offering encouragement when necessary, and above all, being sensitive to the "teachable moment" (Havighurst, 1972). Enhancing self-esteem, then, seems more active than many traditional therapies.

The fifth and final finding about self-esteem enhancement programs is that there is a useful degree of *clinical diversity* present among these systems. For instance, Frey and Carlock's program is extremely flexible. It can be used with many kinds of individuals, providing they are basically healthy, and can easily be done in group or individual formats. Pope and colleagues offer ways to set up highly structured programs, which are helpful in dealing with special populations such as children or specially challenged individuals. And Bednar and associates clear a path to dealing with more serious self-esteem problems that require intensive and lengthy treatment. In being faithful to the phenomenon, then, I have to conclude that there may be a number of ways to enhance self-esteem. Each one seems to show us something about the path to increasing self-esteem and, because each view is perspectival (has its own unique strengths and weaknesses), we probably need them all. Now let us see how this search through the various territories of self-esteem can lead to a comprehensive, practical, credible phenomenological theory of self-esteem.

A Phenomenological
Theory of Self-Esteem

Our investigation of major self-esteem theories found that a comprehensive theory has at least four basic characteristics. First, it is likely to be grounded in one of the major scientific perspectives in the social sciences. Second, a good theory is based on a definition of self-esteem that focuses on worthiness or competence, and a better one is likely to be built on both components. Third, a comprehensive view of self-esteem addresses key aspects of the phenomenon: the fact that there are different types of self-esteem to consider, its developmental nature, and the motivational nature of self-esteem or how it is linked to behavior. Fourth, a fully developed theory takes us back to practice, which in this case means that it will provide the foundations for a systematic self-esteem enhancement program. I have already shown how a phenomenological theory of self-esteem meets two of these criteria: It comes from a legitimate scientific perspective on human behavior (the human science or phenomenological approach) and it is based on understanding self-esteem in relation to both competence and worthiness. Now I can turn to the third requirement and show how a phenomenological theory deals with the major self-esteem findings and integrates them into a genuinely comprehensive framework.

THE FUNCTION OF SELF-ESTEEM AS MEANING MAKING

We can begin by understanding self-esteem in terms of a matrix—a matrix of meaning based on competence and worthiness, as represented in Figure 5.1.

This diagram shows how self-esteem is created by the interaction of worthiness and competence, rather than by either one alone. These two "axes" of self-esteem stand in relation to each other, which gives self-esteem its dynamic character. The horizontal axis can be envisioned as a continuum consisting of a midpoint, a positive range to the right, and a negative range to the left. Competence is placed on this axis, because competent (or incompetent) behavior is easier to observe than an internal state like worthiness, so we can use this line as a way of rating how effective or ineffective an individual's behavior is in many domains of life. For instance, good performance at a particular task,

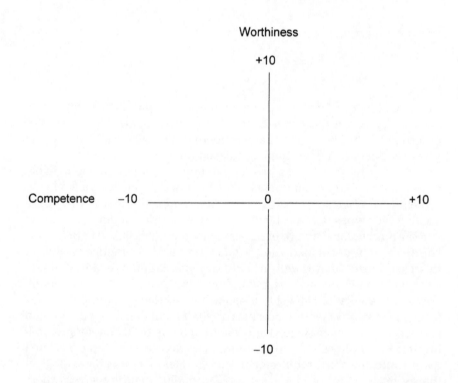

FIGURE 5.1 Self-esteem meaning matrix.

skill, or activity can be assigned a positive value from 0 to 10, and poor performance can range from 0 to −10. The result is a more quantitative continuum of competence ranging from low to medium or average to high as we read from left to right.

We know that the worthiness dimension of self-esteem is much harder to envision, mainly because it is more experiential and deals with more subjective matters, such as self and social values. But values are judgments of merit or worth in a given domain, which means that one either rises above some standard or falls below it. This aspect of worthiness is nicely captured by the vertical axis, because it can be seen as a hierarchy that is characterized by a midpoint and a range that is above it or "higher" in value and one that is below it or "lower" in value. How well or how poorly individuals live up to self-esteem-related values, then, can also be ranked. Those who do well in this regard would be placed in the upper half of the diagram, with scores ranging from 0 to 10, while those who do poorly would be placed in the bottom portion of the hierarchy, with scores ranging from 0 to −10.

Types of Self-Esteem

In the last chapter, we saw that there are four types of self-esteem (high, medium, low, and defensive), and a comprehensive theory must account for them. In order for the fundamental structure to be accurate, then, it must indicate how it is possible for there to be types of self-esteem. There must also be a strong correspondence between the characteristics of the types of self-esteem as formed by the theory and the actual characteristics of each variation as they are described in the research. Figure 5.2 shows that when competence and worthiness are placed in dynamic relation to one another as required by the fundamental structure of self-esteem, the result is the formation of four quadrants, each of which is distinctly different from the others.

It is not accidental that we encountered research on different types of self-esteem: They are inherent to its fundamental structure. The fact that it spontaneously generates four self-esteem possibilities means that there *must* be four types of self-esteem to research unless something is wrong with our understanding of the fundamental structure. Notice how a phenomenological analysis not only incorporates one of the most important self-esteem findings in the field but actually predicts it. Let us see whether or not the characteristics associated with the various types of self-esteem match up in the appropriate ways.

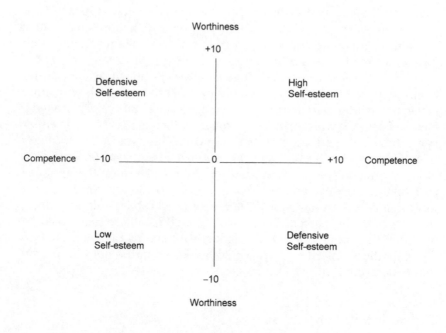

FIGURE 5.2   Self-esteem meaning matrix, continued.

High Self-Esteem

According to the meaning matrix generated by the fundamental structure, people with high self-esteem should have a good degree of both
competence and worthiness. This configuration is found in the upper
right-hand quadrant of the matrix. Individuals who have a developmental history that includes ample supplies of acceptance (being valued) or a personal history of virtue (acting on beliefs) would be placed
on the positive or top half of the vertical axis. Similarly, the more
competently a person deals with the developmental challenges of childhood or adulthood, such as dealing effectively with the tasks presented
by school or by work, the more competence we should expect them to
possess. Such a history would place them on the right (positive) side
of the horizontal axis. The intersection of these two points puts them
in the upper right-hand section of the matrix, which is just where they
should be according to the fundamental structure. Moreover, the matrix
allows for the possibility of a wide range of positive variation between

individuals: The more successful they were in these areas of life, for instance, the farther up the diagonal line of this quadrant they would move. Similarly, some people will have more positive scores in rating competence than worthiness, whereas others will have higher worthiness than competence scores, which would shift their locations in the matrix more toward one side than the other.

In regard to personal characteristics associated with this quadrant, we would expect to see people here who have been successful in terms of meeting the challenges of living over time, because they should be fairly secure about their worth and open to life or risk taking instead of pulling back out of a fear of failure. Their competence should mean that they react to stress fairly well, because their skill at solving problems is generally good, and the worthiness they experience ought to offer them a strong shield to ward off a good degree of stress when it does occur. Similarly, the combination of worthiness and competence should allow the individual the freedom to act in ways that are more autonomous and independent than those who are less sure of their abilities or values. Notice that all of these characteristics are associated with the research on high or positive self-esteem reviewed earlier. Indeed, if we look to the case of someone who is very high in self-esteem, near the +9 and +9 region of competence and worthiness, for instance, we might even expect them to have a harder time understanding what it is like to fear rejection or worry about the possibility of failure. The matrix thus allows us to incorporate the research on the problematical characteristics of high self-esteem.

Low Self-Esteem (Classical Type)

Because low self-esteem is the quadrant that is directly opposite high self-esteem, we should expect to see the converse of many characteristics associated with high self-esteem there. Where those with high self-esteem are open to life, for instance, we should expect individuals who have a low sense of worthiness and competence to be cautious. Instead of risking their self-esteem, they should be expected to behave in ways that conserve it. Thus, the research on self-handicapping strategies seen earlier makes good sense here, as does the finding that, for the most part, both high and low self-esteem groups have the same feelings about the desirability of success, even though they act very differently in terms of taking the necessary risks for attaining it.

The matrix also anticipates the vulnerability of low self-esteem: It is the weakest type of shield, so one ought to feel anxious, uncertain, or doubt-ridden while marching into life's battles under this condition.

Note that all of these feelings are commonly associated with low self-esteem. Similarly, problems with feeling or being competent should result in a reduction of autonomy and an increase in dependence. A history of failure or rejection ought to generate lower expectations about future success and happiness—unless the person is out of touch with reality. Finally, the further one travels down this diagonal line of decreasing competence and worthiness, the more severe or dramatic symptoms should become, which can account for things like clinical depression or worse. Thus, the matrix anticipates the feelings of depression and worthlessness that the literature associates with more severe self-esteem deficits.

Defensive Self-Esteem (Types I and II)

Remember, the research on self-esteem shows us that there is a type of it that involves individuals acting as though they have authentic self-esteem while actually suffering from a serious lack of it. This type of self-esteem is called discrepant, pseudo, or defensive self-esteem. Its primary characteristic is that such individuals may appear as though they feel quite good about themselves or their abilities, but they readily behave in ways not typically associated with high self-esteem, particularly when they are challenged in terms of their competence or worthiness. For instance, the research suggests that some people who seem to feel good about themselves actually act out on others aggressively through displacement when their sense of worthiness is threatened. Others may attempt to compensate for a self-esteem deficit by making excessive claims about their importance or by using success to cover up for feelings of inadequacy.

Notice, once again, that the matrix predicts that this "mixed" self-esteem should occur. The structure of self-esteem requires that both competence and worthiness be present together in order to create genuine self-esteem, so when one component is missing or deficient, self-esteem must suffer, too. In such a case, the resulting behavioral patterns will look better than those of people with low self-esteem because defensive self-esteem involves either positive competence or positive worthiness. The fact is that these kinds of self-esteem problems are just more complicated. For when such an individual is challenged in terms of the component in which he or she is vulnerable, behaviors that are not associated with self-esteem emerge, just as the research suggests. Indeed, the meaning matrix actually goes beyond traditional theories in helping us understand the research more completely, because it indicates that there are *two* ways defensive self-esteem could be lived and expressed defensively.

Defensive self-esteem: Type I. The upper left-hand quadrant of the picture suggests that some people with defensive self-esteem will have a sense of positive worthiness but not one of competence. These individuals, for instance, may be what critics of the self-esteem movement legitimately worry about when they point out the possibility of such programs producing children who think highly about themselves, but who cannot perform age-appropriate academic behaviors competently. Indeed, a child who is raised by a family that accepts low standards of competence concerning his or her behavior does run a risk of becoming an underachiever because the child was never required to develop beyond a certain point. The same result could occur if the child was "spoiled," in that whatever he or she did gained approval, no matter what its quality. In this case, the person might grow up to have unrealistic appraisals about the value of his or her efforts or achievements. Hence, an adult who has difficulties in this area might seem pleased with himself or his work, but there may not be much evidence to warrant such an opinion. Indeed, the matrix would predict that the individual is vulnerable in situations that require the demonstration of competence and that the person will become defensive when challenged in this way. Bragging about minor accomplishments, refusing to see deficiencies in his or her performance, blaming others for problems, and other forms of compensation or denial are all ways that this self-esteem pattern could be lived out and still be consistent with the fundamental structure.

Defensive self-esteem: Type II. The lower right-hand section of the matrix is based on a different kind of arrangement of competence and worthiness. Therefore, although it still represents a self-esteem problem, this type of defensiveness ought to involve somewhat different issues and behaviors than its counterpart. Here competence is positive but worthiness is low, so the individual still ought to be fairly good at doing things reasonably well. The person's history of successes may even be exceptional in any number of areas, such as in achieving goals or in acquiring influence. Much of the time such a person can keep busy enough with the challenges of school, athletics, social activities, earning a living, or managing a career, to avoid the abiding sense of doubt and anxiety usually associated with low self-esteem. After all, sublimation is a socially acceptable and psychologically gratifying way of living out personal conflicts, because others value our productivity or success. Furthermore, being very productive or successful can reflect some fairly neurotic sources of motivation if they are used to mask a self-esteem deficit.

If a person depends on competence to offset a lack of worthiness, he or she is still vulnerable to certain things in life. For example, the individual might become surprisingly defensive when his or her success, or even a symbol of that success, is challenged by a situation or another person. Because such individuals rely on competence to substitute for a sense of worthiness and are often very confident about their proven abilities, they are likely to react to such situations more assertively. Instead of withdrawing or denying the situation or threat, then, they may attempt to push through it much more vigorously than their Type I counterparts might do. Such behaviors may take the form of becoming obsessed with proving their worth through ever greater achievements (the "overachiever" or "workaholic"), using their ability to influence others to get their way (the bully or "pushy" individual), or even being aggressive (attacking others verbally, going for the jugular in any competitive activity, or, in the extreme case, becoming physically intimidating). All of these behaviors can be used to avoid a further loss of self-esteem.

Medium Self-Esteem

At first it may look as if we have run out of possible rankings on the self-esteem matrix to account for medium self-esteem, which probably characterizes most people. However, if we recall that individuals with medium levels of self-esteem have some degree of positive self-esteem, and if we remember that in order for that to be so they must have a certain level of competence and worthiness, then their place in the matrix becomes quite clear. Possessing some competence and some worthiness places an individual with medium self-esteem in the upper right-hand quadrant, but not as far up the scales as a person with high self-esteem. This phenomenon is easily accommodated into the matrix if we simply divide the quadrant into two ranges of self-esteem at the midpoint, as seen in Figure 5.3.

To incorporate the research findings on this type of self-esteem in a consistent fashion, we must remember that there are many more people in the first part of the range (0 to +5) than there are in the second part (+6 to +10). Actually, the matrix accepts this limitation quite well because it is in keeping with the standard distributions of behavior in general, such as intelligence, athletic ability, and personality. The "average" or most frequent type of behavior should cluster toward the middle, whereas the more unusual forms ought to become less frequent

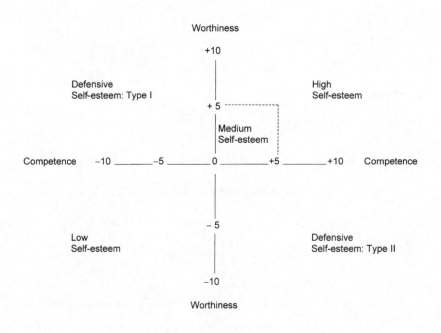

FIGURE 5.3   Basic types of self-esteem.

as we move away from the center. Once again, the matrix shows how well the fundamental structure captures and integrates what research shows us about self-esteem.

The fact that most people will regress or cluster toward the center on a given dimension of human behavior, as well as the fact that more unusual forms of behavior will occur in the extreme part of the range, allows us to refine the matrix of self-esteem. This step can be taken by making the distinction between mild and extreme ranges of behavior in the other quadrants, just as we did in the positive one. In each case, the interior areas are closer to the center of the matrix, so they can be used to represent the more common self-esteem issues people may have associated with the characteristics mentioned above for each respective type. This configuration of the information is represented in Figure 5.4.

Of course, people can usually get through life without working on such nonclinical self-esteem problems, but at the cost of reduced effectiveness or diminished satisfaction and at the risk of increased negative

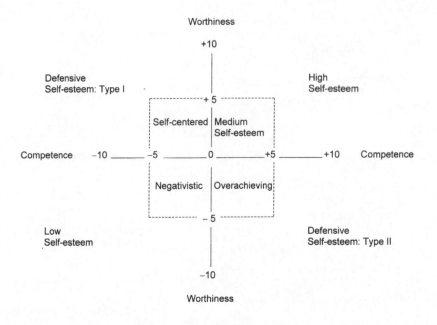

FIGURE 5.4   Nonclinically significant self-esteem problems.

affect or behavior associated with being more vulnerable. I must point out as a clinician, however, that these costs are painful, may be unnecessary, and are likely to respond well to growth-oriented therapies, so there is much value in getting into treatment to work on them. In short, being negativistic (low self-esteem in the classical sense), self-centered (Defensive Type I), or overachieving (Defensive Type II) does not warrant a DSM-IV diagnosis. These problems may take away from the fullness of life, can interfere with relationships, often are painful to live with, and are certainly obnoxious to be around for extended periods. However, they are *not* clinical conditions.

Clinically Significant Self-Esteem Problems

In more extreme forms, pessimism is a neighbor of anxiety and depression, conceit is a cousin of narcissism, and aggressiveness is akin to becoming antisocial, all of which *are* clinical concerns. Such self-esteem problems are presented in Figure 5.5 to show how they emerge from, and fit into, the matrix.

Because a lack of self-esteem is tied to several diagnosable mental health disorders, as I will show momentarily, those with serious self-esteem problems often require professional attention.

High vs. Medium Self-Esteem

It is important to remember that medium self-esteem is much more common than high self-esteem. When we look at normative ranges for standard self-esteem tests, such as MSEI and SEI, for instance, we see that fewer than one fourth of those tested fall within the high range, and some may actually exhibit defensive self-esteem. The bottom quarter represents those with classically low self-esteem, meaning that a good portion of us fall somewhere in between. The characteristics associated with medium self-esteem should involve a sense of worthiness, but not enough to take it for granted. This means that, although people with

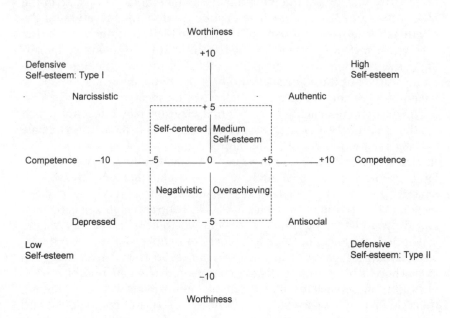

FIGURE 5.5   Clinically significant self-esteem problems.

medium levels of self-esteem may experience some anxiety or insecurity about themselves or their abilities from time to time, their quality of life is generally acceptable if not good. Similarly, it is reasonable to expect that such individuals are fairly confident in some areas of life, but not so much that they are as open to new experiences or as autonomous as individuals with high self-esteem. Although those of us with medium levels of self-esteem have many more good days than bad, we are a bit more vulnerable to life. The research findings also indicate that this state of being is not all bad, because some vulnerability may help make us more sensitive to others.

Because high self-esteem does seem to be qualitatively and quantitatively different from medium self-esteem, it might be useful to give it an identifying term. I prefer the term *authentic self-esteem* for two reasons. First, the word *authentic* suggests that this kind of self-esteem is genuinely high, which is certainly the case statistically. Second, the existential concept of authenticity suggests that such self-esteem is earned, not given, which is a very important distinction to keep in mind in understanding self-esteem. Also, authenticity implies a certain kind of integrity that makes the individual less vulnerable to collapse in the face of threat or adversity, which is supported by the literature on the relationship between intrinsic religiosity and high self-esteem. Note that this type of self-esteem seems to be the "ultimate goal" of much theorizing in this field and that it happens to fall into the extreme upper right-hand portion of the matrix—just where it should be if self-esteem is based on high competence and high worthiness.

The existential meaning of authenticity is especially important when we think about the research associating high self-esteem and violence that we mentioned earlier. The matrix suggests that it is incorrect to think about this connection in a simplistic fashion for several reasons. First, even the authors of such research admit that only those with what they refer to as "inflated" self-esteem are prone to violence in the face of threat (Baumeister et al., 1996). In contrast, high self-esteem is based on a history of competence and worthiness involving realistic self-appraisals. Second, there are plenty of people who face ego threat associated with loss or failure who do *not* resort to violence or aggression. There is no reason to believe that people with a history of worthiness and competence in facing the challenges of living will not be among them. In fact, when self-esteem is defined in terms of competence and worthiness, people with authentic self-esteem are more likely to have the capacity to endure challenges. Third, most of the research cited in this regard concerns work that is based on defining self-esteem in terms of worthiness alone. Not only does this partial, albeit common, definition present a limit to the generality of such findings, but there are better ways of understanding a link between self-esteem and violence than to associate it with high self-esteem, as I shall present momentarily.

In short, if we use the definition of self-esteem based on competence *and* worthiness, we would have to agree with Branden when he suggests that it is no more possible to have too much (authentic) self-esteem than it is to have too much physical health (Japenga, 1996). The only real problems associated with this kind of self-esteem concern the more mundane ones mentioned in the research earlier, such as some difficulty in being sensitive to the vulnerabilities of others with low self-esteem or in being introspective about shortcomings, but certainly not violence.

Low Self-Esteem: Negativistic vs. Depressive Self-Esteem

Moderately low competence and moderately low worthiness surely mean that the individual is vulnerable to challenge and loss. Yet we also saw that such a condition does not typically mean that individuals exhibiting such traits hate themselves or that they cannot function in the world. At low to moderate levels, we would expect people who live this type of self-esteem to display a "cautious" or "conservative" stance toward life, such as that which is associated with self-handicapping strategies and the avoidance of risk. We would not expect to see much in the way of general optimism, as Seligman (1990) noted. People who tend to see their faults more than their strengths, who are anxious because they fear others might perceive them critically, who are more attuned to potential loss or failure than to possible gain or success, but who also function adequately in relation to their families or jobs, are not necessarily depressed. However, because they focus more on negative possibilities than positive, I use the term *negativistic* to describe them. We have all known people who grumble about how unfairly life treats them, who are sure nothing will work out for the best, or who hold themselves back even though they could do more, but who also manage to maintain a good job as well as a meaningful relationship with a partner for years. Those exhibiting such mild but chronically low self-esteem may benefit from counseling or therapy but certainly do not require it.

As we move further down a diagonal line into this quadrant, a lack of competence and worthiness does become genuinely problematical. For instance, clinical significance seems to occur when an individual also develops depressive or anxiety disorders, which are two of the more common conditions we saw associated with low self-esteem in the literature. If individuals use drugs or alcohol to avoid dealing with low self-esteem, depression, or anxiety, then substance-related problems may occur as well. Indeed, I suspect that self-esteem issues are particularly active in the "dual-diagnosis" situation (Evans & Sullivan, 1990) and with so-called codependent relationships. Others extend this line of reasoning to see a relationship between low self-esteem and psychosis, particularly in regard to delusions of grandeur (Epstein, 1985), in that such a state may be seen as a desperate attempt to compensate for feelings of powerlessness or worthlessness. In more acute cases, the lack of competence and worthiness may even help move individuals toward a state of hopelessness when they are depressed. Hopelessness is thought to be a crucial risk factor for suicidality (Durand & Barlow, 1997).

I am not saying here that low self-esteem causes these conditions. Anyone who is familiar with the etiology of mental disorders knows that simplistic causal theories do not explain much of anything when it comes to complex behaviors (Durand & Barlow, 1997). Low self-esteem, then, is but one factor among many in clinical conditions, but few would deny that it is an important factor that should be attended to during the treatment process.

Defensive Self-Esteem Type I: Self-Centered vs. Narcissistic Self-Esteem

The self-esteem matrix shows us that a person with a sense of worthiness but without an accompanying sense of competence is prone to a certain kind of vulnerability in life associated with Type I issues. People who live non–clinically significant versions of these problems tend to feel worthy and competent but believe that others do not see the value of their abilities or accomplishments as being anywhere near as outstanding or significant as they do. Because this discrepancy cannot be admitted by people living this type of self-esteem problem, it must be defended against. Thus, they may underachieve in the workplace, for instance, and exhibit some form of excuse making, such as blaming others. Such self-centered people are often inconvenient or annoying if, for instance, one has to work or live with them, but they are not diagnosable, because the behavior in this part of the quadrant does not reach clinical significance.

If the behavior becomes enduring, inflexible, and a source of impairment, all of which are criteria for clinical significance in the DSM-IV, then we must think about how defensive self-esteem plays a role in the narcissistic personality. People who demonstrate a greatly exaggerated sense of their own importance no matter what their accomplishments may be, who seem to expect others to automatically recognize their specialness (a sense of entitlement), or who react far too strongly when someone questions their accomplishments demonstrate problems with self-esteem severe enough to suggest this personality disorder (Raskin et al., 1991). The particular imbalance between competence and worthiness associated with this quadrant can be so severe that the individual becomes quite vulnerable to relatively mild challenges. This development often means that they can become vigilant in regard to perceiving potential threats, as well as defensive much of the time. Indeed, there are those such as Levin (1993) who feel that increasing self-esteem is central to treating clinically significant narcissism.

If the self-esteem structure of such an individual becomes fragile, then a threat to his or her narcissism could lead to a strong negative reaction. After all, a fall from a high place is a frightening possibility; when emotions are flaring strongly, it is often easier to give in to the impulse to "erase" a threat than it is to face it. In this case, verbal aggression may be used to protect the self from further injury or collapse. Such an individual might even be so vulnerable that he or she resorts to something like revenge or other acts of aggression in order to sooth a narcissistic injury. This type of act can be a way of showing the other that we are, indeed, a power to be reckoned with, while simultaneously showing ourselves that we really can deal with challenges to our sense of worthiness (albeit it in a very sad way).

Defensive Self-Esteem Type II: Overachieving vs. Antisocial Self-Esteem

Earlier it was indicated that, at lower levels, the most common form of defensive self-esteem in our culture is an exaggerated worry over success and failure. This kind of self-esteem problem can be lived as "being insecure," which shows itself as a strong need to achieve or at least to avoid failure. In the case of defensive self-esteem, the related behaviors are based more on a desire to avoiding feeling inadequate than the love of simply doing something well, although both conditions may coexist in a given individual. Overachieving was used as the identifying example for this range of self-esteem problems on the matrix because such behavior exemplifies those who attempt to compensate for a lack of worthiness by doing things well (through successes) or by being approved of by others through the trappings of success (through money, influence, admiration, prestige, etc.). Most of the time overachieving individuals seem to have high self-esteem and would be likely to look that way to many people. After all, we value success so much in our materialistic, achievement-oriented society that we are all to prone to forgive the occasional outburst of anger, ignore seemingly momentary rudeness or indifference to others. This behavior takes away from one's worthiness as a person, so it is a serious mistake to associate it with authentic self-esteem.

If we move further down the diagonal line of this quadrant, however, we can see the basis for a link between defensive self-esteem and genuinely aggressive or even antisocial behavior. For instance, the research cited earlier linking self-esteem and delinquency is relevant here. When the ordinary routes to acquiring or demonstrating competence and receiving recognition of one's worthiness from others are limited, individuals may use aggression to attain recognition even if it violates the rights of others. The suggestion that the antisocial personality disorder involves a problem with self-esteem also makes some sense in regard to this type of self-esteem. The basic idea is that such behavior stems from a sense of self-esteem that is quite fragile. If, for instance, an individual has a low degree of worthiness and tries to compensate for it by being competent or successful at something, then ordinary routes to success may be difficult because they usually require starting out at the bottom, putting up with many frustrations, working hard, and tolerating setbacks, until success finally comes. Under such circumstances, "quicker" routes to success may involve such things as lying, cheating, stealing, and controlling others—all of which involve violating someone's rights. In addition, each time a person is successful using one of these "alternative" strategies, he or she demonstrates a certain type of competence that may be described as feeling like a "rush" or thrill (Samenow, 1989).

Another interesting aspect of this type of self-esteem problem is its relation to violence in general. For example, it is possible to see how defensive self-esteem can be associated with a violent outburst from an otherwise law-abiding person. If a hard-working, upstanding, seemingly "together" individual actually has a poor sense of worthiness, he or she may compensate for it through some form of success (a prestigious occupation, a successful business, a large income, a desirable marriage partner, or even something as mundane as a fancy automobile). Consequently, if that success or one of its symbols is acutely threatened, then the meaning of that threat could be experienced as a direct, intolerable personal assault. Violence always is a possibility in a situation where the individual is threatened with the collapse or loss of something as central as a sense of identity.

For those who are fragile enough in this way, then, a business failure, sudden unemployment, or rejection from a loved one could be interpreted as an attack. In fact, this kind of self-esteem dynamic may help to explain some of the seemingly senseless aggression we see in our society today, from murder-suicide over the end of a relationship, to assaulting a supervisor, and to some "road rage." Notice that I am *not* saying that all or most criminal or violent acts involve a loss of self-esteem. Some people simply choose to violate the rights of others for personal gain or pleasure. Yet it is clear that we can account for some of the violence as a result of defensive self-esteem instead of high self-esteem.

THE DEVELOPMENT OF SELF-ESTEEM

We saw earlier that self-esteem must be understood as a developmental phenomenon. Most of the material on this subject focuses on how self-esteem emerges earlier in life. We see in White (1959), Coopersmith (1967), and Rosenberg (1965), for instance, a clear focus on self-esteem in early childhood, middle childhood, and adolescence, respectively. More recently, self-esteem in adults has become a research focus, particularly in terms of the kinds of experiences and situations that affect self-esteem (Epstein, 1979; Jackson, 1984; Mruk, 1983). Integrating this material phenomenologically (i.e., showing how the research findings on the development of self-esteem fit into the general structure of self-esteem) results in a three-stage, life span–oriented developmental model. These stages are early childhood precursors of self-esteem, the emergence of a basic level of self-esteem during childhood and adolescence, and self-esteem as a major developmental theme that runs throughout adulthood and aging. I will discuss the first two stages only briefly, because the focus of our work here is on adulthood.

Early Childhood and "Pre-Esteem"

Because self-esteem is defined as a sense of competence and worthiness, and because these things require some degree of self-awareness, then it is going to be some time before individuals grow to the point at which they consciously "have" self-esteem. Moreover, relatively little hard research has been done on the development of self-esteem in early childhood (until about age 4 or 5) for several good reasons. For one thing, most experience is preverbal during this time of life, which makes what we know about self-esteem at this stage largely a matter of observation and inference. For another, even when children can use words and symbols to communicate effectively, the self (or at least some of the cognitive functions needed to think about oneself) is as yet largely unformed. Thus, I like to talk about the early childhood foundations of self-esteem as involving "developmental precursors" of self-esteem rather than self-esteem per se.

The worthiness dimension of self-esteem seems to precede the competence component, because by the time the infant appears on the scene, he or she is already surrounded by a value-laden environment that structures what is perceived as being good, desirable, attractive, or worthy (or unworthy, for that matter). The infant is also more passive than active at this time of life, and being exposed to values requires much less effort than actively exploring them. Gender is a good example of a similar dimension because, although the infant has nothing to do with it, he or she is labeled "male" or "female" upon his or her arrival into the world. Gender also announces a whole range of categories, values, and expectations that others bring to the infant, who can only respond to them.

It is also important to recognize that each perspective understands the development of worthiness from a different angle. White (1959) talked about "loveworthiness" and identification with parental figures or objects. Coopersmith (1967) connected worthiness to various patterns of parenting. Humanists speak of being accepted either "conditionally" or "unconditionally" (Rogers, 1961), as having a major impact on our worthiness, and so on. The fact is that the infant or very young child is influenced by how significant others react to his or her very presence, as well as by his or her particular behaviors. In a certain sense, then, the first source of worthiness we encounter, and perhaps the first source of self-esteem, is being valued by others. Later on we will have to accept ourselves, a task that is much easier if we have had "good enough" acceptance in the first place. Competence is also a part of infancy, but it seems to appear just after worthiness and takes much longer to develop. Although it is impossible to know exactly what the infant or toddler experiences while engaging in actions that require some degree of competence, it is possible to observe the parents' facial expressions when an infant does something successfully: The smiles of parental delight are sure to stand as a profound source of acceptance and approval concerning the child's worthiness as a unique and special human being.

Middle Childhood and the Emergence of Self-Esteem

Although some might argue that self-esteem forms in early childhood, I would point out that this position is not descriptively accurate, because it does not include the most important period for the development of competency. For instance, although children and their families are often fairly accepting of themselves and their abilities in the early years, the world of middle childhood is an unforgiving place by comparison. It is filled with evaluations of motor, social, intellectual, personality, and behavior characteristics. The classroom, the playground, and all the peer-related activities after school are arenas for a comparison of abilities and traits according to the external, and usually less accepting, standards of teachers and peers. For instance, who has not experienced being picked first—or last—for a team? The latency period may even be the most crucial stage for the development of self-esteem, because this is when children discover, become known by, and eventually identify with their abilities and characteristics. No wonder self-esteem work with children often involves evaluating their functioning in the social, athletic, and cognitive domains. These trials of "industry versus inferiority," as Erikson (1983) would have it, set the foundations for competence and the other half of self-esteem.

Age seems to be important during this period in the development of self-esteem. Each year seems to bring with it a range of new challenges at living and more sophisticated standards of worthiness at play, with friends, in class, and so on. During this extended developmental time, the child has many successes and failures, both great and small. Eventually, certain patterns develop and the child finds that he or she is relatively competent in certain kinds of tasks or areas and less so in others. Some of these skills are valued as being more worthy than others, which means that there is also plenty of individual variation in what could otherwise seem like a regimented process. By the end of this stage of self-esteem development, the individual comes to have what the literature refers to as a basic or global level of self-esteem. We must keep in mind that these relationships and processes are always reciprocal. The child's sense of worthiness, growing competence, and developing sense of individuality all play important roles in shaping his or her perception and experience. Consequently, past experiences with being valued or competent (or, conversely, being rejected or incompetent) influence how the child perceives risk, evaluates chances, determines his or her level of motivation, and so on.

By now, the developing child is well on the way to acquiring his or her own self-esteem type or style. The material we considered on the development of self-esteem indicates that an individual can run into three kinds of problems in this stage of self-esteem formation. First, a child can already have encountered major obstacles or problems in the early development of worthiness or competence. For example, such factors as early childhood behavioral problems, learning disabilities, unsupportive or abusive parenting, and social-economic deprivation may affect the development of self-esteem in ways that impede its movement toward a positive direction. Second, the child's natural competencies may not be relevant to the skills required for success in a given environment, or the opportunities for developing such skills may be limited, either of which could create a situation in which the child's chances for failure outweigh those of success. Third, there can be a conflict of values. A child, for instance, may want to try something new and exciting but may also have a strong preference for that which is familiar, friendly, or nonthreatening.

Various factors that help or hurt this situation include the nature of the gene/environment fit between a child and the world into which he or she is born, how observant the parent is, how caring a teacher happens to be, and how supportive or rejecting other children are. Those who find circumstances favorable because of one positive factor or another may move forward in their growth more easily, whereas those who do not may acquire the beginnings of a problematical self-esteem theme. In either case, this phase of the development of self-esteem appears to end with adolescence, which adds the final ingredient of identity and self-awareness. Although the adolescent appears to be somewhat open to fluctuations in self-esteem at the beginning of this process, the level of self-esteem acquired by the end of this period seems to be the basic sense of competence and worthiness with which the individual can begin to face the challenges of living in adulthood (Harter, 1993).

I have only sketched out how competence and worthiness work together to create self-esteem developmentally in childhood and adolescence because this topic is complex enough to be examined in its own right and because my focus is on the development of self-esteem in adulthood. However, there are many important developmental aspects of self-esteem that need to be explored. For instance, I find the possibility of a relationship between resilience and self-esteem to be promising. How is it, for example, that some children can come from genuinely terrible childhood environments and still become psychological healthy individuals as well as productive citizens? These individuals seem to thrive in spite of their harsh developmental histories, not just survive them. Similarly, there are complex self-esteem puzzles presented by the development of self-esteem during adolescence. On the one hand, for instance, Susan Harter, who is a leading figure in this area, points to an intricate dance between the formation of self-esteem in childhood, a reworking of this material through the developmental tasks associated with identity achievement, and the reemergence of self-esteem for adulthood (1990; 1993). Judith Harris, on the other hand, appears to attribute self-esteem largely to peer groups and other social factors affecting adolescence, while minimizing the roles of early childhood experience or parental influence (1998). I think there may be some ways of using integrated description to understand how both kinds of processes may be active in the development of self-esteem, but that is the work of another edition if not another book.

However, it is possible to give an example of how competence and worthiness can be affected by various events in early life. There are many potential examples to use in this regard, but I want to use one that also addresses a serious clinical issue that we mentioned briefly: We can use the meaning matrix to understand the ways in which sexual abuse can have a negative impact on the development of self-esteem and behavior. One of the most impressive studies supporting the position that such abuse does have powerful developmental, behavioral, and clinical implications for a developing person is found in the work of Swanston, Tebbutt, O'Toole, and Oates (1997). An advantage of pointing to this study is that it is one of the very few that involves a good number of well-stratified subjects (68), a comparable control group that did not experience abuse, and a longitudinal design that compared the two groups of children over a 5-year period. In addition to confirming the general finding that sexually abused children suffer increased rates of several types of mental health problems such as low self-esteem, depression, anxiety, binge eating, and self-injury, this study found that the difficulties continue over time. Such a finding is important because it supports the idea that sexual abuse can go beyond "just" creating a problem: It may become a developmental influence itself.

The authors also indicated that the findings are consistent with Finkelhor and Browne's (1985) model of traumatization. This view identifies four "traumagenic dynamics" that are associated with the "categories of psychological injury experienced by children who have been sexually abused" (p. 605). They are sexual traumatization (learning age-inappropriate sexual behavior), betrayal (feelings of depression, hostility, or isolation associated with the abuse), powerlessness (described as anxiety, a decreased sense of personal efficacy, and an increased risk of victimization in the future), and stigmatization (a sense of self-blame or shame).

These findings and this understanding of sexual abuse are quite consistent with the self-esteem matrix in several ways. Most important, the impact of such experiences can affect the development of competence or worthiness in ways that are likely to affect or distort the matrix over time. For instance, the first possible consequence is sexual traumatization, which means that one's ability to develop loving relationships characterized by mature modes of sexual expression may suffer long after the event. If this occurs, then one's competence as a sexual being is compromised. Similarly, being betrayed by someone who is stronger, trusted, or respected could affect one's sense of worthiness at any age. In childhood, being used as an object for the pleasure of another can also confuse the meaning of such basic concepts as "good" and "bad," "right" and "wrong," and thereby undermine the very sense of worthiness itself. The experience of powerlessness that may come with being threatened verbally, forced physically, or dominated psychologically could surely detract from one's competence at living, no matter what defensive maneuver one uses to blunt the pain. Being stigmatized, feeling "different," blaming oneself for one's plight, or experiencing a deep sense of shame in regard to such events could certainly detract from one's sense of worthiness or, even worse, create an abiding sense of unworthiness. Just as with any other childhood difficulty or trauma, which particular problem one may develop in relation to such an event depends on such variables as the identity of the abuser, the frequency of abuse, its severity, one's age and level of developmental maturity, the degree of social support present, an individual's personality, and one's resilience. These factors work together to determine whether or not a negative self-esteem theme is likely to develop in response to being abused. The same factors also determine the particular form the self-esteem problem would take in terms of low or defensive self-esteem and so forth, as well as whether it will be clinically significant or not.

Self-Esteem in Adulthood

We see how dynamic the development of self-esteem is even early in life. Even so, it is largely reactive in the first two stages because of the biological and cognitive constraints of childhood and early adolescence. But research shows us that self-esteem is a phenomenon we can be quite aware of in adulthood. We know that as adults, we are confronted by situations that evoke, are experienced in terms of, and have consequences for self-esteem. As adults, however, we also have some control of the outcomes such self-esteem moments come to have. Living up to important self-values (or failing to do so) and working through problems that challenge our abilities (or failing to do so) are situations that adult life may bring to us at any time. In fact, we can anticipate some of the more common self-esteem moments, such as developing mutually satisfying interpersonal relationships or losing them, either of which can affect our sense of worthiness. Similarly, we can anticipate the need to acquire certain behavioral competencies, such as those required by most kinds of jobs or for simply dealing effectively with the increasing responsibilities of adulthood. Setbacks in these areas, which include such things as a lack of progress in career development or financial difficulties, pose threats to our self-esteem that have to be managed. The major change between how self-esteem is lived in the first part of the life span compared to how it is alive in adulthood may be captured by thinking of the former in terms of *developing* self-esteem and the latter in terms of *managing* it. For although self-esteem can be increased in adult life, it can also be lost, and a good deal of what happens to this vital resource for living depends on the way we face the challenges of living over time.

Epstein has probably done the broadest work on the more typical kinds of self-esteem moments in adult life, particularly in his article entitled "A Study of Changes in Self-Esteem in Everyday Life" (1979). He began this study in the "natural laboratory" of life by asking 19 female and 10 male subjects to keep a record or journal of the events that they experienced in a given period of time in their life and to monitor them for fluctuations in their self-esteem. The volunteers were instructed to describe one experience that enhanced their self-esteem and one that decreased it once per week for several consecutive weeks. This data generation and collection procedure resulted in a large pool of self-esteem-related experiences. These narratives were then analyzed according to certain parameters of experience, such as the type of situation that triggered the response, the kinds of emotions experienced during the event, their relative intensity, and behavioral manifestations of the experience. Epstein found that two such experiences seemed to affect self-esteem most directly.

He described one such self-esteem moment in terms of success-failure experiences. Typically, these are situations in which individuals found themselves facing some problem or issue with which they had to deal. The relationship between the outcome of that situation and their self-esteem fell in the expected directions: Successes were associated with an increased sense of self-esteem, and failures were linked to decreases in it. The other type of self-esteem moment Epstein noted appears to be interpersonal in nature and involves what he termed "acceptance-rejection." Family, peer, and romantic relationships are the typical situations in which one is accepted or rejected in a way that affects self-esteem. Once again, these situations affected self-esteem in the expected directions. Finally, Epstein found that for both acceptance-rejection and success-failure,

[e]ach of the 10 dimensions describing feeling states was significantly associated with changes in self-esteem. When self-esteem was raised, high levels were reported for happiness, security, affection, energy availability, alertness, calmness, clear-mindedness, singleness of purpose, lack of restraint, and spontaneity. When self-esteem was lowered, high levels were reported for unhappiness, anger, feelings of threat, weariness, withdrawal, nervousness, disorganization, conflict, feelings of restraint, and self-consciousness. (1979, p. 62)

This kind of research is important for several reasons. First, it helps justify talking about the meaning of self-esteem instead of just its measurement. Second, such work demonstrates the value of using qualitative methods in addition to quantitative ones: Natural laboratories are different from sterile ones and there is value in using them. Third, experientially oriented work can help us to see the connections between self-esteem and various affective or behavioral phenomena that statistical analysis seems to be unable to detect.

It is important to note that Epstein's findings are consistent with the phenomenological framework. If we examine them in terms of the self-esteem meaning matrix, for instance, it is clear that the success-failure experiences are competence based and therefore can be located on the horizontal axis. Successes may range, then, from small (represented by a +1) to large (+10). Failure would range in the opposite direction. We would expect varying degrees of positive affective states to accompany increases and negative ones to be associated with decreases on the scale because of the pleasure associated with mastery and the pain associated with failure. Likewise, the way acceptance-rejection affects on self-esteem is compatible with the worthiness-unworthiness dimension of the matrix. The beginning and ending of a love relationship, for example, could be an example of such a situation, and its significance for self-esteem could be scaled on the vertical axis of the matrix.

Finally, the meaning matrix can integrate one more dimension of these self-esteem experiences. Epstein found that trends in self-esteem-related experience can be associated with gender: "Females reported more experiences involving acceptance and rejection, particularly acceptance, than males, and males reported slightly more experiences involving success and failures than females" (1979, p. 62). Because we noted earlier that other authors have corroborated such small but real gender-related correlations, we must account for this phenomenon in terms of the matrix. In this case we would say that, just as society influences other values, the forces of socialization can influence which component of self-esteem is most important for a given group in a particular culture. Hence, there seems to be a slight shift toward competence for men and toward worthiness for women in the matrix. Epstein's results also tell us that each gender needs *both* competence and worthiness to develop, have, and maintain self-esteem. Thus, we are talking about a matter of degrees, and not necessarily a large gap between men's and women's levels of competence and worthiness.

The self-esteem meaning matrix actually predicts that if individuals are limited in their ability to access either competence or worthiness, then they are more vulnerable to suffering self-esteem problems, because both components are structural necessities. Indeed, this situation does seem to exist in some people, although it might be more true of past generations than current ones. Sanford and Donovan (1984) pointed out, for instance, that the historical and cultural forces collectively referred to as sexism have acted to limit women, particularly those from traditional backgrounds, preventing them from acquiring sufficient competence-based self-esteem experiences to deal effectively with modern realities. This would mean that in addition to overvaluing being worthy as a source of self-esteem, many so-called traditional women fail to develop competence in the skills necessary for being successful outside the home. It is important to point out that the consequences of sexism in society also include the likelihood of a negative impact on men. Overvaluing the skills necessary for success and underappreciating the importance of caring for others, and being cared for by them, are damaging to self-esteem because they cut people off from the worthiness component. Blocking access to either component of self-esteem, then, is a significant problem for both sexes. It may be especially important to keep this limitation in mind in light of popular literature, which suggests that we are moving toward a society that emphasizes success for both men and women more than it does caring and nurturing (Sigelman & Shaffer, 1995). If this proves to be correct, then we ought to expect to see in the future more self-esteem problems associated with a lack of worthiness or caring than competence or succeeding.

Other significant life events can also affect self-esteem. For instance, in another study entitled "Experiences That Produce Enduring Changes in Self-Concept," Epstein (1979) used his ecological method to study personality changes by examining situations or experiences that act as a turning point in an individual's life. Here he asked some 270 volunteer college students to describe in writing "the one experience in their lifetime that produced the greatest positive change in their self-concept and the one experience that produced the greatest negative change in their self-concept" (1979, p. 73). The analysis of this data, which were gathered from almost equal numbers of men and women, identified that there are three types of such experiences that occur most often in adult life: having to deal with a new environment, responding to changes in circumstances that requires the person to acquire new responses, and gaining or losing significant relationships. Unfortunately for us, Epstein concentrated his efforts on understanding how these kind of situations lead to significant changes in self-concept, and thus went into the larger context in which self-esteem is nested: namely, the development of personality. Yet, because these situations affect other dimensions of the self-structure, it is safe to assume that they are likely to have a similar impact on self-esteem. Harter's work on adolescents (1993) also supported the idea that there are naturally occurring opportunities to change self-esteem associated with transitional periods in life.

Another set of self-esteem experiences to receive significant research attention focuses more directly on how self-esteem develops in adulthood. The experiences seem to involve a uniquely powerful kind of self-esteem moment that occurs only in situations with two key characteristics (Jackson, 1984; Mruk, 1983). First, these self-esteem moments begin with a fairly ordinary conflict in the everyday world of a given individual. Second, these conflicts mobilize problematical self-esteem themes that seem to follow one into adulthood. When both types of conflict become active at the same time, self-esteem appears to be put "at stake" in a way that means it can be either won or lost. Jackson (1984) likened these self-esteem conflicts to Freud's notion of the repetition compulsion, meaning that we are doomed to repeat them until we get them right. But as I hope to show momentarily, we can also understand the underlying dynamics of such situations phenomenologically as a part of the meaning-making function of self-esteem.

As mentioned in chapter 1, I investigated the phenomenon of problematical self-esteem themes using 20 subjects who represent a fairly stratified sample of American adults (Mruk, 1983). Let me briefly elaborate on that work in order to help us understand the importance of these naturally occurring moments for self-esteem in adulthood. The participants were asked to describe two experiences in detail: a time when they were pleased with themselves in a biographically crucial way and a time when they were displeased with themselves in this fashion. The experiences spontaneously chosen by all the subjects can be described as breaking through a personal difficulty or limitation (which resulted in being pleased) and failing to do so (which resulted in being displeased). Three of the subjects were then interviewed about their descriptions, which resulted in six research protocols (three instances of both types). The transcripts were subjected to a phenomenological analysis based on Giorgi's (1975) version of the method described in chapter 2 for two reasons: This technique is probably the most representative or standard format in American phenomenological psychology and it is a step-by-step process, so independent researchers can use the method to verify findings. The complete set of data, which may be called extended narratives, was then examined in terms of meaning units (meaningful transitions in the data) depicted in the subjects' stories of their experiences. These units, in turn, were analyzed for similarities across the subjects and the resulting empirical regularities were then used to identify essential components of the phenomenon or its "constitutive" elements. Such findings became the building blocks to develop the underlying general structures of each type of experience and eventually led to my first articulation of the fundamental structure of self-esteem (Mruk, 1983).

If you will recall the examples from chapter 1 of the men and women dealing with certain self-esteem-related problems in their lives, you will remember that these experiences show how a current situation can challenge an individual's competence and worthiness in his or her current life, but also reopen the individual's history concerning an unresolved self-esteem theme. Another example not mentioned earlier concerns a person who is desperately afraid of leaving the safety of the first floor in a building and will not go to higher floors under any circumstances. One day this individual's best friend suddenly comes down with a particularly life-threatening illness and is being treated on the 38th floor of a large medical facility. The subject describes driving around the hospital for hours before making a decision as to whether to "do the right thing" and overcome the lifelong phobia in order to be with the friend. The suffering soul drives and drives and drives. . . . I do not include the end of this story or the gender of the subject because I want to emphasize the fact that these conflicts are painful to people regardless of gender, ethnicity, culture, or economic background. It could be you, me, or anyone at all, because these are human dilemmas in which we have a strong desire to do that which is worthy, but seem to lack the competence to do so. In one way or another we all "drive around" them, not knowing what the outcome will be until we actually enact our decision and face the challenge, authentically or otherwise.

The identifying characteristic of these self-esteem moments is their dual nature: A situation that requires competence and worthiness in the present (the surface conflict) opens up an unresolved conflict from the past (the source conflict). In addition, the immediate or surface conflict always seems to involve a solution that is clearly "better," that is, more healthy, mature, competent, and worthy. For example, it is usually better to stand up for one's rights, overcome a fear, treat one's body with respect, face loneliness, or be there for your loved one than it is to avoid these things. Yet the underlying source conflict goes beyond the immediate situation in that it means doing precisely what one has become very skilled at avoiding due to a historically painful lack of competence or worthiness. In other words, the individual finds himself or herself at a crossroads of self-esteem. He or she sees an uncertain, untrodden, pro-self-esteem path leading in one direction and a secure, well-known, safe, but ultimately anti-self-esteem road leading in another. All the while the surface conflict relentlessly demands making a decision—right now.

The study (Mruk, 1983) found that there are six steps or stages that a person must live through in order to resolve such self-esteem dilemmas. The first three stages that a person goes through in becoming pleased or displeased with himself or herself are the same, so I will only describe them once. The last three stages are very different for each experience, so I will describe them separately. Being pleased or displeased with oneself begins when a person comes to a situation that can be called a biographical *fork in the road*. Typically, it begins when life forces the individual to choose between two alternatives. One of them is clearly worthy but requires a certain degree of competence. The other is less worthy or even unworthy but does not involve demonstrating higher or new forms of competence. The person hesitates to make the decision because, besides the fact that one alternative is more difficult to execute than the other, the individual now faces a personally troublesome, historically significant self-esteem theme concerning competence and worthiness that has been awakened by the situation. Notice here that since the person's history is involved, the surface nature of the problem need not be terribly difficult. Most people, for instance, can speak in public even if they are nervous about it, and visiting a sick friend in a hospital is usually experienced as a caring moment rather than a terrifying one. The second stage is a particular kind of *choice and conflict*. Here the individual becomes acutely, but not necessarily fully, aware that he or she *must* make a choice and that the decision is a much larger one than it appears to be on the surface.

The third stage is one of *struggling, movement, and action*. It is by far the most complex part of the process, primarily because the individual now finds himself or herself engaged in two conflicts: one which is situational and one that is historical. Moreover, the alternatives creating the conflict have competing motivational structures. One solution is positive and worthy: It calls the individual forward both in terms of handling the immediate situation competently and in terms of wanting to overcome repeating the unworthy and incompetent behaviors of the past. These forces are counterbalanced by those associated with the other alternative, which is negative in that it encourages protective, repetitive, avoidant, or inauthentic behavior. Here, the individual is "pulled" back toward historically familiar but ultimately constricting domains of incompetent behavior and unworthy experience. As the individual struggles between the options, he or she becomes more inclined toward one choice, based on what is going on at this point in the individual's life and the unique characteristics of the situation itself. Although gradual (dialectical) shifts occur during the process of struggling with the self-esteem challenge, the outcome could go either way until the very end, when the individual acts and begins to live one reality over the other.

Although either outcome occurs after a painful struggle, coming to the more positive resolution seems to be associated with how long and how deeply the individual engages in the process of struggling. It seems that the more the person understands what is actually at stake at both levels of the conflict, the more he or she is motivated to take the pro-self-esteem stand. Although other factors may be at play, such as how much social or environmental support the person has at the time, we shall see that this stage presents important possibilities for therapeutic interventions.

The fourth stage of being pleased involves moving into what I describe as *release, relaxation, and being pleased*. It is characterized by the individual's immediate feelings of release (the affective response), relaxation (a more bodily reaction), and a conscious sense of being satisfied (a cognitive response) with his or her performance in the face of this particular challenge at living. This step gradually gives way to the fifth stage, *meaning and affirmation*, when the individual experiences the consequences of the way he or she resolved the conflict and the meaning of his or her behavior. The surface or immediate level usually involves a sense of acceptance and responsibility for the task at hand, whereas the source or historical level is experienced as a shift in the competence and worthiness of the self-esteem meaning matrix. The result is that the individual comes to appreciate *already* being more competent at living and *already* more worthy to do so, because he or she has just demonstrated that fact both situationally (in the here-and-now) and biographically (in terms of the person's history).

Finally, *learning and settling* occur in the sixth stage, when life moves on and the entire situation begins to fade into the person's history. But it does so in a way that alters the story of the individual's problematical self-esteem theme in a positive way. Although personal history can never be erased, it can be modified, sometimes even transformed, and thereby lived in a more positive fashion for the future. The self-esteem matrix is thus affected by the meaning of this event; this kind of behavior is "added" to the individual's position in terms of competence and worthiness. The experience also stands as a landmark reminding the person about how to face such conflicts in a pro-self-esteem way in the future.

In contrast to becoming pleased, the fourth stage of becoming displeased with himself or herself in a biographically crucial way begins when a person ends the struggling, makes a decision, and acts in the unworthy mode of avoidance. The result is *relief, tension, and being displeased*, which means that instead of being released from the conflict and free of it, the individual experiences only a temporary sense of relief from having escaped the need to face the underlying conflict—this time. Rather than the relaxation and openness to life that accompany being pleased, the person encounters the tension and constriction associated with failure and missed opportunity in regard to both the surface and source levels of the situation. Often, this painful state is met with more defensive measures, so such displeasure may be buried, suppressed, denied, or acted out, none of which is to any avail in the long run and some of which can even make things worse.

As the individual moves toward the fifth stage of becoming displeased, which is one of *meaning and disaffirmation*, he or she begins to reengage the ordinary tasks of living. This particular situation and its challenge to self-esteem begin to fade, but in doing so they become a part of the problematical self-esteem story and may even strengthen or deepen it through reinforcement. Once it is psychologically safe, however, the individual tends to report genuine remorse, guilt, or at least regret over missed opportunities. Eventually, time moves on, and so the sixth stage of this negative self-esteem moment also becomes one of *learning and settling*. This final transition in the process is similar to its counterpart in that the event stands as a self-esteem landmark, which is why the term for the stage is the same. However, an important difference does occur: The event and experience recede from awareness, but they can remain alive as a signpost or reminder of how important it is to act differently—the next time. Therefore, although this increased consciousness can be helpful in dealing with such challenges more effectively in the future, there is no corresponding modification of the self-esteem matrix to help the next time the individual encounters these themes in action.

There is good and bad developmental news in the fact that such self-esteem moments are a part of adulthood. The bad news is, most of us will have these kinds of problematical self-esteem challenges to deal with repeatedly in life. We cannot escape the psychological vulnerability they create because it comes from who each of us is as an individual.

Indeed, most of us have several such self-esteem themes. For those of us with particularly poor self-esteem developmental histories, the cross of self-esteem can be hard to bear. The fact that there is no guarantee that we will resolve our self-esteem issues in a positive way is another piece of bad news. Sometimes life is severely affected by this cruel fact, especially insofar as low self-esteem is related to the clinical conditions mentioned earlier in this chapter.

But the good news is just as potent. For one thing, this aspect of being human is like a kind of psychological karma. We do indeed reap what we sow in terms of competence and worthiness. Self-esteem helps us to be psychologically honest: We cannot get away with bad choices forever. Once we know about the role of competence and worthiness in self-esteem, we have a sense of direction in life, a kind of internal compass that can tell us where to go in difficult times. In this sense, it would be genuinely terrible if we did not have a way of knowing the importance of developing and maintaining positive self-esteem in adulthood. Also, the fact that the fundamental structure of self-esteem is such that it "fates" us to face our particular problematical themes again and again is something to appreciate, not dread. It means that there is hope for the possibility of changing self-esteem in the future. In short, these two kinds of self-esteem experiences can give us a second or even third chance for development during adulthood. Again, I will take up the exciting therapeutic implications of self-esteem's general structure in the next chapter.

In the final analysis, then, self-esteem may be likened to a bucket or container in which we carry substances vital for life, as indicated in Figure 5.6.

Each time we encounter a potential source of self-esteem and take advantage of it, self-esteem is "added" to the bucket. As the research indicated, it does not matter if we find equal amounts of all four sources of self-esteem or not, just as long as some pertains to competence and some comes from worthiness. Of course, a bucket can be spilled, meaning that we can lose self-esteem if we do not husband it properly. Truly, it is up to us to manage self-esteem once we become adults.

REEXAMINING THE LINK BETWEEN SELF-ESTEEM AND BEHAVIOR

The last area to tackle in developing a comprehensive phenomenological theory of self-esteem is to articulate the link between self-esteem and behavior from this perspective. Earlier, we found that the cognitive

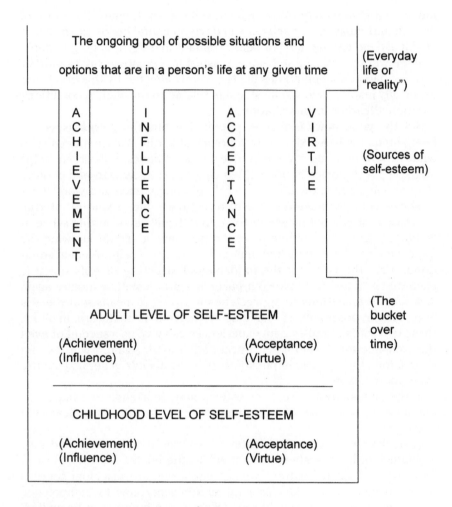

FIGURE 5.6   Self-esteem bucket analogy.

approach, which used the idea of the self-fulfilling prophecy to link self-esteem with behavior, was the most common theory to consider. We saw that one important consequence of viewing self-esteem in this way is understanding it as a kind of self-regulatory feedback loop. If this theory is true, then behavior is simply a function of what those in computer-related fields call GIGO (garbage in, garbage out), which is a way of describing the "dumbness" of computers and the mechanical way in which they work. Over time the "data" of self-experience assume relatively stable forms that are easily recognized by the brain according to the principles of pattern recognition. These patterns, in turn, help organize perception, inform experience, and direct behavior. Eventually the system becomes reasonably stable, then begins to work hard to maintain itself through various regulatory mechanisms and support processes. Change is likely only when these underlying cognitive and behavioral patterns are altered, which is where therapy is directed.

So far, the cognitive approach seems to best explain the link between self-esteem and behavior. In addition to offering useful computer analogies, this approach is capable of dealing with some of the more problematical self-esteem issues seen earlier. For instance, in this framework it really doesn't matter whether the self is real or just a construct. In either case, it simply serves to organize information efficiently for the organism and to do so in a way that provides a high degree of stability. Indeed, I must admit a certain attraction to this approach (Mruk, 1989). In some ways it is genuinely unfortunate that there are several problems that limit its ability to account for all the self-esteem data we have seen, because the view is a "clean" one that looks as if it offers real understanding.

First, in general, this information-processing approach is *reductionistic* (Costall & Still, 1987; Dreyfus & Dreyfus, 1986). That is, likening a human being to a computer, even a sophisticated computer, reduces the fullness of the person and the richness of human experience by making lived processes merely mechanical ones. For example, instead of making a choice, which implies a certain degree of free will, a person is seen from a cognitive vantage point as making a "decision." Even computers can do that on the basis of logic trees, parallel processing strategies, and so forth. Although such an approach certainly results in more measurable or reproducible results, it is not correct descriptively because it fails to consider important but explicitly human factors such as self-awareness and meaning. In other words, the cognitive perspective is fine for describing such things as computational processes and perhaps even modeling how basic organisms work, but to claim that human beings do it the same way is quite a leap.

Second, the fundamental structure of self-esteem tells us that the cognitive version of the self-fulfilling prophecy does not describe how competence and worthiness are actually lived. For instance, the self-esteem matrix does not merely "process" information; it makes information *meaningful*, and meaning, as a whole host of phenomenologists point out, is beyond computation.

Finally, the cognitive approach involves what has been referred to as the "ideology of control," or a fascination with manipulating things (Dreyfus & Dreyfus, 1986), whereas phenomenology always appreciates the fact that life is always richer than our ability to reduce it to mere understanding.

Co-Constitution: A Phenomenological Alternative

The phenomenological alternative to the self-fulfilling prophecy is found in the process of constitution (Husserl, 1970b), which is better discussed in its more contemporary term *co-constitution*. This concept is used to express the dynamic way in which meaning and meaning-making are fundamental, irreducible qualities of human beings. One of the primary advantages of thinking in terms of co-constitution is that it describes what actually happens for the person at the lived level of experience, so let us explore how the meaning matrix works as a constitutive or co-constitutive process linking self-esteem to behavior.

The process of co-constitution consists of three elements: the person, the situation in which he or she currently finds himself or herself, and the relationship between the two. The term *self-world relationship* is used to refer to these three fundamental aspects of behavior. On the "self" side of the existential picture, each person faces the world, which includes others as well as objects and situations, on the basis of the meanings that the individual brings to it from his or her past and present experiences with life. These meaning-making factors include a tendency to perceive events in ways that are compatible with one's cultural heritage, social background, personal identity, and individual preferences (including one's genetic and other biological predispositions); current degree of self-awareness; sense of agency (purpose, motivation, and free will); and, because of the meaning matrix, self-esteem. The "world" side concerns what a particular situation brings to a person in terms of objects, people, opportunities (possibilities), and limits or the constraints of reality. Of course, free will is always limited by reality, which is why some of us prefer the term *situated free will* over the more open-ended understanding of the concept, which is easily criticized by reductionistic points of view. Behavior is represented by the hyphen in the self-world relationship, because it expresses (or is the result of) the interaction between these two co-constitutive dynamics.

Phenomenologists fully appreciate that neither side is more important or real than the other. This is why we cannot be phenomenalists, who tend to emphasize the role of the subject in behavior too much to be faithful to reality. Nor can it be said that any situation announces endless possibilities: We are limited by the structure of our bodies, brains, and so forth, which is why I feel that phenomenologists should resist the temptations of postmodernism and pull back from declaring that inter-pretation is everything. Rather, both sides of the interface between person and world interact to organize, form, create, or in other words co-constitute human realities. This process of interaction is lived much more like a conversation than a feedback loop in that both participants (the person and the world) make room for certain possibilities to occur, shape them over time, and engage in a process of unfolding until they have either played themselves out or flowed into new scenarios. In short, the connection between self-esteem and behavior is *not* simply a matter of information flowing dumbly through circuits, even neurologi-cal ones. Rather, self-esteem is one co-constitutive process, among sev-eral others, and all of them are lived out dialectically. As such, self-esteem may have a statistically weaker link with behavior than tradi-tional psychologists might want to see because of their preoccupation with cause-and-effect relationships, but it is an important connection nonetheless.

Although this interaction may look like a feedback system that perpet-uates itself in the form of a self-fulfilling prophecy, the life-world of human beings is much richer than any mechanistic approach can ever hope to fully capture. Although traditional scientific concepts provide some insight, it is important to remember that they are often analogous ways of understanding being human, not descriptive ones: Information should never be confused with meaning, just as computing machines are not to be confused with living brains. On the one hand, the self-esteem meaning matrix formed by our inevitable developmental con-cerns with competence and worthiness orients us toward the world so that we are ready to perceive, react, and respond to it in these ways. The world, on the other hand, addresses us on a number of levels, some of which mobilize these structures of meaning and experience. When that happens, the situation "captures" us in terms of the meaning matrix and mobilizes us to respond in terms of worthiness and competence, which give self-esteem its motivational power.

Co-Constitution and Global vs. Situational Self-Esteem

One way self-esteem is linked to behavior, then, is as a constant readi-ness to respond to certain possibilities that may emerge at any time: those that challenge our competence and worthiness. Over time, the way we live such openness becomes patterned, stable, or "embodied," which is to say lived without thinking about it consciously. The result is that we become more attuned to certain aspects of situations and more disposed toward certain types of behaviors in response to them. This readiness to constitute situations in certain ways is relatively stable once we pass childhood and is lived as the "global" self-esteem various instruments seek to measure. However, we also know that self-esteem is only one force among many in most situations, some of which are more powerful in a given context, such as peer pressure or basic needs. Thus, it is not surprising that self-esteem can be involved in complex behaviors like school performance, relationships, coping with stress, and mental health, without necessarily being the most important or measurable factor.

By the same token, we have seen that self-esteem can have paradoxical qualities. One of them is that it can be a strong factor in certain situations. These include situations that involve dramatic changes in identity and those that invoke important biographical themes related to competence and worthiness. Self-esteem is thus both global and situational because the meaning matrix is less or more active, respectively, at any given time depending on how the situation is co-constituted for a particular individual. Indeed, I wonder what would happen to its level of statistical significance if traditional researchers measured self-esteem during what we have been calling self-esteem moments, instead of the contrived situations often used in attempting to assess it in relatively meaningless situations like the laboratory.

Understanding self-esteem as a small but steady force seems to account for more of the research than does trying to conceive of it as a pivotal or statistically significant variable. The latter depiction is poor phenomenologically in that it is not faithful to lived reality. That is, rather than being a readily identifiable or statistically powerful force in life, self-esteem acts like drops of water over time. Although its power is usually not significant at any one moment, a small but steady drip can wear its way through the hardest concrete. Indeed, a sufficient accumulation of small drops can eventually cause a flood. A phenomenological understanding readily accepts the fact that self-esteem is only one factor shaping behavior, but it accommodates the possibility that sometimes situations that evoke self-esteem can be meaningful events for an individual. In other words, self-esteem moments can either have a cumulative effect on identity and behavior, like single drops of water over time, or occasionally act as turning points that alter the psychological and behavioral landscapes very dramatically, as floods do in nature. In either case, the only true (phenomenologically descriptive) way to appreciate self-esteem would be to understand it over the course of a lifetime. Ignoring such a long-term process in nature would be considered poor physical science. Why should it be any different in a social science?

Co-Constitution and Stability vs. Change

The last issue we need to address before moving on to showing how a phenomenological theory can be applied at the practical level concerns understanding how self-esteem can be both relatively stable and yet open to change. We know that research concerning the development, assessment, and modification of self-esteem indicates that, once established, it becomes fairly stable. Self-esteem thus exerts a steady influence on perception, experience, and behavior in many kinds of situations. Yet we also saw that self-esteem can change fairly dramatically under certain circumstances, such as when large-scale change occurs in a person's life or in regard to certain kinds of crucial challenges. This situation is one of the key self-esteem paradoxes mentioned in chapter 2.

The term *lived status* (of one's competence at dealing with the challenges of living in a worthy way over time) was chosen because it captures the possibility of both conditions. *Status* implies a certain degree of stability, such as the relationship between income and social status. A state of being can be a fairly steady state if sufficient forces work to keep the phenomenon stable. The status of one's competence and worthiness on the self-esteem meaning matrix is relatively stable in this way, which is to say that it provides us with a "global" level of self-esteem in traditional terms. Yet status also connotes the notion of *relative* position, in that states of being can change if that which supports them is altered. The meaning matrix shows us how this possibility occurs at the lived level. First, there are situations in life that challenge our competence and worthiness. These occur with enough regularity that we can count on them to happen in the future. Second, if we do manage to respond to these situations in ways that demonstrate competence and worthiness, or at least more competence and worthiness than we usually do, then this action becomes a part of our living self-esteem history. Our old perceptual patterns and behavioral inclinations undergo the processes of adjustment in order to accommodate this new reality, and change occurs. Although we can never erase the past, we can transform it—but only by making different kinds of choices. Lived status, then, is a living status, which means that in addition to reflecting developmental stability, it is tied to the current state of our development and the world in which we live, both of which are inherently open to new possibilities. Thus, while a given individual may be primarily oriented toward maintaining self-esteem or protecting it, he or she is also always called to the possibility of enhancing self-esteem through growth. Consequently, what at first appears to be a paradox is actually just a description of reality.

The meaning matrix allows for two possibilities of changing self-esteem: in small increments and in large leaps. Although we strive to co-constitute the world so that it makes sense to us given our particular historical and social circumstances, the world can make maintaining stability difficult at times. It brings to us new people, different opportunities, or unexpected situations, all of which can disturb existing understandings. A few of them will speak to us in terms of our competence and worthiness and do so in ways that place additional demands on the forces that maintain stability. Challenges that are not too threatening are relatively easy to deal with, even welcomed, because they do not require a large degree of change. This is probably one reason why the research on changing low self-esteem suggests small incremental increases may be better than larger or sudden ones (Bednar et al., 1989) for people with extremely low levels of self-esteem. Indeed, we all can afford to grow and change in this way. But qualitative research shows us that situations can evolve in ways that force us to confront our own problematical self-esteem themes more directly and more powerfully, which means that they also present an opportunity for major or dramatic change.

Advocates of the cognitive approach who see the dynamics of self-esteem as a self-fulfilling prophecy often attempt to explain change by bringing an independent need structure into the self-esteem picture, usually some variant of the pleasure/pain principle (Epstein, 1980). The idea is that people are motivated toward higher levels of self-esteem because success is more enjoyable. This approach can easily accommodate the first possibility for change: Small victories can be incorporated into our self-esteem system fairly easily because they do not threaten it and because they feel good. Change is both enticing and reinforcing under such conditions.

But these kinds of dynamics do not account for the second type of situation, which involves sudden or dramatic change. One limit of a cognitive explanation is that once a certain level of global self-esteem is established, stability is a more powerful motivational force than change because other systems, such as identity, depend on it. If one system changes, then others must change, too, which creates a state of considerable resistance. It is true that if the self-system is overwhelmed by pain, then it might become reorganized at a higher level later on. Those who use this argument must concede that the results of such an event, particularly when it occurs without the benefit of a psychotherapeutic relationship, as is usually the case in real life, are just as likely to lead to depression, regression, or even acting out, rather than growth. Another factor weighing against traditional arguments is that pain is usually a more powerful motivator than promise, and we know that self-esteem dilemmas present very painful conflicts and struggles. Indeed, the biographic themes that make such situations possible are based on the denial or avoidance of underlying anxiety concerning conflicts with competence and worthiness. Furthermore, the pain is strong enough so that the promise of change has *never* been enough to allow the person to undertake it in the past, so why should the present be any different, especially if there is no such thing as free will? In this case, the pleasure/pain motivational argument would actually work in such a way as to help close off the possibility of enduring the additional suffering that comes with facing personal limits and giving up the security of the familiar for the additional anxiety of the unknown.

A faithful description of what happens in powerful self-esteem moments includes the fact that the world can generate situations that, on occasion, bring the past to the present and in so doing gives the individual the opportunity to alter the future on both levels of existence. Understanding the link between self-esteem and behavior in terms of co-constitution automatically brings with it a recognition of the full range of motivational factors involved in self-esteem, which means the possibility of growth as well as self-protection. Growth is a steady positive influence toward change, but it does not have to prevail; pain usually leads to protective responses, but it does not always have to do so. There is no need to reduce the dilemma any further because it is reality and the individual makes the choice concerning which path will be followed. It is important to realize that making a choice is a complex act. It involves an intense process of conflict and struggle as well as varying degrees of awareness. Making such a choice is not like a computer moving through a series of if-then computations.

In concluding this chapter, it is important to note two things. First, this phenomenological theory seems to meet the requirements for a legitimate approach: It is based on a tradition of psychological work, it uses a definition consistently, and it is capable of being comprehensive in regard to the data, sometimes even data that appear contradictory to other perspectives. Second, the ability of a phenomenological approach to integrate diverse findings on self-esteem makes it a fairly

Enhancing Self-Esteem
Phenomenologically

We are finally in a position to use research and theory to develop a practical, phenomenologically based self-esteem enhancement program. Remember, we must comply with the major design principles uncovered by the analysis of what constitutes a good program if that goal is to be reached. Basically, the program needs to be consistent with its own theoretical foundations and it needs to be systematic, which means that its design must include focusing on the processes of increasing one's awareness of self-esteem, assessing it for each participant in order to individualize the program, enhancing self-esteem through a structured series of activities, and helping the participant to maintain self-esteem gains after the program ends. There are good clinical and research reasons for building a program on these foundations. For instance, a theoretically consistent, well-structured approach gives the client and facilitator common ground for their work together. Such a format protects the consumer, because it requires the therapist to offer a specific set of guidelines and procedures instead of simply calling his or her work self-esteem enhancing, as I have seen some therapists do, or of just putting together a collection of human growth and development techniques and calling the package a self-esteem program, as I

have seen other clinicians do. Unlike more open-ended or general therapies, the steady focus provided by a structured program helps us to
avoid becoming overwhelmed by, or bogged down in, the developmental
and clinical complexities associated with self-esteem and its problems.
Hence, while a good program is flexible enough to allow us to deal with
issues like depression or defensiveness along the way, it is clear and
sequential enough to keep the sessions moving in a specific direction.

A theoretically consistent, well-structured program also lends itself
to more systematic attempts to gather experience and information about
it. One advantage of such consistency is that it allows us to observe
how people move through more or less the same process time after
time. This feature of the program means that I can get a sense of what
to expect as a therapist, when to expect it, and sometimes even from
whom to expect it. Such information can be useful in making the group
run that much more smoothly in the future. Occasionally, for example,
there is a certain kind of person, interpersonal response style, learning
style, or personal characteristic that can interfere with the group process (Burns, 1993b). In such cases it is advantageous to have a sense
of when that is likely to happen or to have a sense of what might work
best in a particular kind of situation. Similarly, running a reasonably
well-structured program has teaching value: It helps us to develop ways
of training other therapists better because we can identify common
stumbling blocks to learning in advance of when they are likely to occur
and offer suggestions to help people deal with them more effectively.
Finally, the consistency of a well-structured program has research value:
It makes building a database about the program possible, which allows
us to evaluate the effectiveness of a particular therapist or the program
itself. We will talk more about researching this system at the end of
the chapter.

Finally, if structured activities are a clear path for the facilitator,
providing a look at them in advance is like having a map for the participants. Thus, I give people an outline for the program at its beginning:
This "map" lets them know where they will be going and what self-
esteem challenges they will be facing along the way. Doing so seems to
help the provider and the consumer begin to see each other as partners
interested in the same quest, even though they play different roles. In
the following pages, then, we will walk through each part of the program
as it is sequenced from beginning to end. The handouts for the steps
that constitute this way of searching for self-esteem are found in the
appendix. It might be a good idea to turn to that section now and
become familiar with the material.

ENHANCING SELF-ESTEEM IN THE GROUP SETTING

The group version of the program is the major format for this enhance-ment system, so I will be talking mostly about running the program in this way. It can be offered as a psychoeducational group for nonclinical populations or as a therapeutic group for clinical ones. I will point out distinctions between the two when necessary and suggest guidelines to help structure them appropriately for each population. Both forms of the group are designed for about 6 to 15 people, plus a leader or two cotherapists. It is a good idea to keep a group designed to enhance self-esteem for clinical populations near the middle of this range as other issues are likely to crop up more frequently with this population. Com-bining nonclinical and clinical populations into one group is not recom-mended, because the latter often move at a much slower pace than the former. In either case, I have had the most success with groups by having a male and female working as cotherapists, but this practice is not necessary in order for the program to work. My cotherapists have been social workers, counselors, and substance abuse specialists, so the program is set up for use by a number of mental health professionals.

The other general parameters of the program are as follows. First, its basic structure consists of a series of five meetings, each of which is about 2 hours long. This length of time for sessions is within recom-mended limits for group psychotherapy (Vinogradov & Yalom, 1989). Such a period is long enough to allow people to warm up to the session comfortably and engage in some real encounter or dialogue, and to allow some "working through" to occur. Dividing the session into ap-proximately two 1-hour blocks with a short break between them seems to be a good idea for most groups. I have not run the group with people under 16 years old, nor have I run it with clients who have less than average intelligence. It may be that such populations would do better with shorter and more frequent sessions, as Pope and colleagues (1988) found with their program for children and adolescents.

Second, the minimum number of two-hour sessions is five. They should be spread evenly over time, such as by having five meetings at a rate of one per week. The number can be expanded, particularly if one wants to include assertiveness training or a follow-up session (I often include the latter). However, 5 weeks seems to be optimal in terms of making a compromise between having enough time to work on self-esteem in a way that allows for some change to occur and maximizing attendance in an outpatient or educational setting. On the one hand, we know that changing self-esteem takes consistent time and effort for it to have an effect. On the other hand, the simple fact is that most adults have busy lives and going beyond a limited number of sessions is likely to create problems with attendance, which would impede the group processes and diminish results. I present the program as if it is being run in 5 weeks, then talk about the possibility of a sixth session as a follow-up meeting.

For most populations, it is more realistic to create a self-esteem program that is brief and well structured rather than long and informal. This framework also means that we are best served by employing a few solid therapeutic activities rather than a large range of them. (We know that there are simply not very many proven self-esteem enhancement activities to consider, anyway.) People can always go through the program more than once if they have such a need or interest. It takes time to learn anything well, so marathon or weekend workshops are not recommended unless one is dealing with a motivated, high-functioning audience. I have also found that care should be taken to do some prescreening, whenever possible, even if it is only a referrals-only approach. Self-esteem is a very popular topic, and programs on it may draw people with much more serious issues. Such individuals may slow down or disrupt a general population group, so it may be more appropriate to refer them to a clinical or individual offering of the program. Finally, clinical groups, which often move at a slower pace and can go on for a longer time, may be modified somewhat by adding a few extra sessions to make sure that everyone gets a chance to process the activities and experiences.

With these general comments out of the way, we can now go through the program 1 week or session at a time. For each one, I will indicate the basic *goal* for a given week, identify what *materials* are to be used during that period, then present a step-by-step *procedure* to use as a method of reaching those goals. The handouts and materials are presented in the appendix instead of being included in the text so as to make them easier to use. You may want to modify the handouts where it is necessary in order to meet the needs of your particular agency or program. After doing so, it is possible to use the material for overheads or to distribute them to participants as a kind of self-esteem workbook. It is always necessary to provide the appropriate citation for these tools when copying them. The one exception is the MSEI self-esteem test, which must be ordered separately. At the time of this writing, the address is Psychological Assessment Resources Inc., Box 998, Odessa, FL 33556; telephone 813-968-3003. It may be possible to use another instrument such as Coopersmith's SEI or Battle's Culture-Free Self-Esteem Inventory, and such an alternative would be necessary should the MSEI go out of print. I have not researched the use of these instruments in the program as thoroughly as the MSEI, so making such a substitution would take some careful thought and would require some modifications that I will mention later.

The following information is organized according to the week of the program being discussed, so I will refer to each one by its title as it is discussed below. You can reference each handout quickly by turning to the appendix.

Week 1: Focusing Phase

Goal

The first week may be the most important, because people usually make the decision about whether or not to come back at this point and because it sets the general tone for the program. Therefore, we have two objectives here. One is building the foundation for a focused, supportive group. This means facilitating a sense of interest, comfort, and purpose so that individuals feel relatively safe but ready to work. The other is to raise consciousness of self-esteem and its role in our lives, which the research shows us to be the first task in any good, systematic self-esteem enhancement program. Ideally, the result of this initial meeting is to come to a common ground in terms of what definitions are being used in the program and what kinds of work we will be doing together. I want each member to leave the session feeling stimulated to learn about self-esteem and excited about coming back to find out more the next time.

Materials

The following sections of the workbook will be covered this week in the order in which they are presented. Note that the leader can create a cover page if desired.

1. Week 1—Handout 1: Self-Esteem Enhancement: Program Announcement. This statement simply makes it known that the program is available. It can be circulated among colleagues, to potential patient populations, or to the general population, depending on the setting in which one is going to be working. The announcement makes it clear that we are working on self-esteem and not other issues. It can be written on professional stationery and modified as needed.

2. Week 1—Handout 2: Activity Schedule. This handout is the basic "road map" of the program in that it allows people to see where they will be going if they participate in the program.
3. Week 1—Handout 3: Group Guidelines and Expectations. This handout consists of the rules governing the group and the interaction between its members. The guidelines are intended to help establish a supportive, respectful code of conduct. They can also be helpful in confronting and limiting destructive or inappropriate behavior. The information is intended to facilitate the group process, encourage pro-self-esteem behavior, and address some possible legal/ethical issues in advance.
4. Week 1—Handout 4: Defining Self-Esteem. The first stage of an enhancement program concerns increasing one's awareness of self-esteem. This exercise does that by helping us to think about what self-esteem is and by taking some time to focus on competence and worthiness as we actually live them in daily life.
5. Week 1—Self-Esteem Journal. The facilitator can either hand out notebooks or ask participants to buy one to use exclusively for this purpose. I recommend providing a notebook to the clients, as that tends to make the program seem more professional and may actually motivate people to keep such a journal.
6. Week 1—Multidimensional Self-Esteem Inventory. (The MSEI is currently available through Psychological Assessment Resources Inc. at the address mentioned earlier.) This test, or something like it, is essential to the program. The leader should order this instrument well in advance. Its cost is relatively low, and its format can easily be worked into a group setting. Those who do not care for this test for whatever reason should consider using Coopersmith's Self-Esteem Inventory, because its questions can be divided into those that concern competence and those that concern worthiness. This test is much easier to use, but it lacks a scale for defensiveness. Therefore, using it would require modifying some tasks in the program in ways that I have not tested thoroughly.

Procedure

This is a busy session because it serves several important functions, such as organizing the group, taking care of various administrative tasks, and beginning the program. I usually find it helpful to develop a brief program announcement, such as the Self-Esteem Enhancement: Program Announcement (Week 1—Handout 1). This simple device is a convenient way of letting an agency or other therapists know that I am starting a new group and when it will be running, so that they can refer appropriate patients to it. The handout can also serve as a recruitment instrument.

After the group has been announced and is gathered together for the first time, I ask everyone to sit in a semicircle so that we all may see each other. The materials are then distributed to each person. The room is always equipped with an overhead projector and chalkboard (or a flip chart with lots of blank pages), as we will need such tools to do some of the exercises. I typically introduce myself first and offer the participants a warm welcome to the "exciting search for self-esteem that we will embark upon together over the next 5 exciting weeks." This introduction includes letting them know a little about my credentials, background, and preference for a scientific approach to enhancing self-esteem. I usually close with some information about my own self-esteem issues and the work I am doing on them so they can know I struggle with self-esteem, too. The use of humor whenever possible is beneficial, and I often use cartoons to illustrate points about self-esteem and its importance. However, humor must be used tastefully, especially with respect to issues concerning age, gender, and cultural diversity.

Step 1: Introducing the program. We begin by sitting in the semicircle and looking at the Activity Schedule (Week 1—Handout 2). This outline is used to preview the program, a practice that is beneficial in several ways. In addition to providing a sense of the lay of the land, so to speak, it can put people at ease. Many individuals are a little apprehensive, even anxious, about being in the group. Sometimes they have peculiar ideas of what to expect from a psychotherapeutic or psychoeducational group. Also, more experienced participants may expect too much from a group. Another important point is that many people who attend such groups usually have self-esteem problems. They may feel unworthy of group attention or may be unskilled, so it often helps them to know in advance what to expect and what is expected of them.

Part A is a general introduction to the psychology of self-esteem. I usually begin by sharing some of the more important research findings concerning self-esteem and enhancing it. The aim is to dispel some of the myths that are a by-product of the popularization of self-esteem and to give the participants a few key findings that they can trust. Although any facilitator is free to select the findings he or she feels are most important, it is often useful to stress the self-esteem fallacy so that participants will not develop false expectations about rapid transformations in their self-esteem or behavior. I do this by using the bad news, good news technique. First, I point out the bad news, which concerns the research findings showing that self-esteem is only one factor affecting any given situation or behavior. This tends to capture the group's attention, because self-esteem has become another buzzword and I appear to contradict my own purpose. I quickly follow up with the good news: Although small in effect, self-esteem is a constant force, meaning that while increasing it may not make a great difference right now, even a small gain can have tremendous power over the course of time, especially a lifetime. The participants usually get this point without too much difficulty and have already begun thinking about self-esteem more realistically.

It is not a good idea to spend a long time going over the research information on self-esteem. To do so takes too long, and the exercise is too academic. A few solid findings are easier to remember than a long list of weaker ones. Focusing on the finding that shows that the better self-esteem programs are systematic is a nice lead-in to Part B of the outline, which is next. This material allows me to emphasize that it is possible to divide a good self-esteem enhancement program into four parts (understanding self-esteem, developing a better awareness of it, nurturing or enhancing self-esteem, and learning how to maintain it) and to identify them on the handout. I also make some attempt to indicate the major activities that we will be doing for each stage, which is why they are included on the overhead or handout. This procedure helps participants to understand the specific steps that they will be making from week to week and that the steps are linked together in a way that has a cumulative effect. Enhancing self-esteem, then, is seen as a process rather than an event. I always end this step by pointing out that we are already in the focusing phase, because we are working on our awareness of self-esteem *right now*.

The next part of the introduction focuses on Group Guidelines and Expectations (Week 1—Handout 3). This material lays the foundation for how we will treat one another in the group. I always try to read the guidelines and expectations aloud in order to stress the seriousness of the enterprise on which we embark. This practice also makes sure that everyone is familiar with the basic rules that govern the group and reinforces them to some degree. The voluntary nature of the program and a statement concerning confidentially are mentioned in the introductory paragraph. Remember, the therapist is obligated to maintain confidentially, not necessarily the client. Therefore, it is important to bring up the issue of confidentiality and to be careful not to promise more than you can deliver. Similarly, respecting limits and differences is absolutely essential to our work, because recognizing the rights and dignity of each individual human being is already self-esteem enhancing. The same applies to the issue of gender, age, and cultural differences.

The comments concerning attendance are important because the program is designed in a stepwise fashion and it is difficult, though not impossible, to recover from missing even one week. In fact, if people anticipate missing even 2 weeks I suggest that they wait until another time to take the program. I encourage people to participate actively in these groups—learning and growing usually occur as a function of how much effort one puts into the process. However, it is important to let participants know that they are not required to do anything that feels uncomfortable to them, and to remind them that they must let the facilitator know when they feel that way. It may be wise to do this part of the program very clearly, as it may reduce some risks associated with liability.

By now, participants are likely to be wondering if I am just going to lecture to them for 5 weeks, so at this point it is useful to engage in some basic ice-breaker activity to help them feel more comfortable and to help them see themselves as a group instead of as a collection of individuals. I typically ask participants to introduce themselves to the other members of the group by stating their names and interest in enhancing self-esteem. There are other standard getting-to-know-you activities that can be used here, but simple ones seem to be the least threatening. After all, it is important to remember that some people are likely to be there because they have difficulties feeling comfortable in social situations. The step takes about 30 to 40 minutes. You can include a 10-minute break for refreshments if you like, but it is a good idea to have the refreshments in the room with the group rather than break it up.

Step 2: Becoming aware of self-esteem. We found that a good enhancement program begins by increasing awareness of the importance of self-esteem in our lives. An excellent way to begin focusing attention on self-esteem, and to achieve a common ground from which the group can work, is by defining it. The first experiential activity of the program is guided by the material found on the handout Defining Self-Esteem (Week 1—Handout 4). It is designed to help the group do its own mini-phenomenology of self-esteem. (I seldom use that term because it is too technical for lay audiences.) I begin by presenting and explaining a simple definition of self-esteem based on competence and worthiness, which is at the top of the handout. In Part A of the activity, participants are asked to examine their own biographies, both recent and past, for experiences in which they found themselves being competent and to describe one of them briefly on the handout. Then, they are invited to examine this experience and ask themselves what it shows about the relationship between self-esteem and competence.

It is important to take the time to ask the group members to share these experiences and what they can learn from them about self-esteem. I usually start it off by sharing an example of my own recent experience, then ask for volunteers to do the same. This activity helps people to see the connection between competence and self-esteem. In addition, the experiences are by and large positive, and sharing them is usually enjoyable. This work tends to help participants relax and brings the principle of positive feedback and enhancing self-esteem into play. The same procedure is repeated for worthiness in Part B of the exercise. This one can be more difficult because worthiness is more abstract, which is why we begin with the competence dimension. Usually someone will give an example, such as an experience of helping someone, and the ball will start rolling.

Often, the effect of this activity is surprisingly strong. First, tying a definition to experience makes it more meaningful. Second, having participants share some of what they experienced or discovered helps those who might be having a hard time with this exercise or with understanding self-esteem as we will be working on it. Third, this activity makes people think about self-esteem and self-esteem moments in their own lives. Fourth, this process of identifying, describing, and thinking about self-esteem is important because it prepares the group to write a self-esteem journal. I also let them know that there are other ways of defining self-esteem, just as a matter of academic honesty.

Now we have shown participants that they can identify, describe, and learn from experiences of competence and worthiness in their own lives. We have also helped them to see that these experiences are connected to self-esteem and to various challenges of living. The group is now ready for its first homework assignment, which is starting the self-esteem journal. There is usually some resistance to this activity at first, probably because it requires work and people do not often write regularly. Once again, I find it helpful to give a blank notebook or at least an attractively bound packet of papers for the journal. This courtesy facilitates taking the journal seriously and adds a professional touch to the program. I also point out that the group has just shown they can do this kind of activity because they described two relevant experiences. They are told that the journal is written the same way and that they should write on any experiences with competence and worthiness they have during the next week. The importance of the journal is emphasized by adding that they will be keeping one for all the sessions, but it will not be graded or collected, so it can be done informally. This step of the program usually takes about 40 minutes, with 20 minutes for each part.

Step 3: Administering (but not interpreting) the MSEI.   Now we are at the end of our first meeting. Sometimes, depending on how large the group is and who is in it, participants will either want to process more about their experiences or feel that they have worked hard enough for one session. Either way, I tell them about the research findings concerning the need to assess self-esteem. At this point, O'Brien and Epstein's MSEI (1988) is administered *but not scored.* The form can be filled out in about 20 minutes, but some people will take longer because of slower reading speed, which is why it is good to do the test at the end of the session when such differences will not require others to wait. (Be sure to have reserved the room you are working in for about 2 1/2 hours to avoid any time crunches, as that may affect results and does not set well with people.) The MSEI is the best instrument for this program because of the test's design qualities and compatibility with the phenomenological model of self-esteem. It is also set up in a way that can help us tailor the program to meet individual needs. Note that if you choose to investigate another instrument, it will be necessary to modify this activity to accommodate the new instrument. It is important to have the testing done this first week because it stimulates participant's curiosity about themselves and encourages them to come back, if only to find out their "results." We do a lot of work in this session, which usually takes about two hours, although it is sometimes necessary to wait a while longer for someone to finish the MSEI.

Week 2: Awareness Phase (Appreciating Self-Esteem)

Goal

The second week continues the process of increasing awareness as a first step toward enhancing self-esteem. The goal is to raise consciousness concerning the nature of self-esteem, its value, and the sources of this vital psychosocial resource. Our objectives in this work include becoming aware of the basic types of self-esteem, appreciating their related problems, and identifying individual self-esteem strengths and weaknesses.

Materials

1. Week 2—Handout 1: Self-Esteem Types and Problems. This handout is used as a general introduction to the self-esteem meaning matrix (or cross of self-esteem, depending on which metaphor is more suitable for a particular group). It is designed to introduce how problems with competence and worthiness affect self-esteem.
2. Week 2—Handout 2: Applying the Multidimensional Self-Esteem Inventory (MSEI) Scales. This handout is designed to help participants make sense of their scores on the MSEI, especially as they apply to the program. It would have to be modified if any other instrument is used to assess self-esteem.
3. Week 2—Handout 3: Finding Sources of Self-Esteem. This worksheet is based on the research findings concerning the four major sources of self-esteem. It is set up to help participants get in touch with how the sources are potentially available to them.

Procedure

Step 1: Reviewing. I usually begin this session by creating an opportunity for group members to share experiences and reflections from their self-esteem journal of the past week. Someone always seems to get the ball rolling, but sometimes it is helpful to model (an established self-esteem enhancement principle) by sharing my own experience. Reviewing in this way reinforces the importance of focusing on competence and worthiness as components of self-esteem and allows the group to see that these themes really are alive for themselves and others. All the rest of the sessions begin with a review because it facilitates the development of a cohesive group as a group and offers an opportunity to clarify previous material.

Step 2: Determining self-esteem problems. Becoming genuinely aware of the importance of self-esteem in human behavior also means knowing that there are problems associated with the lack of it. Although it is not necessary to go into great detail about the nonclinical and clinical problems, it does help to become aware of how the lack or loss of competence and worthiness can lessen or impair self-esteem. The self-esteem matrix can be used to do this. One can simply draw the axes or cross on the board to show how competence and worthiness work together to form self-esteem, or use the handout Self-Esteem Types and Problems (Week 2—Handout 1). The focus is on the four basic types of self-esteem, three of which lead to self-esteem difficulties because they involve deficiencies in competence or worthiness or both.

If I am working with a general population group, I focus on the middle (nonclinical) range of problems, but I do mention that there are some clinically significant self-esteem problems. I also add that we are not going to be dealing with the latter in a general psychoeducational group because they take more time to work on than the short-term model we are using allows us. The complete diagram in chapter 5 is useful for showing how this is so, but sometimes including the clinical labels is confusing, so they can be left out for a more simplified version. For instance, you may notice that the sample handout provided in the appendix leaves out differentiating between defensive self-esteem Types I and II in favor of just conveying the idea that defensiveness can reflect a self-esteem problem. The aims are to show how competence and worthiness are related to self-esteem and its problems and to address the learning styles of visually oriented participants. Sometimes there is value in asking people if they can recognize these kinds of self-esteem problems in themselves or others and to list the more common ones, as indicated in Part II of the handout. Although it is necessary to talk about self-esteem problems, I try to keep the group focused on enhancing self-esteem, not on the lack of it, because people are usually already quite good at focusing on negative phenomena and I do not want to reinforce that behavior. It is important to try to limit steps 1 and 2 to the first half of the session. If I am working with a clinical group, I make use of the portions of the diagram that concern clinically significant self-esteem problems, but even then I try to keep it simple.

Step 3: Interpreting the MSEI.   We know that a good self-esteem enhancement program involves assessing self-esteem and that this process can be complex. Fortunately, the MSEI is easy to administer, score, and interpret in a group setting—providing one has the proper credentials to use it and is familiar with the test manual. The MSEI provides both percentage and t-scores on the 11 scales, and the manual shows how to interpret them. Remember, the normative samples are limited, and age and various cultural factors might affect scores (Sue & Sue, 1990), so I *strongly* recommend a simple scoring and interpretive procedure. In the most recent work I have done with groups, I have found it most useful to simply write up a very brief report for each individual, such as the one shown in Applying the Multidimensional Self-Esteem (MSEI) Inventory Scales (Week 2—Handout 2), and hand it to the respective participant. Sometimes I also write a brief description of what the scale "means" according to the MSEI, but that practice is not necessary, as

I always go over the general meanings of all the scales with the whole group just after I return the results. As long as individual names are not used, this procedure is faster, avoids having to explain t-scores, and helps us to focus on a few areas on the test instead of on all 11 scales. The individual practitioner is free to present the results in other ways or to use other forms, but I caution against becoming overly technical with the reports and against getting bogged down in too much detail. Finally, it is important to take the time to make sure that all participants understand what their scores are suggesting about them and to understand that these are only suggestions to consider, not facts.

The MSEI provides several kinds of information about an individual's self-esteem that can be useful in the program. The Global Self-Esteem scale, for instance, is a composite figure that tells us something about the individual's general level of self-esteem. Another general scale, the Identity Integration score, is less useful because identity is such a complex, abstract topic. However, it can give some indication about the likelihood of other psychological issues that may have to be dealt with before self-esteem can really become a project, such as finding out about one's own values (which can be done through values clarification work). Perhaps the most useful, and certainly the most fascinating, scale is the one for Defensiveness. This scale is helpful in identifying individuals who are anxious about their self-esteem in a way that is otherwise difficult to detect. Sometimes, for instance, an obviously rigid or aggressive individual will score very high on all the other self-esteem indicators. However, his or her behavior will be so lacking in self-esteem that it is clear there are some real issues in this regard. If the individual's score is high on the Defensiveness scale, we have something with which to work. For example, we can approach the individual and ask if he or she finds himself or herself having difficulty admitting making mistakes or reacting too strongly to criticism. Of course, sometimes people with high scores simply do have high self-esteem or are unable to deal with their defensiveness, but one can at least be aware of these possibilities using the MSEI.

The heart of the test consists of eight subscales that assess various domains of self-esteem. The basic self-esteem scales (the eight components of self-esteem) can be grouped together as reflecting either competence or worthiness. On the one hand, what the test calls Competence, Personal Power (or influence), Self-Control, and Body Functioning are behaviorally based or action-oriented. Each scale concerns an individual's ability to perform certain identifiable skills that can be evaluated to yield some measure of competence (or the lack of it). On the other hand, the qualities of Lovability, Likability, Moral Self-Approval, and

Body Appearance are more value oriented and range in importance in terms of being worthy (or not) in regard to some personal or social value system. The Defensiveness scale helps to identify those who are dealing with Type I or Type II self-esteem problems. It is crucial to remember that scores on Defensiveness are arranged in a way that is opposite of the others. For example, a high score on the Defensiveness scale indicates some difficulty with self-esteem and low scores are generally positive. I always close this part of the session by offering participants the opportunity to ask questions about their results. If it becomes necessary to use another instrument, then this part of the program will have to be modified to reflect that change; however, the goal of the step should remain the same.

Requiring people to consider both the areas in which they are strong as well as the areas in which they are weak is useful because there is a tendency for participants to pay too much attention to the negative aspects of their self-esteem assessment. Indeed, allowing such a negative drift to occur too often or too long may actually reinforce self-esteem problems. Also, we saw that increasing success is a valid route to self-esteem and it is sometimes better to encourage this by working with a client's strengths rather than weaknesses. Some people suffer such serious self-esteem problems that they can only afford to work on increasing what little strength they have before they can address more difficult challenges. Participants are then instructed to start tracking these positive and negative self-esteem themes in their journals. This homework will help them to increase their awareness of self-esteem as they live it.

Step 4: Finding sources of self-esteem.　Now that we have assessed self-esteem, it is important to become aware of its potential sources, especially those that are most readily available within the context of our own lives. The handout for this activity, Finding Sources of Self-Esteem (Week 2—Handout 3), lists each major source of self-esteem we found in the research, namely, personally significant achievements or successes, evidence of influence or power, acceptance or being valued by others, and virtue or acting on beliefs. After I describe the characteristics of each source, I include an example of a recent experience I have had in an area, then ask for examples from the group. It is helpful to point out that these four sources of self-esteem are based on competence (achievements and influence) and worthiness (acceptance and virtue). Then, the participants are asked to try and identify one or two recent experiences of their own in each of the four areas.

Some people complete this activity quite easily, but others have a hard time with it because they tend to look for only major achievements, influence, actions, or acceptance. Occasionally, people worry that they do not seem to have much material to put in one or another category, so there is some advantage to having members share their work. Sooner or later, a person will say something like, "It makes me feel good about myself when I find my child waiting for me at the door when I come home from work," or "Someone was having a problem doing something at work today and I was able to show him how to do it—that made me feel that I have something to offer." Others in the group will begin to look for small but readily available potential sources of self-esteem in their own lives.

Another factor to be aware of in working with the group is that self-esteem environments vary considerably. For instance, some life situations make one source of self-esteem more or less accessible than others and not everyone is going to be able to readily find all four sources. The point is to let people know that these four basic sources of self-esteem really do exist and that they need to be aware of which ones are most likely to be available in their own set of circumstances. It is probably best to take some time to make sure that each member of the group becomes aware of at least one realistic source of self-esteem that can function as a viable option for him or her, because having one available is necessary for the program to work. Indeed, it may be helpful to make a copy of the "self-esteem bucket" (Figure 5.6) and use it as a handout in this activity.

Finally, we turn to the journal and ask participants to track the ways in which these potential sources of self-esteem manifest themselves during the next week. This information will be used again at the end of the program.

Week 3: Enhancing Phase (Increasing Worthiness)

Goal

The third week marks the beginning of the enhancement phase. As before, it begins with a review of the previous week's homework in order to reinforce the material that was learned and the need to be aware of the importance of self-esteem. Once again, participants are asked to share their experiences. By now they are usually comfortable enough with each other and with the group for me to begin to encourage individuals who seem to need a little help to participate more actively.

volves asking participants to fill in Enhancing Worthiness: Using Positive Feedback (Week 3—Handout 1), which involves writing down 10 positive qualities or attributes about oneself. We then share these lists with each other in the group. I know that the "standard" way to go about this activity is to have participants read the list on a daily basis, but I have found that having each participant read the list *to the group* seems to enhance the technique and bring the group together at the same time. Naturally, no one should be forced to read his or her list aloud.

Occasionally, a person is unable to complete the list. There are two reasons this may occur. For one thing, people tend to look for unusually significant achievements or outstanding qualities. Most of us would have a hard time coming up with 10 of those, so it is important to tell participants that things we easily overlook are also indications of worthiness, such as being a good parent, being faithful to one's word or spouse, and so on. Another thing is that low self-esteem can interfere with a person's ability to perceive or identify worthy or competent things about himself. Sometimes the individual feels so unworthy that he thinks there is *nothing* good to say about himself. I remember one woman who dropped out of a group because she felt unworthy of feeling worthy about herself. (She went back to individual therapy.) Offering the group a small number of realistic examples and giving participants time to reflect on their positive qualities seems to help them complete the activity, although occasionally some will not fill in all the blanks. When this happens, it can be helpful to ask if they heard anything on someone else's list that applies to them and, if so, to add it to theirs.

Reading lists aloud comes next and should be done with considerable sensitivity because some people learn that saying positive things about themselves is "wrong" (a sign of a braggart or a violation of the principle of humility) or they are only used to vocalizing their negative qualities. I usually begin by reading my own list to show participants that it is all right to say positive things about oneself and to get the ball rolling. Then, I ask for volunteers and try to make sure everyone has an opportunity to participate. It is easy to dismiss this exercise as a pop psych gimmick, and I would be hard pressed to prove that doing something like reading a list every morning is going to change self-esteem. But there are at least two good reasons to engage in this activity in the group setting. First, some people feel so unworthy about themselves, or come from environments that affirm them so little, that they may weep when they see that they actually have a number of real, identifiable, positive qualities that they seem to have ignored or forgotten. Many times the rest of the group sees how special this moment is and responds with a comment like "I can see that about you," or they spontaneously give a soft round of applause. These moments can be very moving and certainly are self-esteem enhancing. (Remember the findings concerning being accepted?) Second, although this activity has less empirical support for its effectiveness than others, it is actually a variation of an established self-esteem enhancement technique, in this case using positive feedback. This activity helps us make the transition from mere learning to learning in an atmosphere that involves sharing, camaraderie, and, above all, acceptance, which are necessary for a self-esteem group to be effective.

Step 2: Introducing the concept of cognitive restructuring. The first part of the session takes about a half hour. Next, we turn to Enhancing Worthiness: Introduction to Cognitive Restructuring (Week 3—Handout 2). We already examined the literature about cognitive restructuring techniques and how they work to break up irrational thinking patterns associated with self-defeating behavior. Most mental health professionals worth their salt know about them, so I will not go through it again. However, it is important to remember that this information is often very new to clients. Therefore, it is best to present the information clearly and walk them through it step by step.

First, it is helpful to explain the basic idea behind this cognitive intervention, which is Part A of the handout. This usually involves a discussion about "self-talk," the idea of self-fulfilling prophecies, and the concept of self-defeating behaviors. I use these terms instead of the concept of co-constitution because they are more familiar for most people and the cognitive literature in which this technique is embedded is replete with them. The important things to emphasize are (1) the idea that distorted thinking leads to unwarranted perceptions, negative feelings, and dysfunctional behavior and (2) if we correct such cognitive mistakes, then our perceptions, feelings, and behaviors are likely to change as well. I also have found it helpful to give people an example from my own life of making such errors and what it means to do so. Be careful in what you disclose, however, because it may be similar to what someone in the group is currently working on, which means that you may fall prey to a transference situation, a phenomenon to which I can attest.

The idea is to help individuals become especially aware of the negative patterns they happen to use most often themselves. I put together a list of common thinking errors like the one in Part B of the handout. The list is not set in stone, and you are free to substitute items on it with your own favored terms. Making such a handout for your group is helpful because it provides everyone with a common set of terms that can be used to identify and to understand these slippery self-esteem "gumption traps." I go over my definition of each term (you can modify them if you desire) and try to offer some examples of each one so that the group can have a better sense of how these self-esteem foils work at the lived level. For example, I might tell them about a time when a relationship I was involved in was ended by the other person and how my "self-talk" (or meaning making) at the time helped create (co-consti-tute) a higher degree of pain for me than was actually necessary. "There I sat in my lonely apartment," I might tell them, "convinced that no one would ever love me again because I am such a loser." Then, I ask participants to identify which "gumption traps" I had fallen into as they look over the list. Usually, there are several possibilities to consider. This thought is a good example of what David Burns (1980, p. 40) calls "fortune-telling," because knowing that I would never have a relationship again would require me to be clairvoyant in order for the belief to be realistic. It also illustrates "name-calling," because of the derogatory personal reference. I take some time to point out here that it is usually necessary and appropriate for a person to be sad over a loss; otherwise, participants may develop exaggerated expectations about the value or effectiveness of this technique. The point is that one does not have to suffer unduly over the event, such as by becoming forlorn, depressed, or even suicidal, all of which represent a severe and inappropriate loss of worthiness. I then lead the group in looking at examples of the other traps by asking participants to identify the ones that they are most vulnerable to using. This activity can be done with good humor as well as instruction. Sometimes the session becomes quite lively as we all learn to laugh at ourselves a bit more easily.

Step 3: Using cognitive restructuring.   Now comes the time to show the group how to use the technique to alter patterns that help to co-consti-tute a life of low or defensive self-esteem. First, though, the clinician or facilitator has a decision to make concerning which system to use. There are several to choose from, and it probably does not matter to a great degree which one is selected, as long as it is fairly well structured and supported by research. Often I use David Burns' system, particularly the version found in his 1980 work *Feeling Good: The New Mood Therapy*, but Albert Ellis's approach is just as useful. In either case, the general approach is straightforward. First, it teaches people how to identify ways of thinking that create negative perceptual and behavioral patterns by naming them in simple, easily recognizable terms. Then, it asks participants to practice what amounts to a three-step process that breaks these patterns. They are describing a troublesome situation on paper, identifying the cognitive distortions that occurred in it, then correcting the errors of thinking to see how they change the situation. No matter which system is chosen, the aim is to help the group understand and be able to identify the ways that people deceive themselves, thereby creating pain and unnecessary loss of self-esteem.

Whatever version of this approach is selected by the therapist, it is essential to walk people through the process step by step and to do so several times. David Burns offers two versions of this technique, the standard three-step approach (describe the situation, name the distortion, insert a rational alternative) and a longer six-step method. I use a modified version of the latter in the handout Pattern-Breaking Worksheet (Week 3—Handout 3) for this program because the additional steps break down the process into smaller tasks, which are easier for participants to understand and to work with. After identifying the six steps presented in the handout in Part A, I usually show how they are to be used by working one of my own recent problems in front of the group. I do this by taking the vexing situation or difficulty through the entire system, which is presented as Part B.

Typically, I begin by describing the situation to the group in step 1. Then, I name my strongest feeling and rate its intensity to complete the second step. In step 3, I reflect on what was going through my mind at the time (without embarrassing myself too much) and try to simply state my own thoughts as they actually occurred. Step 4 involves asking the group to help me identify the irrational part of my thinking according to the list of distortions I presented in the previous handout. Now that the group is involved, I ask them to offer a rational alternative for my distorted thinking to complete step 5. I conclude step 6, and the process, by reevaluating my own feelings in front of the group to show that there is a real gain involved in doing this kind of work. I always point out that even a "measurable" reduction in intensity is better than what I was experiencing before we went through the exercise. Sometimes a person will say, "Yeah, but you still have a problem that didn't go away." In that case, I point out that this is a technique to reduce unnecessary suffering, not a magical solution for all of life's problems. Sometimes I will also focus on the "yeah, but" part of the comment as an example of how that particular cognitive distortion keeps suffering going on for longer or more intensely than is necessary.

I emphasize that it is important to outline every step by writing them down on paper because we fall into these "gumption traps" so easily or fool ourselves by thinking it is sufficient to do the steps mentally. It is helpful to point out that, like any bad habit, these cognitive patterns have been learned over the course of a lifetime, so it will be hard to unlearn them quickly. Indeed, as far as I know, the work of writing things down and going through *all* the steps on paper is stressed by all the authors of the techniques whose work has been confirmed by independent research. These habits of meaning making are so well practiced and ingrained that it takes something like writing to slow down cognitive and perceptual patterns, let alone to disrupt them. Changing them requires even more work, which is why the process has to be repeated many times before progress occurs. Being methodical may help reinforce the importance of thinking more reasonably.

To be sure the participants get the point and to ensure that they know how to use the program, I ask them to do the same thing I did and to fill in the Participant's Examples portion of the handout, which is Part C. Building on the self-esteem enhancement principle of hard work and practice, I ask a participant to allow me to help him or her work through the system using a recent experience that created a self-esteem issue. This part of the session is always done with permission from the individual, on the board, in front of the group, and in an accepting fashion. After one or two times, the group typically becomes relaxed. Now people volunteer to have their experience processed, and eventually I have the group tell me what to put on the board as we go through each of the six steps. This part of the process is crucial to the program's success and can be fun. As the handout indicates, the last step of the activity involves a homework assignment, which is to continue to practice the technique and record results in the journal.

Week 4: Enhancing Phase (Increasing Competence)

Goal

The fourth week continues the enhancement phase of the program, but shifts it from working on worthiness to developing competence. This phase may be lengthened to include more activities than I have included here. If, for instance, we were working in a long-term group situation, then we could focus on learning to stand up for ourselves through assertiveness training. However, learning such sophisticated skills usually takes several weeks (Rakos, 1990). Therefore, the fourth session aims to round out the enhancement phase by increasing competence in other ways.

Materials

These materials are designed to continue our work on enhancing self-esteem and not just feeling good about ourselves, which is the major criticism of the anti-self-esteem movement mentioned earlier. We do this by remembering that the fundamental structure of self-esteem shows us how competence balances worthiness and vice versa. Thus, the next set of activities focus on the behavioral dimensions of self-esteem, or how we *earn* it.

1. Self-esteem journal data.
2. Week 4—Handout 1: Enhancing Competence: Problem-Solving Method.
3. Week 4—Handout 2: Enhancing Competence: Problem-Solving Worksheet.

Procedure

Step 1: Review. The session begins with a review of the cognitive restructuring technique. I start by asking the group to share examples from their journals, but this time I also diagram the situations on the board so that the whole group works through the experiences with me from beginning to end. I repeat this procedure until I am sure everybody knows how to do it. There are several reasons for beginning this way. One is that we are trying to help people acquire a new skill that needs to become a habit to work effectively. Such learning takes time and people often make mistakes in the early stages, just as any novice might. Also, the old habits are so powerful and so automatic that people are likely to be trapped by them again and again despite attempts to intervene. Repeating the process reinforces new ways of dealing with these old self-esteem traps. Finally, by going over them publicly, participants get to see that someone else in the group actually found relief using this method. Often, hearing others talk about how they broke out of a trap, even if momentarily, lends credibility to the technique, gives hope for the future, and underscores the program's value.

It should be noted that some of the cognitive (co-constitutive) distortions we commit that perpetuate our misery are trickier to deal with than others. Working through a participant's problem on the board allows us to use our professional expertise to help with some of the trickier self-esteem traps. I find that one of the most difficult distortions with which to deal is that of a person who co-constitutes a situation through what Burns (1980) calls "emotional reasoning." I like to call this particular form of that type of distortion "yeah, butting," which is a phrase a student of mine once coined when she noticed that those seem to be the words people use most often when they are engaged in emotional reasoning. Let me illustrate this phenomenon here because it can be disruptive to the group process if it is not dealt with successfully.

Typically, emotional reasoners will present a situation that is genuinely unpleasant. They will work what happened through the six steps but see only a slight reduction in feeling intensity. Rather than just accepting the fact that the situation is simply an uncomfortable one, or instead of being satisfied with a realistic reduction in negative affect, they start up all over again. Usually, such individuals will offer superficial agreement by saying something like "Yes, I see what you mean, but . . . " then slip right back into the distortion. Having them work each "yeah, but" through the cycle (this process can take several repetitions) often helps them to understand how they are distorting the situation to keep it more painful than it needs to be. For example, someone might keep going back to being betrayed in a relationship again and again and again because the feeling of anger allows him or her to avoid the feeling of loss that comes with endings. "If only this . . . or if only that . . . " is another variation on this theme that can be used to achieve the same distorted end. When a participant manages to realize the nature of this particular trap in the session, the event can be a powerful lesson for the individual as well as for the group, because it shows that even the most stubborn distortions can be broken.

Step 2: Enhancing competence through problem solving. The second activity of the session, which usually comes after the break, continues to follow the phenomenological theory of self-esteem by building on the connection between self-esteem and competence. The goal is to help participants learn a skill that increases their ability to better deal with the challenges of life. The most powerful tool for this purpose is probably learning to solve problems effectively. After all, increasing this ability should increase an individual's chances of success in a variety of situations, which, in turn, should lead to a greater demonstration of competence over time. As indicated in the handout Enhancing Competence: Problem-Solving Method (Week 4—Handout 1), the way we are going to go about enhancing competence is by using a modified version of the training process developed by D'Zurilla and Goldfried (1971) whose work Pope and colleagues (1988) adjusted to help children enhance self-esteem. This method is chosen because it is theoretically sound, nicely compatible with our phenomenological theory, reasonably well researched, and relatively simple. Although the temptation is to go directly to the problem-solving steps listed in Part B, I do spend some time on the theory of the technique in Part A. This helps participants appreciate that feeling, thinking, and behaving are distinct parts of the process, which is important because sometimes they have trouble with one or more areas. For instance, I still find that men tend to have more difficulty than women in recognizing their own feelings, which often means that men have more trouble detecting early signs of when a problem is developing. All too often this tendency means that things have to get worse before they can get better.

The next part of the session consists of walking the participants through the steps of the problem-solving process format presented in Enhancing Competence: Problem-Solving Worksheet (Week 4—Handout 2), much in the way that we did with cognitive distortions. I usually begin by listing in order all the steps and procedures from Part A on the board. Next, I take a problem I am facing in my own life (that is not too personal or complex) and work it through the process step by step. In other words, I first identify a problem, list it, and describe how I came to recognize it as a problem. Then I stop and think about it with the group and try to articulate what is really bothering me about this problem. I ask the group to help me decide what my *realistic* goal would be in dealing with this problem.

Next, we think about potential solutions to this particular problem and do some brainstorming to generate a number of possibilities. This step is a little tricky, because people tend to want to evaluate the relative merits of each possible solution. Someone, for instance, will often say, "Well, that sure won't work," and I will have to remind the group that we are not yet evaluating solutions, just trying to list as many possibilities as we can. After writing all the possible solutions on the board, we move to the next step, where we evaluate the alternatives individually. The typical approach is to think about the likely consequences for each one. Putting them in some kind of order in terms of what a solution will "get me" versus what it will "cost me" is helpful. Next, I select the best solution, which is usually the one that has the highest gain for the amount of work or responsibility I am willing to accept. It is important to take the time to make a realistic plan of how to implement the decision I made. Paying close attention to detail is important here, because people will usually make plans that are doomed to fail. Therefore, I ask the group to help me identify each step necessary to implement the solution. Finally, I add a step that is not on most of the other versions of the list—the need to practice problem solving before deciding on whether or not it works.

After going through this practice run, we make the exercise more realistic by asking for people to volunteer problems in Part B. Of course, we work each one out on the board by asking the group to process the problem each step of the way. As the facilitator, I clarify their responses and write them on the board for all to see. Usually, someone agrees to think about what has been done here, use the technique, and report back to us on his or her experience of the problem at the next meeting. The same procedure is repeated until we run out of time, then the whole group is instructed to practice using this technique for the next week and to record their experiences in their self-esteem journals. Participants often seem to be very pleased to receive training in problem-solving, and even the most skeptical tend to see it as a tangible benefit of the program that is readily transferable to real life.

There are some points to remember in working both the cognitive restructuring and the problem-solving activities. For one thing, it is helpful to model them for the group, which in this case is done by the facilitator's working through a problem and by working through problems from the group. Modeling not only shows each step of the process more clearly but, as we have already seen, is itself a valid self-esteem enhancement technique that is tied to competence. Standing up before others and trying things out also allows us to help dispel certain kinds of self-esteem traps. In terms of cognitive restructuring, for example, participants might say that even though their pain or uncomfortable feelings have been reduced, they still feel bad. At this point it is necessary to emphasize that the goal is to be *realistic*, which means that sometimes situations are simply uncomfortable, and even then a reduction in pain or anxiety or suffering is a net gain and that itself justifies using the techniques. The same happens with problem solving in that some people will say something like "OK, I've done what you want, but I still have a problem . . . " or "None of the alternatives are good ones." It is often necessary to remind participants that these techniques are not magical, just rational, and that they at least help us find the best ways to deal with problems or challenges of living.

Finally, we must consider the fact that the principle of practice is more important at this point in the program than ever before. By this time, people tend to groan about the journal writing (and sometimes that does fall off). However, by now they also see the importance of doing the actual work, so I often try to reinforce the value of practicing by using an analogy. The idea is to compare learning how to restructure one's thinking and response patterns to other forms of learning that participants can relate to more easily, like weight lifting and joining an exercise class: One starts out slowly and the first few attempts are crude and uncomfortable, but gains will come—if one sticks to the activity for a reasonable length of time. In other words, increasing self-esteem is just like any other complex learning activity—it takes time and work. I conclude by asking once again, Why should they expect anything else when so many years have gone into learning to develop a self-esteem problem?

Week 5: Management Phase (Maintaining Self-Esteem)

Goal

The fifth week deals with two related issues. First, the group is coming to an end. Any experienced clinician knows about the importance of dealing with issues such as termination, separation anxiety, and the sadness of losing something. Second, and more important, ending the group means that its members will no longer be able to count on the discipline or structure offered by weekly meetings to help them focus their awareness or to reinforce the gains that have been made during the program. We know that complex learning takes time and that we have invested only a few weeks. The finding we uncovered showing that good programs must deal with the problem of maintaining self-esteem turns out to be very wise indeed, so this concern becomes the focus of the last regular meeting. I use the term *managing* instead of *maintaining* self-esteem because management is much more active, dynamic, and future oriented than maintenance, which implies holding ground more than making advances.

Materials

The fundamental structure of self-esteem was found to consist of not just competence and worthiness. However, the relationship between them is a factor, perhaps the most crucial one, in developing and maintaining self-esteem. Consequently, the following materials are designed to bring together the work that we have done on worthiness and competence over the past 2 weeks or sessions.

1. Self-esteem journal data.
2. Week 5—Handout 1: Building a Self-Esteem Project.
3. Week 5—Program Evaluation Sheet (clinician's design).

Procedure

Step 1: Reviewing. As usual, the session begins with a review of what the members of the group did over the past week with the material from the last meeting. It is a good idea to examine what participants did with the problem-solving technique since the last session. Usually, one person presents a positive experience and another presents an example in which the technique failed. Both experiences are good grist for the therapeutic mill: The former is reinforcing as any testimonial tends to be, and the latter gives us an opportunity to practice. At this point, I have the group tell me what steps should be used as we walk through the particular problem. This kind of review reminds participants to use the method correctly and is an opportunity to reinforce the learning process. This step should take no more than 45 minutes.

Step 2: Introducing the concept of managing self-esteem. We are attempting to provide a way to build on the work done to date so as to extend it beyond the life of the group. Key aspects of this endeavor include offering a way of continuing to be aware of self-esteem as a vital psychosocial resource in everyday life, finding individualized ways of becoming more worthy as a person and more competent at living, and remembering how important it is to manage self-esteem effectively rather than poorly because self-esteem can be won or lost in life. One way to help participants is to show them how to make self-esteem an ongoing personal project, which can be done by developing a "self-esteem action plan."

The activity for this week, which is presented in Building a Self-Esteem Project (Week 5—Handout 1), is divided into two parts. Part I is a visual representation of the idea of a self-esteem action cycle. I organize this information as a cycle to show people how maintaining or increasing self-esteem works conceptually. Also, the diagram is helpful in explaining the process before we go through its steps. Thus, as the chart indicates, the participants are told that the current (or lived) status of their self-esteem is where we must start, no matter where it is. Moving clockwise, the next step is to identify one self-esteem issue to work on that is especially important or appropriate *right now* in one's life. Once such a goal is identified, we can use the information acquired from other parts of the program to build an individualized self-esteem project. This means targeting a source of self-esteem that is capable of increasing worthiness or competence, or both, and setting up a plan to get there by using our problem-solving skills. We can work on reaching that goal through practice, which eventually results in new learning and growth regarding this particular self-esteem theme. Because acquiring more competence and more worthiness is cumulative (Harter, 1993), completing the cycle in this way can shift our position on the self-esteem matrix in a positive direction. I point out that one can always repeat the process and that keeping a self-esteem project "going" at least maintains our awareness of self-esteem over time.

Step 3: Building a self-esteem action plan. Now we move to Part II of the handout and walk participants through the steps one at a time in a way that requires them to build a plan. There are two reasons for doing so. First, this allows us to check the work to see if participants really understand the cycle. Second, the exercise is really much more: Ideally, the self-esteem project they develop becomes the first one they decide to work on by themselves once the group is over. The worksheet is set up to be done in a stepwise fashion under the direction of the facilitator, who acts as teacher, coach, and troubleshooter.

Part II-A asks group members to identify a self-esteem area that they wish to improve. Now our work with the MSEI on identifying two self-esteem strengths and weaknesses becomes important again. A person whose self-esteem is relatively healthy may be best served by building a project around a content area from the test that is low. Such an individual is likely to be able to tolerate looking at shortcomings without becoming defensive or discouraged, and reducing a self-esteem deficit may be a "fast track" toward being more competent and worthy. Certainly, doing so would at least open up an area for growth and development. However, a person with a more serious self-esteem problem already focuses on his or her vulnerabilities, so that individual may be better served by taking another track. In this case, working to improve functioning in an area where one is already doing at least moderately well may be more effective. Taking this approach may lead to a speedier increase in the kind of self-confidence that success brings with it, which could help the person to move on to more complex tasks. I usually leave the choice up to the members, but I do suggest these basic guidelines to them in targeting an area for improvement. Having a choice in the matter is also the reason I had them identify their chief self-esteem strengths and weaknesses in the assessment phase.

Next, members are instructed to match the nature of their self-esteem theme with an appropriate source of self-esteem by using the four basic sources they worked with in Week 2—Handout 3. This information is to be written in Part II-B on the worksheet so as to focus awareness. The activity also helps participants to build an efficient program because they can begin to look for the kinds of self-esteem opportunities they need to make a given project successful. Individuals who suffer from difficulties with competence, for instance, might think about increasing various skills that could help them to have more achievements or influence. Possibilities here include learning how to speak more effectively and taking a leadership training course. Those who score lower on worthiness scales might seek out interpersonal opportunities that could lead to being accepted or valued more, such as doing volunteer work. Or they could look for ways to act more virtuously, even if it is just to cut down on a bad habit they would do well to eliminate. Notice that in each case, although either competence or worthiness is emphasized, the other component is active as well. In one case we want the individual to increase his or her abilities but select a worthy goal at which to aim. In the other situation we see the person using his or her existing competencies in more worthy ways.

The next part, labeled II-C on the activity sheet, brings the problem-solving skills work done last session into play. Here, we ask individuals to examine their self-esteem needs, to consider the ways in which the source of self-esteem they are focusing on manifests itself concretely in their own lives, and to generate some goals that are realistic in terms of their own situation and abilities. Once again, the tendency is for people to set their sights a little too high, so I help by asking them to decide on one or two goals that are meaningful and realistic. Sometimes this involves going around the room and asking participants what they are targeting as a goal so that others can get some ideas. The participants can also be asked to pair up and develop self-esteem projects for each partner.

The final part, II-D, is the most difficult and important. Again, it relies on the problem-solving skills learned in the last session. The task is to help members create a practical program, or one that involves clear, realistic steps that result in reaching a reasonable self-esteem-enhancing goal. A good self-esteem project is therefore highly individualized. It must accommodate a personal range of possibilities, take into account various individual qualities, and be able to utilize the environmental characteristics currently present in the person's life. For instance, a self-esteem enhancement project aimed at increasing competence for an individual who is challenged mentally would look very different from one for a person who was doing reasonably well in life but who wishes to do better. In the first case, the goal of learning how to find the right bus home from work might be appropriate. In the second instance, aiming for an award or promotion might be the goal. Sometimes people doom themselves to failure by picking goals that are too high for them right now or by selecting ones that cannot be supported by their current environments. Then, we have to help them make realistic adjustments to their plan. In all cases, developing a self-esteem project is like preparing for a trip, in that the more planning one does, the more likely one is to reach the destination.

In a certain sense, this part of the process is the key to the entire program, and it certainly shows its cumulative, integrated nature. Although participants do seem to increase self-esteem during our 5 weeks together, a phenomenon that I will address later, the rest of their lives lie ahead of them. Therefore, we ask people to write down each and every step they must take to reach the goal they have identified. If the aim, for instance, is to work on bodily functioning (which includes physical functioning as well as body image issues) by developing an exercise program, then the individual is asked to be specific about how this will happen. It might mean trying several sports. If so, then the individual must indicate the steps needed to experiment in this way, such as calling the YMCA, joining a club, or finding a friend involved in a class as the first step. If the individual decides to join the Y, then he or she must call for information, find out how much the program costs, set aside a day to go the gym, talk with a trainer, try a certain number of activities, and so on. If someone makes becoming more likable the goal, then he or she needs to consider such things as becoming involved in a community activity or learning better interpersonal communication skills. Depending on which activity is selected, there will also be a need to develop a list of organizations, contact friends, make phone calls, meet with a few groups, and try out the activity until something suitable is found. Similarly, assertiveness training is a popular project and a well-established self-esteem enhancement activity. But it also means finding a qualified trainer nearby (which itself can take time), seeing how much the program will cost, finding low-cost alternatives if that is necessary, and making schedules compatible.

Focusing on these mundane details is good for all kinds of reasons, ranging from such platitudes as "A journey of a thousand miles begins with a single step," or "Inch by inch, it's a cinch," to the simple fact that small successes can lead to larger ones. At this point, I present my own self-esteem enhancement goals and ask members to help me develop the specific action steps necessary to improve in this area so that they can see how it is done through modeling. Then, I encourage volunteers to present their plans to the group. As before, I put the steps on the board and walk the group through the plans so that we can help improve it and so that I can reinforce the need to be detailed. This process is repeated until about the last 10 or 15 minutes of the session.

Finally, the end of the session nears and I use the remaining time as an opportunity for members to share their experience about the 5 weeks, mention their plans for the future (sometimes they have already acquired the phone numbers of people they have linked up with for further support), and assess the value of the group. The last activity gives me feedback concerning what participants found to be useful or useless and what they would like to have done more or less of in the program. Not surprisingly, I want to remind them of the crucial roles that hard work and time play in increasing self-esteem. Therefore, the last step in the activity is to remind participants that the journal is a way of keeping these important ingredients in mind. The program ends by asking the participants to complete whatever evaluation tool the facilitator wishes to use in order to obtain feedback about their experience. I strongly recommend taking the time to do this step for reasons that will become clear at the end of this chapter.

Week 6 (Optional): Boosting the Program

One last possibility needs to be mentioned. There may be real value in adding a sixth session after the group has ended as a kind of follow-up or "booster" meeting. We know that increasing self-esteem requires hard work and that it can take a long time. But sometimes people start out well intentioned but become discouraged or bogged down for one reason or another. A follow-up meeting may help participants to strengthen their resolve or to see the progress they have made, which itself can be a powerful reinforcer. There are several things we can do during this meeting to reinforce managing self-esteem effectively. For instance, we can ask participants to share their experiences about how they were successful, or had difficulty, so that everyone can see how hard people have to work at managing self-esteem. Material from any of the 5 weeks can be reviewed upon request. Special group attention might be given to an individual self-esteem project or need. The follow-up session can also be used to remind people about the learning curve, how long it took to fall into low or defensive self-esteem, and the need to give change a chance. Finally, for those leaders who are brave, obsessive, or simply research oriented, the follow-up session can involve using the MSEI as a posttest to track significant differences.

Although most of my groups do not include this extra session, there is good reason to invest in this additional time. This meeting can be included in the program from the beginning by making it a 6-week program instead of 5. The advantage here is that attendance is likely to be good. The disadvantage of having only a week lapse before the "boost" is that this time is so near the regular meetings that the potency of the technique may be diminished. However, it is also possible to schedule a 1-month follow-up after the five sessions end. In fact, this arrangement is mentioned in the short-term psychotherapy literature and is purported to have an enhancing effect (Wells, 1982). The risk of going this route is that attendance is likely to be poorer because of such things as time limitations, schedule conflicts, and the resurgence of poor self-esteem habits. I have found that another benefit of having a follow-up session is that clients often seem pleased with the progress they made and wish to share their success.

ENHANCING SELF-ESTEEM IN THE INDIVIDUAL SETTING

There are two ways that the program can be used in the context of individual self-esteem education, counseling, or therapy. One is to structure it on the basis of a planned short-term treatment model (Wells, 1982). This version can be used effectively with mildly clinical and nonclinical populations. The other approach is to include various elements of the program in a longer-term therapeutic relationship. This version can be used with people who have more serious self-esteem and/or clinical problems. Let us briefly examine each option.

The short-term treatment model continues to gain in popularity for at least two reasons: It reduces costs (which seems to please managed care programs) and the literature on the subject tells us that it is reasonably effective, generally speaking. Of course, there are several general characteristics of this approach that distinguish it from longer-term models, the most important of which is that it is a time-limited arrangement. Another important distinction is that rather than being open-ended and general, short-term work is usually very structured and focused. Typically, the client and therapist identify a particular problem or issue that is to be the center of their work and relationship. Of course, long-term problems involving such goals as general personality reorganization or extremely psychotic conditions are not well suited to short-term work (Mann, 1973). Finally, there are psychodynamic, behavioral, cognitive, and even humanistic approaches to doing short-term work, and each has its own set of relative strengths and weaknesses. Therefore, one way of adapting this phenomenological self-esteem enhancement program to individual work is simply by making its steps the basis of a short-term therapeutic contract. In other words, the client and the therapist agree to meet together to work on enhancing self-esteem as the primary goal of their work. In this case, the steps and activities are followed in order, but the five 2-hour group sessions can be broken down into ten 1-hour individual meetings.

There are some important differences to keep in mind between the two formats. For one thing, individual work is likely to be more intensive than group work. For example, the types of risk taking the client experiments with in learning to become competent at the challenges of living in a worthy way may be more acute, because the client feels that there is a more personal, supportive relationship with the therapist to fall back on if things get tough. For another thing, the need for involvement from the therapist is greater in the individual setting. This kind of human encounter is much more existential than pedagogical, which means that both client and therapist are more actively engaged with each other than in the group setting. Similarly, individual work involves a greater focus on the client and his or her self-esteem story. Finally, using a follow-up session may be especially important for individual work, not only to boost self-esteem but to deal with some of the termination issues that arise because of a longer-term, more intensive relationship. The MSEI can be helpful in individual work because it can increase awareness of self-esteem in general, and it allows us to explore more completely how the components of self-esteem are alive in the individual's life. We also have more time to ask questions, explore responses, and develop a much more detailed understanding of the matrix as it is lived in a given client's life. In particular, we can explore various self-esteem themes that are especially important for the person at this time and target one or two as the basis for a mutually created self-esteem project. In fact, the entire idea of individual treatment is to walk the client through the self-esteem activities in a more individualized fashion.

It was mentioned that there is another way to use the program in working with individuals. This alternative is to incorporate the steps of the program into a regular or ongoing therapeutic relationship. In this case, the program will be modified considerably because it either becomes the equivalent of focused long-term treatment, like the program offered by Bednar and associates (1989), or it becomes secondary to another longer-term therapeutic project that happens to involve self-esteem. Although one good reason to work on self-esteem this way is that some people simply have more serious self-esteem problems than the group or time-limited format can address, I do not think that we can regard this approach as a way of implementing the program per se. However, various aspects of it might be helpful to standard forms of longer-term psychotherapeutic work.

Probably the most important difference between the short-term and long-term individual formats is that the latter is positioned to make better use of naturally occurring self-esteem moments, especially those involving problematical self-esteem themes: The longer a client is in treatment, the more such opportunities are likely to arise. This can be beneficial for two reasons. First, we know that the positive resolution of such self-esteem challenges can genuinely modify underlying problematical self-esteem themes in a positive direction. Indeed, qualitative research indicated that this is probably the quickest and most direct route to enhancing self-esteem. Second, the therapy adds new elements to the situation that may make a meaningful difference in their outcomes: The individual does not have to face the challenge alone now, and the therapist can help the person to navigate the challenge in a pro-self-esteem fashion. The idea that the presence of a knowledgeable, skilled helper during such periods can tip the scales in favor of a positive resolution is consistent with the research on being pleased and displeased described earlier. Sometimes, for instance, there is a lack of awareness involved in these challenges in that people fail to see that their self-esteem is really at stake until it is too late. In this case, the clinician can help raise a client's consciousness, which we now know is a key step involved in enhancing self-esteem and related behaviors. Similarly, we can also work to deepen a client's understanding of the biographic self-esteem themes present at such times. Perhaps we can even help a client to work through some portion of personal history that is currently active and resolve enough of it to make a difference *this* time. Even if a client fails, we can help the individual to understand events in ways that improve his or her chances of being successful the next time the challenge occurs.

The group and individual approaches have their respective strengths and weaknesses. For instance, the former has all the wonderful dynamics of the group process to rely on, such as multiple perspectives, spontaneous opportunities, group affirmation, and reduced cost, while the latter offers more personal attention. In either case, the phenomenological program presented here may seem somewhat rigid to those who are familiar with the humanistic overtones of this approach. However, it is important to realize that the program cannot be run successfully in a mechanical way. Indeed, much of the program's effectiveness is predicated on the research that identified the interpersonal attitudes of acceptance, care, and respect for others as one of the primary agents for changing self-esteem. If the quality of interpersonal contact is poor, then the effectiveness of the rest of the program is likely to suffer. Thus, the therapist is not just a good technician, or even just a skilled teacher, in either version of the program. He or she also becomes a primary source of worthiness, which is an important part of self-esteem. Although the program's steps show us where to go, the therapist's presence takes us there in such a way that the technical aspects of the program are intertwined with the interpersonal qualities of the therapist.

One final comment is in order. I am aware that relying on the MSEI makes the program more complicated than some educational or mental health professionals might want it to be. I do think that the SEI (Coopersmith, 1981) or the Culture Free Self-Esteem Inventory (Battle, 1992) could be worked into the program in theory and that doing so would make it easier to run. However, because I know of no published research to support such a substitution, I cannot recommend it now. This alternative certainly stands as the first option to use if the MSEI is no longer available and if all the appropriate modifications to the program that such a change would require are made.

VALIDITY (REVISITED)

We are at the end of our phenomenological search for self-esteem, which means that I can address one more issue one last time. From the beginning I have stressed the importance of empirical support. For example, I tried to show how the program meets the criteria for construct validity in two ways. First, we found that a valid approach to understanding self-esteem must be able to account for genuine insights and findings made by other researchers, theoreticians, and clinicians. The idea was that validity increases in relation to the descriptive power of the approach, in this case the ability of a phenomenological approach to integrate the major research findings on self-esteem. The phenomenological approach actually seemed to do quite well in this regard in that the work on the definitions of self-esteem, the self-esteem paradoxes, and the research findings on self-esteem were all shown to be compatible with the fundamental structure of self-esteem and the meaning matrix. Indeed, this phenomenological framework was able to make sense of otherwise contradictory work. Second, it was said earlier that a valid approach would be one that is theoretically consistent. We just saw how the phenomenological approach uses the definition of competence and worthiness to move from research to theory and end with practice in an extremely consistent fashion.

Ideally, I would like to demonstrate the validity of both the theory and its application with convincing empirical aplomb, in the traditional sense of the term, because that is what our society respects the most about the scientific method. If one accepts data of experience as being empirical, then I think we have already demonstrated the validity of our fundamental finding, which is that self-esteem consists of both competence and worthiness. But the practical aspect of the program means that we are also interested in applying psychological knowledge to human life, which makes validity an ethical as well as a scientific issue. Therefore, as a clinician I must agree with insisting on more traditional forms of empirical validation concerning program effectiveness. Of course, we can never expect the social sciences to reach the same levels of "uncertainty reduction" (Tryon, 1991) as do the natural sciences: Scientific expectations must always be tempered by the fact that things are more complicated at the lived level than they are in the lab. So, although we should be thankful for this basic fact, it does make the situation more complicated. Nevertheless, there have been considerable advances in studying the effectiveness of psychotherapy over the past two decades. Also, I will show that research done since the publication of the first edition of this book indicates that this program does have some quantitative as well as qualitative support.

Traditional forms of empirical evidence that lend credibility to a program consist of reliability and validity. The reliability of a program, or the degree to which it can be implemented in a consistent way by others over time, is important for two reasons. First, clear, specific, well-structured steps are necessary if we are to be sure that the program being offered is, indeed, the same one. In other words, the more loosely constructed a program is, or the more it depends on unmeasurable factors such as personality, then the less confidence we can have in offering it to a broad spectrum of clinicians and clients. Who knows, for example, what actually goes on in unstructured or loosely structured programs? Second, if we want to measure the effectiveness of a program, which is the chief aim of traditional research on therapy, then the need for reliability increases because the program must be standardized for such work to be done. Reliability is the key to data-generating activities, especially if we want to gather quantitative information on a particular phenomenon. Reliability becomes even more important if the information is going to come from a number of settings, through a range of practitioners, or over any period of time, as is the case with clinical practice.

There is good reason to believe that this phenomenological program is very reliable, at least for working on self-esteem in adulthood. For instance, the group version of the program is highly structured in that it involves clear steps that are to be followed in a sequential fashion. The handouts, the testing instrument, and the materials for the activities are all standardized as well, although there is room for clinical flexibility in each area. Next, the same basic program has been used successfully by other therapists. In addition to training mental health therapists in a community mental health system with which I am associated, I have used the program with traditional and nontraditional college populations. Moreover, it has been used by others beyond my control who have simply followed the book and who wrote or talked to me about their experiences afterward. Furthermore, some of these individuals work in diverse settings, from inner cities to college counseling centers. Indeed, the program has been taught to graduate students in psychology and presented at two international conferences. Naturally, I would be happy to share the names of these individuals and organizations upon written request if there is a need for such information to verify these claims. But in short, the theoretical consistency and step-by-step nature of the program does seem to give it a fairly high degree of reliability in both the research and clinical settings.

There is still the question of measured or quantifiable validity to consider. This is most important if we are to apply the program to real lives with any degree of confidence. Some degree of empirical validity is seen in the fact that it was one of the things we looked for when researching the self-esteem enhancement techniques to be used in it. Although the degree of such support for any particular technique varies, all of them have been tested by other authors and have stood the test of time. Indeed, some of the techniques, such as cognitive restructuring and problem solving, have done quite well in the empirically oriented literature on therapeutic efficacy. Even the MSEI has more research accompanying it than most self-esteem tests. Yet there is no substitute for testing the program itself. Fortunately, it has also been subjected to more rigorous examination since the publication of the first edition, and now includes comparison groups, a statistical analysis of effectiveness, and publication in a professional journal (Hakim-Larson & Mruk, 1997).

Although I cannot reproduce the entire article here, let me summarize the work. Julie Hakim-Larson, a faculty member of the graduate Department of Psychology at the University of Windsor, Ontario, Canada, was responsible for the analysis of the data, and I was responsible for its collection. The subjects came from a large, hospital-based, multicounty, comprehensive, community mental services program. The participants ranged in age from late teens to mid-60s and were overrepresented in terms of women and underrepresented in terms of minorities, although some of the participants were men and some of the clients were individuals from minority populations. These parameters are fairly typical of the community mental health environment. The subjects were divided into six medium-sized groups. Each group was led by myself and a different co-therapist. Two of the groups were composed of individuals from the general population who were not in treatment at the mental health facility. Two of the groups consisted of people with nonpsychotic mental health diagnoses who were in treatment at the center. The remaining two groups were from the chemical dependency population (one consisted of people with a diagnosis who were in treatment at the facility; the other, of "co-dependent" family members). All of the participants were given the MSEI at the beginning of the treatment, and all those who completed the program were tested once again at the end. They were also asked to fill out a qualitative questionnaire concerning their experience of the program and changes in themselves related to competence and worthiness.

The research design was not perfect in that we did not have the luxury of using a control group. (Like most "real world" environments, the community mental health system is funded by state and local tax dollars, and forcing people to wait for service is ethically questionable.) However, the conditions in this study were the ones most therapists are likely to encounter in practice. There is considerable literature on the importance of doing research under these conditions using methods similar to ours (Kazdin, 1992; Seligman, 1995a).

The results of the research were surprisingly robust. There were no significant pretest differences between those who dropped out and those who stayed, suggesting that the results were not being influenced by this kind of selection factor. Most important, every MSEI scale for self-esteem showed statistically significant positive changes between pre- and posttesting, which is exactly what we would expect if the program worked. Moreover, the qualitative data corroborated these statistical findings in that the subjects reported a high degree of satisfaction with the program and with positive changes in their self-esteem as it is defined by the program. We also did a follow-up session 6 months later, which is a long time in the community mental health situation, and subjects reported continuing change and satisfaction with the program. These findings and issues concerning doing research in real-life settings are discussed in more detail in the article, and the reader is referred to it if he or she is interested in such matters. More and better work is, of course, necessary and welcome. For example, I would like to see the study duplicated by an independent researcher who does have the opportunity to include a control group in the design. But the point is that these results certainly do offer some traditional empirical support for the program—at least as much as other self-esteem enhancement programs available today and more than most.

Let me say in closing that, although there is always room for improvement, we have uncovered good reasons to take the position that a phenomenological approach to the research, theory, and practice of self-esteem stands up to several qualitative and quantitative tests of

Appendix

Self-Esteem Enhancement: Program Announcement

This 5-week program is a group experience designed to increase our understanding and awareness of self-esteem. Participants will have the opportunity to assess their self-esteem, understand its basic components, and learn how to work on self-esteem issues. You will also create your own self-esteem improvement program and use group exercises to help you work on increasing your self-esteem during the program and afterward.

The program is run by _____, who is credentialed as a _____, and who is interested in helping people increase their self-esteem. The group sessions are based on a psychoeducational format, so learning is emphasized. The program is a focused one, meaning that we will deal with one theme, self-esteem, as the main topic of all meetings and activities. Anyone currently involved in treatment for a mental health condition is advised to discuss with his or her therapist whether or not to be in this program.

We will meet on _____ from _____ for 5 consecutive weeks. Attendance at all meetings is strongly encouraged because the program is designed to move in a step-by-step fashion. We hope to see you there, so please be sure that you reserve a place through _____ who can be reached at _____ before _____ as there are a limited number of seats.

WEEK 1—HANDOUT 2

Activity Schedule

I.   Self-esteem enhancement program steps

A.   Introduction to self-esteem and basic research about it

B.   Procedure:

1.   Focusing phase: Defining self-esteem (1st week)

a.   Discussing basic concepts

b.   Assessing individual self-esteem

2.   Awareness phase: Appreciating self-esteem (2nd week)

a.   Understanding common self-esteem problems

b.   Understanding the sources of self-esteem

3.   Enhancing phase: Increasing worthiness (3rd week)

a.   Understanding cognitive restructuring

b.   Removing cognitive "gumption traps"

4.   Enhancing phase: Increasing competence (4th week)

a.   Introduction to problem solving

b.   Practicing problem-solving techniques

5.   Management phase: Maintaining your self-esteem (5th week)

a.   Planning your own self-esteem action programs

b.   Evaluating the approach: Strengths and limits

6.   Follow-up meeting (6th week, optional)

WEEK 1—HANDOUT 3

Group Guidelines and Expectations

The program is run by _____, who is credentialed as a _____, and who is interested in helping people increase self-esteem. The group sessions are based on a psychoeducational format, so learning is emphasized. The program is a focused one, meaning that we will deal with one theme, self-esteem, as the main topic of all meetings and activities. Anyone currently involved in treatment for a mental health condition is advised to discuss with his or her therapist whether or not to be in this program.

We will meet on _____ from _____ for 5 consecutive weeks. Attendance at all meetings is strongly encouraged because the program is designed to move in a step-by-step or progressive fashion. Naturally, confidentiality among group members is required. Similarly, there are some other rules to follow that will help us create a favorable group experience.

1. Respect: For the program to enhance your appreciation of self-esteem, it is important that all members treat each other with the respect that each unique human being deserves. Although we may have differences of opinion, it is essential that all group activities be carried out in an atmosphere of good will and sensitivity toward others, which means appreciating differences.

2. Attendance: Group and seminar processes cannot work well if a good number of people are not present or if attendance is sporadic. Each of us depends on all the others in this regard. While no one can predict the occurrence of unforeseen emergencies, participants in a group do have a responsibility to one another to be there whenever possible.

3. Participation: The benefits of most therapeutic or psychoeducational activities are related to how much you participate in the process. However, you are not required to do anything that you do not feel comfortable doing, other than to follow the above rules. At the end of the group, you will have an opportunity to give feedback to the facilitator about your experience.

WEEK 1—HANDOUT 4

Defining Self-Esteem

I. Self-esteem as competence and worthiness in dealing with the challenges of living

    A. Experience of competence

        1. Describe such an experience briefly.

        2. What did the experience show you about competence?

    B. Experience of worthiness

        1. Describe such an experience briefly.

        2. What does it tell you about worthiness?

II. Keeping a self-esteem journal

WEEK 2—HANDOUT 1

Self-Esteem Types and Problems

I. Self-esteem types
II. Common self-esteem problems (to be discussed)

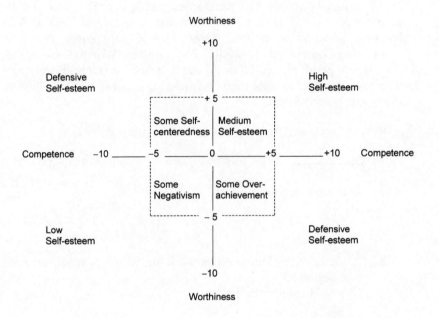

WEEK 2—HANDOUT 2

Applying the Multidimensional Self-Esteem Inventory (MSEI) Scales

Self-Esteem Report for _____   Date _____

The MSEI has 11 scales. The scales describing overall levels of self-esteem are Global Self-Esteem, Identity Integration, and Defensiveness. Competence-related scales are Competence, Personal Power, Self-Control, and Bodily Functioning. Worthiness-related scales are Lovability, Likability, Moral Self-Approval, and Bodily Appearance. The test results focus on the two highest and two lowest areas, which for you are:

A. Current self-esteem strengths (Most positive scores)

1. _____ (The positive scale on which you scored highest.)
    This scale suggests that:

2. _____ (The positive scale on which you scored second highest.)
    This scale suggests that:

B. Potential self-esteem growth areas

1. _____ (The scale on which your lowest score occurred, including defensiveness if that was high.)
    This scale suggests that:

2. _____ (The scale in which your second lowest score occurred, including defensiveness if that was high.)
    This scale suggests that:

WEEK 2—HANDOUT 3

Finding Sources of Self-Esteem

List examples and the values that they imply.

I. Personal achievements or successes

II. Evidence of influence or power

III. Acceptance or being valued

IV. Virtue or acting on beliefs (doing the "right thing")

WEEK 3—HANDOUT 1

Enhancing Worthiness: Using Positive Feedback

A. List positive features. Modified from Sappington, A. (1989). *Adjustment: Theory, Research, and Personal Applications.* Pacific Grove, CA: Brooks/Cole.

1. _____

2. _____

3. _____

4. _____

5. _____

6. _____

7. _____

8. _____

9. _____

10. _____

B. Group sharing (reading aloud)

WEEK 3—HANDOUT 2

Enhancing Worthiness: Introduction to Cognitive Restructuring

I. Common self-esteem gumption traps

    A. Concept: Mistakes in thinking and perceiving that keep us stuck or in pain

    B. A list of common traps. Modified from Burns, D. (1980). *Feeling Good: The New Mood Therapy.* New York: Signet; and Ellis, A., & Harper, R. (1977). *A New Guide to Rational Living.* North Hollywood, CA: Wilshire Book.

        1. CATASTROPHIZING (Exaggerating the negative meanings of an event)

        2. OVERGENERALIZING (Extending the negative meanings of an event beyond the situation in which it occurred)

        3. FILTERING (Focusing attention on the negative aspects of a situation or event and ignoring the positive possibilities)

        4. JUMPING TO CONCLUSIONS (Skipping steps that would be necessary to justify drawing a particular, usually negative, conclusion about the meaning of an event or situation)

        5. MAGNIFYING (Exaggerating the negative meanings of an event or situation beyond their real significance)

        6. "YEAH, BUT" or "IF ONLY . . . " (Thinking emotionally or stubbornly holding on to a belief because it justifies a negative feeling like anger or because it helps to avoid facing a painful feeling like being hurt)

        7. SHOULD STATEMENTS (Believing that things MUST go a certain way or one will be "inferior," a "failure," or a "bad person")

        8. NAME CALLING (Calling someone, especially oneself, a negative name like "stupid," "ugly," or "loser")

        9. PERSONALIZING (Being too sensitive about an incident, event, or disappointment)

      10. FORTUNE-TELLING (Predicting that future events will be bad because a past or recent one was unpleasant)

WEEK 3—HANDOUT 3

Pattern-Breaking Worksheet (Used in conjunction with Week 3: Handout 2)

I. Implementation of the cognitive restructuring process

A. Six-step method. Based on Burns, D. (1980). *Feeling Good: The New Mood Therapy*. New York: Signet. (modified for self-esteem work)

1. *Describe the situation* that lessens self-esteem.
2. *Identify your strongest feelings* in the situation and rate their level of intensity on a scale of 1 to 10 (or 1 to 100).
3. *Describe the thoughts* or perceptions you were actually having in the situation as accurately as possible.
4. *Select a term* from the list of thinking errors to identify the distorted, irrational, or dysfunctional aspect of these thoughts or perceptions.
5. *Correct the error* by substituting a realistic thought or perception for each thinking error you made.
6. *Evaluate your feelings* about the situation as they are now on a scale of 1 to 10 (or 1 to 100) and compare them with the results of step 2.

B. Facilitator's example (work all the steps on the board)

1. The situation was or is
2. On a scale of 1 to 10 (or 1 to 100), my feelings were or are
3. My thoughts at the time were or are
4. The type of thinking error being made at the time was or is
5. A realistic substitute would be to think
6. On a sale of 1 to 10 (or 1 to 100), my feelings right now rate

C. Participant's examples (work problems offered by the group on the board)

II. Practice (in the self-esteem journal)

WEEK 4—HANDOUT 1

Enhancing Competence: Problem-Solving Method

Based on D'Zurilla, T., & Goldfried, M. (1971). "Problem solving and behavior modification." *Journal of Abnormal Psychology, 78*, 107–126; Pope, A., McHale, S., & Craighead, E. (1988). *Self-esteem enhancement with children and adolescents*. New York: Pergamon Press.

A. Problem-solving theory: basic ideas

   1. Feelings: let us know that a problem needs to be solved

   2. Thinking: helps us to understand the problem better

   3. Actions: allow us to solve the problem

B. Problem-solving steps

   1. Realize that there is a problem

   2. Stop and try to understand it

   3. Decide on a goal

   4. Think about possible solutions

   5. Think about their likely consequences

   6. Choose the best or most realistic solution

   7. Make a detailed plan for carrying it out

   8. Practice!

WEEK 4—HANDOUT 2

Enhancing Competence: Problem-Solving Worksheet

A. The problem-solving process

Step	*Procedure*
1. Is there a problem	Look for emotional cues
2. Stop and understand	Ask, What is the problem?
3. Decide on a goal	Ask, What do I want here?
4. Think about solutions	Brainstorm possibilities
a.	
b.	
c.	
5. Think about likely consequences	What will happen if this occurs?
a.	
b.	
c.	
6. Choose the best one	Which can I best accept?
7. Make a plan	What to do, step by step
a.	
b.	
c.	
8. Learning	Practice, more practice!

B. Select examples from class and work through each of the steps.

WEEK 5—HANDOUT 1

Building a Self-Esteem Project

I. *Self-esteem action cycle*

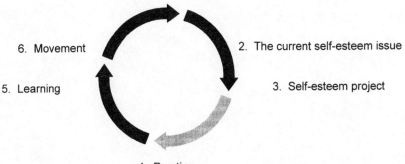

1. Current self-esteem

6. Movement

2. The current self-esteem issue

5. Learning

3. Self-esteem project

4. Practice

II. *Self-esteem action plan: Increasing and maintaining self-esteem*

    A. Identify a self-esteem strength or weakness to work on

        1.

    B. Match the issue with the four sources of self-esteem

        1.

    C. Identify realistic goals

        1.

        2.

    D. Write specific, workable action steps for each goal

        1.

        2.

        3.

References

Aanstoos, C. (Ed.). (1984). *Exploring the lived world: Readings in phenomenological psychology* (Vol. 23). Atlanta: West Georgia College.
———. (1995). From the editor's bookshelf. *The Humanistic Psychologist, 23,* 121.
Adler, A. (1927). *Understanding human nature.* New York: Fawcett.
Alberti, R. E., & Emmons, R. L. (1982). *Your perfect right: A guide to rational living* (4th ed.). San Luis Bispo, CA: Impact Publishers.
American Association of University Women. (1991). *Shortchanging girls, shortchanging America.* Washington, DC: Author.
American Psychiatric Association. (1994). *Diagnostic and statistical manual of mental disorders* (4th ed.). Washington, DC: Author.
Back, K. W. (1984). Psychology and sociology. In M. Bornstein (Ed.), *Psychology and its allied disciplines* (pp. 207–236). Hillsdale, NJ: Lawrence Erlbaum.
Bandura, A. (1997). *Self-efficacy: The exercise of control.* New York: W. H. Freeman & Co.
Battle, J. (1982). *Enhancing self-esteem and achievement: A handbook for professionals.* Seattle: Special Child Publications.
———. (1992). *Culture-free self-esteem inventories* (2nd ed.). Austin, TX: Pro-ed.
Baumeister, R. (Ed.). (1993). *Self-esteem: The puzzle of low self-regard.* New York: Plenum.
Baumeister, R., Smart, L., & Boden, J. (1996). Relation of threatened egotism to violence and aggression: The dark side of self-esteem. *Psychological Review, 103,* 5–33.
Beane, J. (1991). Sorting out the self-esteem controversy. *Educational Leadership, 49,* 25–30.

Bednar, R., & Peterson, S. (1995). *Self-esteem: Paradoxes and innovations in clinical theory and practice* (2nd ed.). Washington, DC: American Psychological Association.

Bednar, R., Wells, G., & Peterson, S. (1989). *Self-esteem: Paradoxes and innovations in clinical theory and practice.* Washington, DC: American Psychological Association.

Bhatti, B., Derezotes, D., Kim, S., & Specht, H. (1989). The association between child maltreatment and low self-esteem. In A. M. Mecca, N. J. Smelser, & J. Vasconcellos (Eds.), *The social importance of self-esteem* (pp. 24–71). Berkeley: University of California Press.

Blaine, B., & Crocker, J. (1993). Self-esteem and self-serving biases in reactions to positive and negative events: An integrative view. In R. Baumeister (Ed.), *Self-esteem: The puzzle of low self-regard* (pp. 59–85). New York: Plenum.

Block, J., & Thomas, H. (1955). Is satisfaction with self a measure of adjustment. *Journal of Abnormal and Social Psychology, 51,* 257–261.

Bradshaw, P. (1981). *The management of self-esteem.* Englewood Cliffs, NJ: Prentice Hall.

Branden, N. (1969). *The psychology of self-esteem.* New York: Bantam.

———. (1983). *Honoring the self.* Los Angeles: Tarcher.

———. (1987). *How to raise your self-esteem.* New York: Bantam.

———. (1994). *The six pillars of self-esteem.* New York: Bantam.

Brockner, J., Wiesenfeld, B., & Raskas, D. (1993). Self-esteem and expectancy-value discrepancy: The effects of believing that you can (or can't) get what you want. In R. Baumeister (Ed.), *Self-esteem: The puzzle of low self-regard* (pp. 219–241). New York: Plenum.

Burns, D. (1980). *Feeling good: The new mood therapy.* New York: Signet.

———. (1993a). *Ten days to self-esteem.* New York: Quill.

———. (1993b). *Ten days to self-esteem: The leader's manual.* New York: Quill.

Campbell, J., & Lavallee, L. (1993). Who am I? The role of self-concept and confusion in understanding the behavior of people with low self-esteem. In R. Baumeister (Ed.), *Self-esteem: The puzzle of low self-regard* (pp. 4–20). New York: Plenum.

Clark, J. (1994, August). Adolescents in post divorce and always married families: Self-esteem and perceptions of father's interest. *Journal of Marriage and the Family,* 56.

Colaizzi, P. (1973). *Reflection and research in psychology: A phenomenological study of learning.* Dubuque, IA: Kendall/Hunt.

Cole, C., Oetting, E., & Hinkle, J. (1967). Non-linearity of self-concept discrepancy—the value dimension. *Psychological Reports, 21,* 56–60.

Conlan, R. (Ed.). (1986). *Artificial intelligence.* New York: Time-Life Books.

Cooley, C. H. (1909). *Human nature and the social order.* New York: Scribner.

Coopersmith, S. (1959). A method for determining types of self-esteem. *Journal of Abnormal Social Psychology, 59,* 87–94.

———. (1967). *The antecedents of self-esteem.* San Francisco: Freeman.

———. (1975, 1981). *Adult form SEI Coopersmith inventory.* Palo Alto, CA: Consulting Psychologists Press.

————. (1981). *Self-esteem inventories.* Palo Alto, CA: Consulting Psychologists Press.

Costall, A., & Still, A. (Eds.). (1987). *Cognitive psychology in question.* New York: St. Martin's Press.

Crocker, J., & Major, B. (1989). Social stigma and self-esteem: The self-protective properties of social stigma. *Psychological Review, 96,* 608–630.

Damon, W. (1995). *Great expectations: Overcoming the culture of indulgence in our homes and schools.* New York: Free Press.

Diggory, J. (1966). *Self-evaluation: Concept and studies.* New York: Wiley.

Dreyfus, H. L., & Dreyfus, S. E. (1986). *Mind over machine: The power of human intuition and expertise in the era of the computer.* New York: Free Press.

Durand, V. M., & Barlow, D. (1997). *Abnormal psychology: An introduction.* Pacific Grove, CA: Brooks/Cole.

D'Zurilla, T. J., & Goldfried, M. R. (1971). Problem solving and behavior modification. *Journal of Abnormal Psychology, 78,* 107–126.

Ellis, A., & Harper, R. (1977). *A new guide to rational living.* North Hollywood, CA: Wilshire Book.

Epstein, S. (1979). The ecological study of emotions in humans. In K. Blankstein (Ed.), *Advances in the study of communications and affect* (pp. 47–83). New York: Plenum.

————. (1980). The self-concept: A review and the proposal of an integrated theory of personality. In E. Straub (Ed.), *Personality: Basic aspects and current research* (pp. 83–131). Englewood Cliffs, NJ: Prentice Hall.

————. (1985). The implications of cognitive-experiential self-theory for research in social psychology and personality. *Journal for the Theory of Social Behavior, 15,* 283–309.

Erikson, E. (1983). *The life cycle completed.* New York: Norton.

Evans, K., & Sullivan, J. M. (1990). *Dual diagnosis: Counseling the mentally ill substance abuser.* New York: Guilford Press.

Finkelhor, D., & Browne, A. (1985). The traumatic impact of child sexual abuse: A conceptualization. *American Journal of Orthopsychiatry, 55,* 530–541.

Fischer, C. (1986). *Individualizing psychological assessment.* Belmont, CA: Wadsworth.

Fitts, W. (1988). *Tennessee self-concept scale.* Los Angeles: Western Psychological Services.

Freud, S. (1957). *On narcissism: An introduction* (standard ed.). London: Hogarth Press. (Original work published 1914)

Frey, D., & Carlock, C. J. (1989). *Enhancing self-esteem* (2nd ed.). Muncie, IN: Accelerated Development.

Frey, D. E., Kelbley, T. J., Thomas, J., Durham, L., & James, J. S. (1992). Enhancing self-esteem of selected male nursing home residents. *Gerontologist, 32,* 552–557.

Gergen, K. J. (1991). *The saturated self: Dilemmas of identity in contemporary life.* New York: Basic Books.

Giorgi, A. (1970). *Psychology as a human science: A phenomenologically based approach.* New York: Harper & Row.

———. (1971). Phenomenology and experimental psychology: I & II. In A. Giorgi, W. Fischer, & R. Von Eckartsberg (Eds.), *Duquesne studies in phenomenological psychology* (Vol. 1, pp. 6–28). Pittsburgh: Duquesne University Press.

———. (1975). Convergence and divergence of qualitative and quantitative methods in psychology. In A. Giorgi, C. Fischer, & E. Murray (Eds.), *Duquesne studies in phenomenological psychology* (Vol. 2, pp. 72–79). Pittsburgh: Duquesne University Press.

———. (1984). Towards a new paradigm for psychology. In C. Aanstoos (Ed.), *Exploring the lived world: Readings in phenomenological psychology* (Vol 22, pp. 9–28). Atlanta: West Georgia College.

Gurwitsch, A. (1964). *The field of consciousness.* Pittsburgh: Duquesne University Press.

Hakim-Larson, J., & Mruk, C. (1997). Enhancing self-esteem in a community mental health setting. *American Journal of Orthopsychiatry, 67,* 655–659.

Harris, J. (1998). *The nurture assumption: Why children turn out the way they do.* New York: The Free Press.

Harter, S. (1990). Self and identity development. In S. Shirley & G. Elliot (Eds.), *At the threshold: The developing adolescent* (pp. 352–387). Cambridge, MA: Harvard University Press.

———. (1993). Causes and consequences of low self-esteem in children and adolescents. In R. Baumeister (Ed.), *Self-esteem: The puzzle of low self-regard* (pp. 87–111). New York: Plenum.

Hathaway, S. R., & McKinley, J. C. with W. G. Dahlstrom, J. R. Graham, A. Tellegen, & B. Kaemmer (1989). *The Minnesota Multiphasic Personality Inventory-2.* Minneapolis: University of Minnesota Press.

Havighurst, R. J. (1972). *Developmental tasks and education* (3rd ed.). New York: McKay.

Heatherton, T., & Ambady, N. (1993). Self-esteem, self-prediction, and living up to commitments. In R. Baumeister (Ed.), *Self-esteem: The puzzle of low self-regard* (pp. 131–145). New York: Plenum.

Heidegger, M. (1962). *Being and time.* New York: Harper & Row. (Original work published 1927)

Heisenberg, W. (1950). *Physical principles of quantum theory.* New York: Dover.

Howard, G. (1985). *Basic research methods in the social sciences.* Glenview, IL: Scott Foresman.

Husserl, E. (1970a). *The crisis of European sciences and transcendental phenomenology.* Evanston, IL: Northwestern University Press. (Original work published 1954)

———. (1970b). *Logical investigations II* (J. Findlay, Trans). New York: Humanities Press.

Jackson, M. (1984). *Self-esteem and meaning: A life historical investigation.* Albany: State University of New York.

James, W. (1983). *The principles of psychology.* Cambridge, MA: Harvard University Press. (Original work published 1890)

Japenga, A. (1996, July/August). What goes up must come down. *Health,* 45–46.

Johnson, K. (1998, May 5). Self-image is suffering from a lack of esteem. *New York Times*, p. F7.

Jung, J. (1994). *Under the influence: Alcohol and human behavior.* Pacific Grove, CA: Brooks/Cole.

Kaplan, H., Martin, S., & Johnson, R. (1986). Self-rejection and the explanation of deviance: Specification of the structure among latent constructs. *American Journal of Sociology, 92,* 384–441.

Kazdin, A. (1992). *Research design in clinical psychology.* Needham Heights, MA: Allyn & Bacon.

Kernis, M. (1993). The roles of stability and level of self-esteem in psychological functioning. In R. Baumeister (Ed.), *Self-esteem: The puzzle of low self-regard* (pp. 167–182). New York: Plenum.

Kitano, H. H. (1989). Alcohol and drug use and self-esteem: A sociocultural perspective. In A. M. Mecca, N. J. Smelser, & J. Vasconcellos (Eds.), *The social importance of self-esteem* (pp. 294–326). Berkeley: University of California Press.

Krauthammer, C. (1990, February 5). Education: Doing bad and feeling good. *Time*, p. 78.

Kuhn, T. S. (1962). *The structure of scientific revolutions.* Chicago: University of Chicago Press.

Leo, J. (1990, April 2). The trouble with self-esteem. *U.S. News and World Report*, p. 16.

———. (1998, May 18). Damn, I'm good! *U.S. News and World Report*, p. 21.

Levin, J. D. (1993). *Slings and arrows: Narcissistic injury and its treatment.* Northvale, NJ: Aronson.

Mack, F. (1987). Understanding and enhancing self-concepts in black children. *Momentum, 18,* 22–28.

Mann, J. (1973). *Time-limited psychotherapy.* Cambridge, MA: Harvard University Press.

Marcel, G. (1964). *Creative fidelity.* New York: Noonday Press.

Masters, K., & Bergin, A. (1992). Religious orientation and mental health. In J. Schumaker (Ed.), *Religion and mental health* (pp. 221–232). New York: Oxford.

McCann, I., & Pearlman, L. (1990). *Psychological trauma and the adult survivor: Theory, therapy, and transformation.* New York: Brunner/Mazel.

Mead, G. H. (1934). *Mind, self, and society.* Chicago: University of Chicago Press.

Mecca, A. M., Smelser, N. J., & Vasconcellos, J. (Eds.). (1989). *The social importance of self-esteem.* Berkeley: University of California Press.

Merleau-Ponty, M. (1962/1945). *The phenomenology of perception.* New York: Humanities Press.

Miller, T. (1984). Parental absence and its affects on adolescent self-esteem. *International Journal of Social Psychiatry, 30*(4), 293–296.

Mruk, C. (1983). Toward a phenomenology of self-esteem. In A. Giorgi, A. Barton, & C. Maes (Eds.), *Duquesne studies in phenomenological psychology* (Vol. 4, pp. 137–148). Pittsburgh: Duquesne University Press.

———. (1989). Phenomenological psychology and the computer revolution: Friend, foe, or opportunity? *Journal of Phenomenological Psychology, 20,* 20–39.

————. (1994). Phenomenological psychology and integrated description: Keeping the science in the human science approach. *Methods: A Journal for Human Science* (annual edition), 6–20.

Newman, B., & Newman, P. (1987). *Development through life: A psychosocial approach* (4th ed.). Chicago: Dorsey Press.

O'Brien, E. (1985). Global self-esteem scales: Unidimensional or multidimensional? *Psychological Reports, 57,* 383–389.

O'Brien, E., & Epstein, S. (1983, 1988). *MSEI: The multidimensional self-esteem inventory.* Odessa, FL: Psychological Assessment Resources.

O'Brien, E., Leitzel, J., & Mensky, L. (1996, August). *Gender differences in the self-esteem of adolescents: A meta-analysis.* Poster session presented at the annual meeting of the American Psychological Association, Toronto.

Pallas, A. M., Entwisle, D. R., Alexander, K. L., & Weinstein, P. (1990). Social structure and the development of self-esteem in young children. *Social Psychology Quarterly, 53,* 302–315.

Pettijohn, T. F. (1998). *Sources: Notable selections in social psychology.* Guilford, CT: Dushkin/McGraw-Hill.

Piers, E., & Harris, D. (1969). *Piers-Harris children's self-concept scale.* Los Angeles: Western Psychological Services.

Pirsig, R. (1974). *Zen and the art of motorcycle maintenance.* New York: Morrow.

Plummer, D. L. (1985). *Help seeking as a function of perceived inadequacy level and self-esteem.* Unpublished doctoral dissertation, University of Georgia, Athens.

Pope, A., McHale, S., & Craighead, E. (1988). *Self-esteem enhancement with children and adolescents.* New York: Pergamon Press.

Rakos, R. F. (1990). *Assertive behavior: Theory, research, and training.* London: Routledge.

Raskin, R., Novacek, J., & Hogan, R. (1991). Narcissistic self-esteem management. *Journal of Personality and Social Psychology, 60,* 911–918.

Rathus, S. (1996). *Psychology* (6th ed.). San Francisco: Holt, Rinehart & Winston.

Rogers, C. (1961). *On becoming a person.* Boston: Houghton Mifflin.

Rosenberg, M. (1965). *Society and the adolescent self-image.* Princeton, NJ: Princeton University Press.

————. (1979). *Conceiving the self.* New York: Basic Books.

Rosenberg, M., & Simmons, R. G. (1971). Black and white self-esteem: The urban school child [Monograph]. *Social Psychological Implications IX,* Rose Monograph Series. Washington, DC: American Sociological Association.

Ross, A. (1992). *The sense of self.* New York: Springer.

Samenow, S. (1984). *Inside the criminal mind.* New York: Times Books.

————. (1989). *Before it's too late.* New York: Times Books.

Sanford, L., & Donovan, E. (1984). *Women and self-esteem.* New York: Anchor Press/Doubleday.

Sappington, A. (1989). *Adjustment: Theory, research, and personal applications.* Pacific Grove, CA: Brooks/Cole.

Scheff, T., Retzinger, S., & Ryan, M. (1989). Crime, violence, and self-esteem: Review and proposals. In A. M. Mecca, N. J. Smelser, & J. Vasconcellos (Eds.),

The social importance of self-esteem (pp. 294–326). Berkeley: University of California Press.

Schneiderman, J. W., Furman, M., & Weber, J. (1989). Self-esteem and chronic welfare dependency. In A. M. Mecca, N. J. Smelser, & J. Vasconcellos (Eds.), *The social importance of self-esteem* (pp. 294–326). Berkeley: University of California Press.

Seligman, M. (1990). *Learned optimism: How to change your mind and your life.* New York: Simon & Schuster.

———. (1995a). The effectiveness of psychotherapy: The consumer's report study. *American Psychologist, 40,* 965–974.

———. (1995b). *The optimistic child: A proven program to safeguard children against depression and build lifelong resilience.* New York: HarperCollins.

Sigelman, C. S., & Shaffer, D. R. (1995). *Life-span human development* (2nd ed.). Belmont, CA: Brooks/Cole.

Singelis, T. M., Bond, M. H., & Lai, S. Y. (1995, July). *Self-esteem, and embarrassability in Hong Kong, Hawai'i, and mainland United States.* Paper presented at the Fourth European Congress of Psychology, Athens, Greece.

Skager, R., & Kerst, E. (1989). Alcohol and drug use and self-esteem: A psychological perspective. In A. M. Mecca, N. J. Smelser, & J. Vasconcellos (Eds.), *The social importance of self-esteem* (pp. 248–293). Berkeley: University of California Press.

Smelser, N. J. (1989). Self-esteem and social problems: An introduction. In A. M. Mecca, N. J. Smelser, & J. Vasconcellos (Eds.), *The social importance of self-esteem* (pp. 294–326). Berkeley: University of California Press.

Snyder, C. S. (1989). Reality negotiation: From excuses to hope and beyond. *Journal of Social and Clinical Psychology, 8,* 130–157.

Snygg, D., & Combs, A. (1959). *Individual behavior: A new frame of reference for psychology* (2nd ed.). New York: Harper.

Steffenhagen, R., & Burns, J. (1987). *The social dynamics of self-esteem.* London: Praeger.

Strauman, T. J., Lemieux, A. M., & Coe, C. (1993). Self-discrepancy natural killer cell activity: Immunological consequences of negative self-evaluation. *Journal of Personality and Social Psychology, 64,* 1042–1052.

Sue, D. W., & Sue, D. (1990). *Counseling the culturally different: Theory and practice.* New York: Wiley.

Swanston, H. Y., Tebbutt, J. S., O'Toole, B. I., & Oates, R. K. (1997). Sexually abused children 5 years after presentation: A case-control study. *Pediatrics, 100,* 600–608.

Tennen, H., & Affleck, G. (1993). The puzzles of self-esteem: A clinical perspective. In R. Baumeister (Ed.), *Self-esteem: The puzzle of low self-regard* (pp. 241–263). New York: Plenum.

Tice, D. (1993). The social motivations of people with low self-esteem. In R. Baumeister (Ed.), *Self-esteem: The puzzle of low self-regard* (pp. 37–54). New York: Plenum.

Truscott, J. W. (1985). *Effects of in-patient treatment on selected personality dimensions of depressed alcoholics.* Unpublished master's thesis, Marywood College, Scranton, PA.

Tryon, W. (1991). Uncertainty reduction as valid explanation. *Theoretical and Philosophical Psychology Bulletin, 11,* 2.

Vaillant, G. (1995). *The wisdom of the ego: Sources of resilience in adult life.* New York: Belknamp.

Vinogradov, S., & Yalom, I. D. (1989). *A concise guide to group psychotherapy.* Washington, DC: American Psychiatric Press.

Weissman, H., & Ritter, K. (1970). Openness to experience, ego strength and self-description as a function of repression and sensitization. *Psychological Reports, 26,* 859–864.

Wells, E. L., & Marwell, G. (1976). *Self-esteem: Its conceptualization and measurement.* Beverly Hills, CA: Sage.

Wells, R. A. (1982). *Planned short-term treatment.* New York: Free Press.

Werner, E. E., & Smith, R. S. (1992). *Overcoming the odds: High-risk children from birth to adulthood.* Ithaca, NY: Cornell University Press.

Wertz, F. (1984). Procedures in phenomenological research and the question of validity. In C. Aanstoos (Ed.), *Exploring the lived world: Readings in phenomenological psychology* (Vol. 23, pp. 9–28). Atlanta: West Georgia College.

White, R. (1959). Motivation reconsidered: The concept of competence. *Psychological Review, 66,* 297–333.

———. (1963). Ego and reality in psychoanalytic theory: A proposal regarding independent ego energies. *Psychological Issues, 3,* 125–150.

Winnicott, D. (1953). Transitional objects and transitional phenomena. *International Journal of Psychoanalysis, 34,* 89–97.

Wood, J., Giordano-Beech, M., Taylor, K., Michela, J., & Gaus, V. (1994). Strategies of social comparison among people with low self-esteem: Self-protection and self-enhancement. *Journal of Personality and Social Psychology, 67,* 713–731.

Wylie, R. (1974). *The self-concept* (Vol. 1). Lincoln: University of Nebraska Press.

Index